The Trouble with Lavinia

The Trouble with Lavinia

Vená Bartlett & Peggy Feltham

The Pentland Press Limited
Edinburgh • Cambridge • Durham • USA

© Vená Bartlett & Peggy Feltham 1995

First published in 1995 by
The Pentland Press Ltd.
1 Hutton Close
South Church
Bishop Auckland
Durham

All rights reserved.
Unauthorised duplication
contravenes existing laws.

British Library Cataloguing in Publication Data.
A catalogue record for this book is available
from the British Library.

ISBN 1 85821 289 8

Typeset by CBS, Felixstowe, Suffolk
Printed and bound by Antony Rowe Ltd., Chippenham

FOREWORD

Many years ago – at the start of the swinging sixties – I watched a pop group (that's what they were called in those days) playing in a pub at Lewes, in Sussex. Afterwards the drummer asked me for my autograph and he said, *'Do you think our group will make it?'* I said I thought they would. His name was Ringo Starr. They were the Beatles. And they did!

Some time later, a girl called Diane Keen asked me if I thought she would make it as an actress. I said yes and she did.

Many, many years later, a lady called Peggy Feltham wrote to me from Portsmouth and enclosed part of a manuscript she and her friend had written. It was from a book entitled *The Trouble With Lavinia*. She asked me if I thought it was good enough to publish.

I said yes – and they have!

I think it is funny and moving and I hope that it is as successful as the Beatles and Diane Keen. And I look forward – as I'm sure you do – to reading this, the completed version.

Fred Dinenage
Southampton
February 1995

INTRODUCTION

It seemed straightforward enough for us to relate the peculiar chronicles of Vená and Peg and combine them into a coherent package - but little did we know! It all started quite a few years ago when Vená was holding forth on the topic of camping to a young colleague at the laboratory where we worked, and Peg's ears pricked up in amazement.

'Weeeee!' came a squeal from young Sally. 'What do you mean - sheets and pillow cases and *pillows*? How can you carry all that?'

Sally and her husband were the sort of campers that travel extremely lightly with a tin kettle bobbing about on a backpack and probably slept in their day clothes in a flimsy tent. Obviously there were two differing conceptions of the term 'camping' here and Peg listened with growing interest.

Vená listed the essentials for a camping expedition that included everything bar the proverbial sink while Sally's mouth dropped open and her eyes almost popped out of her head. It was when 'the small vase for wild flowers' entered the inventory that Sally and Peg became hysterical and Sally said:

'Oh Vená! You ought to write a book - you really should!'

She had no way of knowing that she was talking to Lavinia!

It was at least fifteen years later that the V. & P. team lightheartedly talked about pooling our limited brain power to take up Sally's quip, and then set to work with a will. Just the two of us - at first - and then we became conscious that a third entity was muscling in. Vená can't help but admit that she has two sides to her nature: (a) called Vená, who is very nearly normal; and (b) Lavinia, who is anything but. Vená complains that Lavinia has all the enjoyment while she has to deal with the mundane and sometimes nasty things in life, to which Lavinia would reply, 'Rubbish! Where would you be without me? [A good question.] And I cheer you up, you miserable toad.' This is an indisputable fact that all three of us agree upon. Peg has to rely upon her single and inadequate personality and, therefore, has no-one else to blame or praise for disasters or very minor achievements. This is a shame for her; it would be very nice, she feels, to dash off something quite outrageous or brilliant and then swan airily away.

Perhaps it's for the best as there could well be friction between bossy Lavinia and a rival, and then God knows what would happen!

We found that Lavinia (fondly imagined as wearing a becoming floppy hat and a long romantic scarf) simply bulldozed her way past the V. & P. team, rolled her sleeves up and in very short order had taken over the whole proceedings. Not that we actually remember her doing so, it just happened. Now you see her, now you don't, sort of thing. So for better or worse, there we have it: two mature and slightly battered would-be writers, urged on by one unfettered and blythe spirit making the waves for our frail craft to sail upon.

Next came the awkward question as to how we should combine our two separate sets of experiences and, after much head scratching and furrowed brows, came to no sensible conclusion. At this point Lavinia elbowed her way in and decided to direct matters herself.

'It's simple, fools,' said she. 'We'll have Vená's interesting part first and keep people amused enough to read Peg's boring bit when they're fed up with laughing.'

And while one of us was rather hurt, we couldn't fault her line of reasoning and decided to humour her - just this once.

We aren't quite sure if our husbands have equally enjoyed being involved in our venture and have to admit that on rare occasions they have been subjected to a little inconvenience. On the whole, however, they don't appear to object too strongly to our absence at typewriters, absentmindedness and sudden bellows of laughter. Vená's husband Roy has been known to laugh out loud at some reminiscence or other, while Keith, Peg's husband, once fleetingly suffered from a twitch of the lips before returning to a stuffy old technical journal, which means he was quite amused, and that was most encouraging. There is no doubt, however, that they have generously supported our efforts and for that we love and thank them.

PART ONE

*VENA'S INTERESTING PART - ACCORDING TO
LAVINIA*

STARTER

'Just look after Raymond for a couple of minutes, Vená, while I pop up the road,' said Aunty Lilly. I was twelve years old at the time and felt very flattered and important to be put in charge of young Raymond, aged two (as they insist upon saying in all the papers), even if it was for only a couple of jiffs. I smiled winningly at him and he rewarded me by asking, 'Will you thing me a thong, pleath?' while climbing upon my knee and looking pleadingly into my face.

'How sweet,' I thought and, 'What a dear little boy.' A slight pause while I considered what would be suitable for these young and innocent ears, and decided that the hymns I had just learned in the church choir would fit the bill admirably. I trilled my way through 'Lead us, Heavenly Father, lead us' and then 'Thy Hand, oh God, has Guided'. I knew there were several more in my repertoire, and gave him the full treatment with my healthy and vibrant tonsils quivering with love and wonderment at this angelic little face staring up at me so appreciatively. As my last note died away, he said, 'DAMN AND BLAST YOU, COUSIN VENÁ!', jumped down and kicked the cat.

Well! To say I was shocked would be an understatement, to say the very least. In those more polite days this was the equivalent to '— off, you silly cow' and something that I would never have dared to utter at the ripe old age of twelve, let alone at two. Where had he picked up such dreadful language? Surely not from his mother, Aunty Lilly; that was inconceivable. On the other hand, he might just have been in the company of Naughty Gran, and that would explain everything.

It made a big impression upon me, and fifty years later it is still used as a family expletive when all is not well, which is quite often!

CHAPTER 1

During the early years of my life I listened avidly to the oft repeated chronicle of THE DAY I WAS BORN, as described by my maternal great-grandmother. Naturally, being the star of the show, I was wildly interested in this absorbing topic, and consequently it is etched upon my memory almost as if I had witnessed this dramatic event instead of merely joining the human race.

The witness sees her mother in a bedroom filled with daffodils, glowing coals and snapping flames in the small bedroom fireplace and snow drifting past the window. Her layette is spread out to collect the warmth, awaiting her arrival, and then the midwife arrives and takes command from Great-Gran. The actual birth details must mercifully have been withheld, because she then sees Great-Gran rushing to the door shouting exultantly to her father, 'Harold, Harold, it's a little girl!' and the tired, red-faced midwife with the rolled up sleeves muttering, 'My God! You'd think she'd done it all on her own.'

I was christened 'Vená' and later, at the age of fourteen, changed it slightly with a French accent as that sounded terribly chic and suitable for the beautiful young lady I imagined I was. I suppose I haven't changed very much over the years as nowadays my name is 'Lavinia' when I am engrossed in something I fondly consider to be cultured and/or artistic, though Peg did say once that 'Lavvy' was far more appropriate, taking into account my taste in humour.

You may be a little puzzled as to why my great-grandmother attended my birth. The reason was that my grandmother was missing entirely from the family, having walked out on her husband and children many years before my advent. Known to the youngsters as 'Naughty Gran', she held a certain glamour for us as reports filtered through of her wayward lifestyle, like spending most of her days in the local pub and getting pie-eyed on whisky and gin and dancing on the table tops. The latter activity was very popular with the male patrons who used to crowd around the table in the hopes of getting more than a glimpse of her long-legged bloomers. Obviously Mum and I were much safer in the kind and gentle hands of Great-Gran.

My brother, Roy, was six years older than myself and played an important part in my young life. He taught me many things that are vital to a boy's existence and by the time I was four I was skilled in such useful occupations as Meccano and model making. I have no doubt that I was spoiled to death by my besotted family who, I now realise, were thrilled to bits to have a little girl suddenly in their midst. I should think it is fairly unusual to be petted by an older brother but, with hindsight, he obviously did love and care for me and I have a letter written by him at the age of about ten wherein he refers to 'that delicate little Vená'. This brings forth screams of laughter from my insensitive family viewing my middle-aged body and grey hair. Well, no matter, you are as young as you feel, I say, though can back-fire on grotty days, of course.

My father was a Physical Training instructor in the Royal Navy and when I was three he was transferred to Rosyth, accompanied by his family. Being so young, my memories of life in Scotland are few, but I do remember having to start school at the ripe old age of four. I also recall that I had to wear long black stockings which promptly earned me the title of 'Liquorice Legs' from that brother I have just said such nice things about.

Mind you, he had his problems at this time as he was bullied by local lads for being English in a foreign land and would frequently arrive home after school bruised, bloody, but unbowed. Dad took action after a while when it became obvious that Roy would probably have to go through life sporting a cauliflower ear and a bent nose if the situation was not taken in hand. He therefore presented himself at the school and insisted that Roy should fight each bully separately with himself as referee. This worked wonders. No more packs of young hooligans waiting to set upon him; in fact, a grudging admiration emerged and peace (more or less!) reigned. I admire Roy's courage. It must have been a thoroughly miserable and frightening period in his schooldays and very cleverly solved by my canny father.

I can remember another cunning plan effected by Dad. In the Rosyth garden stood a crab apple tree, and one midwinter I kept grizzling for its non-existent apples. One morning, however, I discovered a big, round, rosy and thoroughly beautiful apple hanging on one of the lower branches. Hardly believing my eyes, I flew indoors to tell my family about this phenomenon and we all trooped back to pick the wondrous harvest. It must have taken Dad quite a while to tie the apple on with cotton and make it look natural, but I suspect his Navy training came in handy for this sort of emergency.

My first big adventure happened at the outbreak of war in 1939 when I was 9½ years old. The schools in my home town were issued with leaflets to be sent to all parents advising them that evacuation of the children to country areas would be the best means by far of keeping them safe. Our particular location was bound to be a potential target because of its Naval connections and high density population. Naturally this fell as an advance bombshell upon the thousands of homes in the city and caused much heartbreak and worry for all concerned. My parents were no exception and my mother was distraught at the prospect of 'that delicate little Vená' and her son being wrenched away from her. However, Dad persuaded her that it would be the correct thing to do, despite the agony of parting with the children, and might possibly save their lives. That argument couldn't be countered and the die was cast.

So, at 9.00 a.m. on a grey September day, fleets of double-decker buses arrived at most of the schools to collect the subdued and rather frightened children to deliver them to the town station. We each had a name tag firmly pinned to our coats and carried a brown paper carrier bag which contained a bar of chocolate, a bag of nuts and raisins, a tin of corned beef and a tin of condensed milk. In theory we were to hand over the bag intact to our new guardians, but I doubt very much if many of them got a glimpse of the chocolate and nuts. It could be that this little ploy was deliberate to interest the children with prospective naughtiness on the journey and, if so, it worked very well. If not, it was remarkably stupid.

My destination was a small village in Wiltshire called Zeals and I, along with my friend Mavis, was handed over to a dear couple named Fry. In my childhood memory they are really old, but as Mr Fry was head gardener at the Big House, he couldn't have reached retirement age and was probably a poor old thing of about forty. He and his wife lived in a beautiful old cottage in the grounds and suddenly had to come to terms with two extremely homesick youngsters, literally doubling the population of their small cottage. They were remarkably kind and, given time, I feel both Mavis and myself would have settled down happily in this new and completely different environment. Potted impressions recall masses of Michaelmas daisies, heaps of lovely red tomatoes and - the lavatory at the bottom of the garden! We were astonished by the lavatory which was operated merely by sitting on a wooden bench with a hole strategically placed over a pit that had chemicals sprinkled into it to counteract the pungent aroma (rather unsuccessfully) and which was emptied once a week. Peg would probably say, trust you for remembering that bit! Mrs Fry looked after us very well and we couldn't wait for meal times as there was always beautifully cooked home grown produce and certainly more than enough to satisfy our enormous appetites.

It was unfortunate that Mavis and I had to walk 2½ miles to the village school and about midway was a large Army camp. Not that we were ever accosted or approached in any way, but as I inadvertently mentioned this fact in a letter to home, my father decided that the long walk unescorted with winter darkness just around the corner was taking unnecessary risks.

The joy of going home and seeing Mum and Dad again is something I have never forgotten. In a dramatic situation such as the evacuation of children, the focus is obviously the children themselves, but now, as a mother and grandmother, I can feel pain for the deprived parents, about whom little has been recorded.

It was, therefore, just two weeks after my sorrowful and scared departure from home that I returned to it, wonderfully happy and, knowing myself, probably a bit cocky as well. More drama was about to unfold, though. This was the 'Phony War' period and a false sense of security prevailed so that Christmas was spent happily. In January 1940, despite my mother's reluctance to part with me once again, it was arranged that I should go to a family in Exeter (of all places) as it seemed to be a fairly safe spot as far as bombing was concerned. And once again I was tearfully delivered to a new home. At first I settled down well enough, but it gradually came about that I became an outsider, receiving less and less as time went on. I was hungry and miserable and very, very homesick for my dear Mum and Dad. As my letters home were always censored they were entirely unaware of my plight and I could think of no way to let them know. Until, that is, the evening when I had written my weekly letter and had it inspected by my new guardian and a providential knock at the front door took her out of the sitting room. Providence also arranged that she had got as far as folding the letter and putting it in the envelope, but as yet it was not stuck down. With the quickness born out of desperation, I tore a small fragment of paper from a book and scribbled 'I hate it here', and poked it into the envelope, seconds before she returned. I was terrified that she might forget she had read the letter or that the scrap might drop out on to the carpet before sticking down the envelope, but luck was with me and I breathed again.

It says much for the Royal Mail, especially in wartime, that the letter was posted that evening and the very next day my loving father was standing on the doorstep. There were no recriminations; he simply said that my mother was missing me and so he had come to take me home. Laughing and crying I shoved my clothes into a suitcase, said 'Thank you' (at Dad's instigation) and 'Goodbye' to my hostess, and together we sped hand in hand to the station. Years later I learned that when Mum had opened the letter the little piece of paper had fluttered to the floor. Picking it up and reading 'I hate it here' caused her to scream 'GO AND GET THAT CHILD AT ONCE, HAROLD!' with the above blessed results. It occurs to me that fifty years later it takes very much longer to get anything done – what's gone wrong?

So much for attempt No. 2 at 'being safe'. Shaken by the sight of their daughter really looking 'delicate' this time, they abandoned the whole idea of evacuation as far as I was concerned. Roy had settled very happily into his new country home so that there was no question of disturbing his education by bringing him home. I missed him, of course, but was so grateful that I had escaped the clutches of the Exeter family that this was something I could easily bear.

Not long after my rescue, I surprised my mother on arrival home from curtailed school time (lack of teachers during war-time) by announcing, 'I am one of the chosen five and you must come to school and see Miss Kitson, the Headmistress.'

I can almost hear Peg laughing at this as she accuses me of being over-dramatic!

'Whatever is the child on about?' asked my bemused mother.

'God knows!' said Dad. 'You'll have to go and find out.'

The events that followed this cryptic bit of conversation had a momentous effect on my childhood and, I feel sure, shaped my future. This is what happened. My mother duly went to see Miss Kitson to find out what on earth her daffy offspring was so smug about, and discovered to her considerable amazement that I had indeed been selected along with four other children to be evacuated to a boarding school in the Mansion House at Clarendon Park, near Salisbury, subject to my parents' approval.

Slightly punch-drunk by this incredible offer and taking my previous track record into account, they talked long into the night, weighing the pros and cons. It appeared to be a marvellous opportunity; the boarding school had fifty-six children from London and my own town; the area was certainly much safer than home; I would be accompanied by four friends; and supervision would probably be of a high standard. Really, it was an opportunity not to be equalled and the following day we all three agreed that I should go.

This third time of leaving my loved ones was high-spirited and full of excitement for me. The Exeter nightmare had receded into the background and I doubt whether I spared much thought for my parents missing and worrying about me. The great day to leave came eventually and we five little girls left home to experience a life quite unlike anything we could have imagined.

The boarding school was in a multi-acre estate owned by the immensely rich Mrs Christie-Miller and her family. Her husband had died some years before and her sons were all away on active service. Her daughters and daughter-in-law lived with her in the mansion along with their children, of whom we became slightly envious as they had governesses, ponies and puppies. Mr Dunstan, the Headmaster, and his wife were in over-all charge of all the evacuee children with the diligent assistance of Miss Murdock and Mr Smith, the two teachers. There were four or five helpers – lovely plump ladies who reminded us all of our mothers – and that comprised the school team. We lived over the stables and kennels which had housed the estate grooms and their families pre-war: in addition to the horses and dogs, of course. The head gardener's bungalow was made available for the five eldest girls and the five youngest boys: a system that sounds odd but worked very well.

The lessons took place in the library at the mansion and in our recreation room; there were usually three or four per day, plus good old religious instruction which was given by the priest from Alderbury Church. Mr Dunstan was a deeply religious man which meant that we had lots of contact with the village church and in fact I was confirmed at Alderbury Church by the Bishop of Salisbury in 1941. All the older children were members of the choir and – this must have been quite a sight – all fifty-six children with teachers and helpers formed a crocodile two abreast, and wound the long, long walk to the Church every Sunday.

It must have been a massive operation feeding this perpetually hungry brood. We were all at the age when it is impossible to feel full up and satisfied for more than a few minutes, but this was war time and food rationing was in force. We started the day with an enormous dollop of porridge, cooked in the Big House and delivered by the cooks in a great metal pan. Looking back, I see that we were well nourished really, with rabbit stew once a week, plenty of fruit and vegetables, and the infamous and stodgy rice pudding which surely must have lined our stomachs with a cement-like coating! Hunger always overcame hatred of this awful dish and we all survived and grew. A bright spot in our lives was our Tuck Tins and once per day a whistle blew once for 'Girls' Tuck' and twice for 'Boys' Tuck'. How wonderful a sweet tasted then. It was a strict rule that all sweets sent from home had to be shared and as there were fifty-six of us, it was not often that we were actually sucking our own sweets. I was particularly unfortunate in this respect as I had an uncle in the Merchant Navy who used to send me exotic goodies from America and I rarely managed to get my hot little hands on even one.

Another welcome whistle signal was one blast for Girls' Free Time and two for Boys'. This meant that we tumbled outside to play and had free range of the drives and the playing field. We were also allowed to use the shrubbery with its many trees. One particular tree, known as Taryam's Tree, was a favourite of the boys and by the time we left Clarendon it was completely bare from much misuse and had to be pulled down. Still, it probably saved the lives of the other trees and perhaps should have been called the Sacrificial Tree.

Being one of the older girls I lived in the bungalow and was allocated a dear little boy of five to chaperone. I was charged to listen to his prayers at bed time, make sure he washed behind his ears and bath him once a week; sometimes I wonder where he is now and if he is embarrassed by the thought of a strange older girl sploshing him heartily with a sponge all over! Another ritual that we had strictly to adhere to was marking the chart with a tick that hung on the back of the lavatory door every time we had a poop. This was a pretty neat method of keeping tabs on the internal goings-on of fifty-six children and should have received an award for ingenuity and efficiency, I feel.

Christmas at Clarendon. Just writing these words starts a sort of belated excitement and a few pangs of nostalgia and I wish every child could have such glorious memories of childhood Christmases. Nowadays Christmas begins at the end of August for buying cards and ends dead on Christmas Eve after the stores have closed to make way for travel brochures. We were deeply involved in carol singing, Nativity plays, parents' visits, and an invitation by Mrs Christie-Miller to the library where, upon her instructions, the highest Christmas tree on the estate had been felled and now stood decorated and stacked with our presents. These were sent in advance by our families and the pile grew as high as our expectations. My dear Mum had made me an enormous stocking in which she had sacrificed a whole month's ration of sweets, oranges that she had queued for for four hours, and many lovely little things that would have been close to a little girl's heart. We also had roasted chestnuts which we (the girls, that is) tucked up our knicker legs to eat later when cosy in bed.

It was during the first Christmas at Clarendon that a new and thrilling dimension unfolded for me: I landed the plum role of the Angel Gabriel in the Nativity play. What bliss! It was as if I'd waited all my life for this momentous event and I learned my few lines so thoroughly that I can accurately remember them now. I suspect that the actual performance presented to our families may have been more funny than serious, though at the time we Artistes assumed that the tears in the audience were due to raw emotion, not mirth. It was probably a mix of both, coupled with relief that we all looked so well and happy. The success of the Nativity play obviously went to my head as 'Theatre' dominated all my spare thinking time and I became a producer. Lots more bliss! My first production was 'Snow White and the Seven Dwarfs', the second was 'The Wizard of Oz' and the last a musical. Naturally I cast myself in the starring role in each, being the obvious choice – but also because one doesn't argue with the star or the producer, and so I could do exactly as I wished with the cast, artistically speaking of course. Just to hear one of the tunes from the shows I produced so ably wafts me instantly back across the years to Clarendon and my companions, and I have to brush away a silly tear and blow my nose heartily.

Every child joined the Brownies, Scouts or Guides, which were taken very seriously. Our leader was Lady Betty from a neighbouring castle, doing her bit for the war effort. The Brownies and Guides were most envious of the Scouts who had 'adventures' and did what looked like dangerous things while we were taught the more mundane skills of cooking over an open fire and tying strange knots.

The long summer holidays were magical. We had plenty of freedom and our help was enlisted by the estate farmers to weed ragwort, harvest potatoes and pick fruit. I suppose it was a good idea to let the children loose in acres of warm and luscious blackcurrants, etc., but we certainly augmented our usual meals with a vengeance, thereby pencilling an alarming increase in ticks on the lavatory door list. Not surprising, really, as I remember cupping both hands to scoop up blackcurrants and the purple juice that ran down my greedy little chin. We weren't very keen on the bean crop, however; they had to be shelled for drying which was quite arduous and besides, they were no good for eating and that made all the difference. By the end of the summer we were as brown as berries and very fit owing to working outdoors and the vast amount of illicit and delicious fruit. We were also allowed to have picnics and were sent off on each one with a parcel of sandwiches that always proved to be door-stop outsides and gruesome beetroot inside. Nevertheless, awful or not, we ate them while grumbling, in an effort to fill that bottomless pit. Just think of it – fifty-six bottomless pits to be catered for; what a Herculean task and how well the cooks provided for us despite those horrible picnic sandwiches!

The awful mechanics of war hadn't touched us as we lived a fair distance from any town and the authorities saw no need for air raid shelters, though they did insist upon dug-outs to be covered with sheep hurdles. These were used once only when a German fighter must have spotted our Sunday crocodile and maybe mistaken us for troops. We scattered in fright from the drive and into the shrubbery and while we were doing that a friendly Spitfire or Hurricane shot the swine so severely that he crash-landed by the Alderbury Gate. Once the fright was over we were wildly excited and rushed about trying to find spent cartridge cases before being quickly rounded up by the adults who then ushered us into the dug-outs. The boys loved this, but for the girls it was the worst part of the whole affair as there might have been worms or spiders lurking in the depths. I have since wondered why these dug-outs were on the beautiful front lawns of the mansion and if they ever got back to smooth green sward after the war.

The main drive, called the Main Drive, was 2½ miles long and flanked with beech, elm and chestnut trees that glowed with warm orange, yellow and browny shades in the autumn. Half-way down the Drive stood a thatched cottage that we called Snow White's house. This was the residence of the estate gamekeeper and, complete with bee hives, looked perfect to our town-accustomed eyes. In the spring the Drive came alive with millions of daffodils under the trees and looked delightful to us. Wild strawberry time in early summer was very popular as they were large, sweet, and so plentiful. And then, if winter obliged us with some snow, another wonderland was ours; one might say that the Main Drive was an all-seasons source of pleasure to us all, each providing its particular delight. We loved the treasure trails that our teachers would lay for us, sometimes extending about five miles. The 'treasures' weren't worth much but finding them was beyond price and we were usually mighty tired by the time we got back to base and kicked off our muddy wellies and struggled out of raincoats. We were so lucky.

Every so often Mrs Christie-Miller would hold a party for important people and on these occasions we were charged to stay indoors. Nevertheless, we derived much excitement from watching the great limousines sweep around the drive in front of the Big House, especially when we spotted such notables as David Niven and Sarah Churchill. When the children of the House (Sarah, Nicholas, Henrietta, Camilla, and a set of twins) had a birthday party we also had to keep out of sight while watching the young guests arrive accompanied by Nanny or Nurse in sumptuous cars. We were so impressed as we watched open-mouthed and amazed and, funnily enough, it didn't occur to us to be jealous in our awe of this other species of mankind.

And so time went on pleasantly; school exams had to be faced and, if possible, passed, which we mostly did; our physical health was robust to a degree and our spirits certainly high. All experiences end eventually and in 1942 the older children began to drift back to their home towns. I was no exception, and though it was good to be back home, I found I was just a little homesick for Clarendon and missed the bustle and rumpus of everyday routines. It was strange, suddenly living without my vast family, the kind teachers and their helpers and - Lavinia in particular - pined for the rarified atmosphere of living (even if slightly humble compared with the Big House) on this superb estate.

I recently attended the first reunion of the Clarendon Girls and Boys and we all had a tremendous wallow in nostalgia. It was made even better by the presence of our old headmaster, Mr Dunstan, then aged ninety-four and only a little fragile. He recognised many of us and remarked:

'You are all beautiful, but not quite as beautiful as you were in 1940.'

Looking around at our middle-aged faces I could see what he meant!

CHAPTER 2

My home town was subjected to many terrible bombing and fire bomb raids that killed thousands of its citizens and destroyed whole streets and areas. Because there was so much suffering we received several visits from Their Majesties King George and Queen Elizabeth who walked calmly through the rubble and smoking ruins to comfort those that had lost maybe everything. Their presence and concern was deeply appreciated by the townsfolk and did much to stiffen backbones and keep chins up in the midst of chaos and horror. So used were we to spotting Their Majesties that on one occasion when my parents were walking through a badly bombed road to visit my grandmother they inadvertently caused a stir amongst a group of small children. My father was dressed in Naval uniform and my mother wore a rather nice dress, coat and hat, all in blue, and to their intense amusement the children cried, 'Ooh look! There's the King and Queen.' Responding to this greeting with gracious smiles and dignified waves, they walked sedately on until they reached the next corner where it was safe to have a good laugh unobserved. It so happened that Gran had run out of tea and Mum drew the short straw that meant she was the one to go to the nearby shop and replenish stores. The small children were obviously dismayed to see 'The Queen' without her husband and called anxiously, 'Where's the King, where's the King?' With kindly smile and great courtesy she replied, 'He is having a cup of tea,' in a newly acquired genteel and refeened voice which, apparently, allayed their fears enough to enable them to get on with the serious business of play. Fortunately they didn't appear to notice that 'The Queen' was carrying a packet of tea, otherwise questions might well have been asked!

My dear father died when he was forty-two years of age and, upon my return from Clarendon Park, the Admiralty took it upon themselves to finance my further education. This was undertaken at a local Commercial College which was of a Catholic persuasion and opened my eyes to many things that I hadn't realised existed. Firstly, I very quickly learned to respect utterly the Roman Catholic belief – it probably appealed to my taste for drama – and I mingled with some extremely interesting people, including a friend who was a classical pianist and a truly beautiful young Jewess. The

Lavinia part of me was in her element mixing with these exciting new people and, of course, I joined in and tried to be exciting myself. I don't suppose I succeeded for a moment. What on earth a young Jewess was doing in a Roman Catholic College, I have no idea, but perhaps all barriers were down in war time. Secondly, and much more important than firstly, I discovered boys. Not brother-type boys, you understand, but ones that gave me funny looks and went all silly. However, I must have applied my mind to studying despite the distractions, as I passed the necessary examinations and was 'finished off' at a very well thought of Secretarial College. I have much to thank the Admiralty for, and in a way it was a legacy from my father. I wonder, do they look after their bereaved families as well today as they did when we needed help? I do hope so.

The Secretarial College was the main source of well-trained secretaries and shorthand-typists locally, and a newly fledged but untried young business lady was offered the amazing sum of £1 5s.0d. in return for a 5½ day working week. Students were well rehearsed on how to present themselves at interviews by the College and it was dimmed into our dizzy heads that this was the *Gateway to a Career* and should be taken very seriously. Consequently, I attended many an interview clad in a neat grey suit, with hat, gloves and handbag in matching colours and - if available - silk stockings. Usually they were, as my Merchant Navy uncle was still crossing the Atlantic and nearly always turned up trumps with a pair at the last minute. Good old Uncle Harry, even if they were of a bright ginger hue.

My very first job through the 'Gateway' didn't really require matching accessories. My boss was a very kind builder who did all in his power to make me feel at home but the work was so boring and dead-endish that I decided before long that I would try another 'Gateway' interview. And, anyway, I disliked working on my own and missed the chatter and companionship of other girls. Out came the suit, etc., and off I went to a furniture store where the management were so impressed that I procured Job No. 2. This was much better as I had six other girls to work with and time sped merrily by.

I met a girl at Commercial College who was very good looking and built on Amazonian lines. Of course she was very popular with boys, and as she and I became friends, it followed that we two girls would shortly be approached by two boys when displaying our charms for their benefit. It never failed; two boys sidling up to us, one handsome and strapping who couldn't take his eyes off Barbara's generous figure, and one shorter than me with homely looks. I offer no prizes for guessing who got which on every occasion. Not that I minded all that much because she was such a magnet and, let's face it, I had far more fun with Barbara's rejects that I would have done if left to my own resources. Besides that, we were really fond of each other and it didn't matter too much that I was small of bust and had skinny legs while she resembled Jane Russell.

As we were at that remarkably silly age, we spent hours in front of the mirror experimenting with the cheaper brands of cosmetics and fell violently in love with every boy that looked at us for about a week. When that particular romance bit the dust we repaired to a beach shelter to cry and sing the hits of the day in mournful voices. Favourites included ' Embrace me, my sweet embraceable you', 'Long ago and far away', and 'I paid for the lie I told you'. It strikes me now that any passer-by should have been convulsed with laughter or thought perhaps we were being murdered, but it was the meat and drink of life and we enjoyed every moment. During the caterwauling sessions we kept a sharp eye open for any likely lads heaving into view and, if they appeared, dabbed another layer of lipstick on our already brilliant lips and, in my case, hastily adjusted the hankies I had stuffed into my bra. In spite of these early mini-frolics we were incredibly innocent. We vaguely knew what sex was about and guarded our virginity with our lives, mostly because we wouldn't have dared to go home and confront our mothers afterwards. To be fair, none of our boy friends pushed us too far as they seemed to be just as ignorant as we were and probably scared by not knowing how to do it, apart from not daring to go home afterwards, like us! A today's child of five appears to know more about the facts of life than we did as teenagers; I rather wonder which is best.

Being very nearly flat chested at the early teens stage, I was more than a little jealous of Barbara's magnificent big boobs and stuffed hankies in the small bra that I insisted upon wearing. While this padding made me look slightly more interesting to the boys, it wasn't entirely satisfactory as occasionally it would slip out of one cup or the other, leaving a rather odd profile that must have puzzled my would-be admirers. Another cause for a twinge of jealousy was a contemporary who had very nicely rounded breasts and walked along with her chest stuck out for further effect. I was much cheered one day when I observed (to my delight) that she was suffering from the same fate as me with the slipping hankies and was hurrying to the toilet with bowed shoulders and one caved in breast. It later transpired (under grilling) that she craftily used bread rolls in her bra and I was furious that I hadn't thought of that. Funnily enough, it didn't occur to me to enquire just where and when the bread roll had tumbled out of her dress and probably bounced on the ground – so much more embarrassing than a genteel hankie fluttering like a butterfly to the floor. She would have been hard put for a plausible explanation of the unmoored bread roll, so that's okay!

While this growing up process was happening, I began to notice a boy of about my own age who lived in a nearby street. Like all the others he tended to hang around street corners with his friends and do a little showing off, like posing while straddled across a stationary bike. Once he treated me to a piercing wolf whistle which made my legs wobble and my hair to toss haughtily while pretending that I didn't even acknowledge his existence. I was definitely interested though, and secretly thrilled to his dark eyes and merry face.

Barbara and I discovered a new meeting venue that was considerably warmer than wandering along the roads and seafront. This was a pin table room and there were boys aplenty to meet and flirt with. One evening, however, a group of young lads came in which included my wolf whistling hero. His appearance had changed rather; instead of sloppily straddling his bike on a street corner, he moved confidently into the throng and commanded attention. The reason for this was because he was wearing an off-white trench coat, a green polo-necked jumper and a large brown trilby hat. His eyes were slitted in the approved Humphrey Bogart fashion and he tried hard to keep up a slight sneer at us lesser mortals. I was instantly smitten with love everlasting, followed by the terrible thought, 'Supposing Barbara wants him! No, no, she mustn't!' I knew I didn't stand the remotest chance if she too was bowled over by the glamorous newcomer and my elated heart sank without trace. As it happened she was about six inches taller than Humphrey, even with the trilby, and the first faint flicker of interest faded from her eyes and he was mine. This is literally true as we later married, had children and then grandchildren. Isn't that romantic and doesn't it make your heart want to sing?

While my free time was so absorbing I was getting restless in the furniture store and decided to sponge and press my 'Gateway' suit for when the opportunity presented itself. This happened fairly soon when I spotted an advertisement requiring a junior shorthand/typist-cum-cashier at a local building society. Not in the least like the huge concerns of today, this one was housed in an ordinary private dwelling in a pleasant street. It was nice and homely and I was delighted when the manager told me I'd got the job. It was hard work, which I like, and my colleagues were all helpful and friendly and we were soon the best of comrades. As my romance with the Humphrey Bogart look-alike, called Roy, was making heady progress, life, I reckoned, was pretty good.

There was great excitement when it became known that HRH Princess Margaret would be visiting our town and would actually be driven past our premises, and even more when we were asked if we would like to decorate the front of the house in her honour. Gosh, would we! The decorations consisted of miles of bunting that had been stored for years in some obscure corner and looked more suitable for a funeral than a joyous visit by a member of the Royal Family, so my friend Jean and I volunteered to stay behind one evening to give it a good old wash in the bathroom. Jean nicked her mother's packet of a new-to-the-market washing powder and I borrowed my mother's iron, and we couldn't wait for the office to close so that we could get started on the grubby old rags. At long last the front door closed on the last member of staff not concerned with this important project and the pantomime could begin.

Having filled the bath with hot water, tipped a goodly quantity of washing powder in and swished it about, we bundled the bunting into the suds and retired to the kitchen to make beans on toast and a pot of tea. All the gas fires were going full blast and chairs arranged for us to dry our laundry. My desk was covered with towels in readiness for ironing – and here I should mention that the desk was a brand new one and much envied by my colleagues who had to put up with grotty old bashed-about ones – and then, feeling rather virtuous and holy, we enjoyed our supper.

Rather later than intended we went, barelegged and shoeless, to the bathroom to tread the suds and bunting in the bath. No problems at this stage. It may have been that we trod suds a little too enthusiastically or maybe we didn't understand these new-fangled detergent powders and put too much into the bath, but in the midst of jumping up and down and giggling we were surprised by a fast rising tide of bubbles that threatened to overwhelm us. Horrified and a little frightened by this strange phenomenon, we scooped buckets full of bubbles and shook them into the toilet, pulled the chain which made fountains, screeched in panic and tried hopelessly to shovel back the foam into the bath as it cascaded over the sides. It was beyond understanding; the more we rinsed them away the more appeared, and we feared the whole house would be set in a jelly of bubbles, to say nothing of two shorthand/typists-cum-cashiers. There was only one thing to do: have hysterics and then get on with it. Suppose one of the bosses came back to see how we were getting on! That thought caused more wild shrieks of laughter and then we settled down to the near impossible task of restoring the bubble-filled bathroom to something approaching normal. In desperation we tried the newly invented theory of 'bubble-disposal-by-urine' but all that achieved was revoltingly yellow streaks mingling with the pristine white quivering mountain. We did win eventually, but it took two hours and even then we left it rather damp (but smelling pretty) with little heaps of bubbles peeking coyly from behind the loo and in all the corners.

Right, that was Stage 1. Stage 2 was the drying part but we had no time for that and went straight on to Stage 3 – the ironing. The kitchen soon looked like a steamy swamp as we battled away, but after what seemed hours the bunting was hanging over the chairs to dry. Exhausted and with a weak cry of triumph, I whipped the soggy towels off the desk top – along with the top layer of varnish. This was the last straw and I was certain I'd get the sack. The jolly jape had turned into a horror story and the tears rolled down my cheeks. Jean said.

'Don't worry, Vená. If we put the filing basket here, and the typewriter here, and these papers here, and the pen and pencil thing here, it won't show.'

She added reassuringly that she would bring her mother's special furniture polish so that we could do a quick repair job. With this consoling thought we put the damp office to bed and staggered home.

We were back again very, very early the next morning and hastily applied the magic solution. Nothing happened. We tried some more, and still nothing happened. Feeling frantic, we rubbed on brown sauce, strong black coffee, tea and shoe polish, and it looked much the same and also smelt funny. As 9.00 a.m. was fast approaching we had no alternative but to replace the typewriter, etc. and try to look composed. At last something worked as no-one noticed the strange desk top and we were congratulated on the good job we had done on the dampish bunting. I only hope that Her Royal Highness took note of the fluttering and brighter decorations that welcomed her to our town. My God, it was hard and dangerous work!

Some months later (and I should have known better) Jean and I were involved in another little scrape. Millions of insurance notices had to be sent out and this again meant that we would be working in the evenings as we had volunteered our services, strictly for the extra money that would be most welcome. Beans on toast and tea was the menu once more, and having filled the inner man, we set about filling the out tray. Gradually the massive pile in the in tray shrank while we worked and chattered and at last it was empty. Hooray, we thought, not noticing that time had sped faster than we gave it credit for, and decided that as we'd been such good girls we would wander home past our shopping centre and see what we should spend our overtime money on. This also took longer than anticipated and was further extended by a visit to the coffee shop to round the evening off.

While we were enjoying our silly selves, there was great consternation at our respective homes. Having been given an approximate time of return that evening, both families became a little anxious after we were overdue to the tune of about an hour, and when two hours had elapsed our mothers became slightly frantic. Jean's father was a Special Constable and was more aware of the awful things that might have happened to us, and so, after phoning our office and receiving no reply, he immediately got in touch with the police and reported us missing. Having taken this drastic step he then called at our house to inform my mother and also to see if, as he hoped, we had arrived in the interim. No luck there, so he tried to cheer my mother up by saying that no-one in their right senses would want to kidnap two incredibly daft girls like Jean and Vená, and made matters much worse. Roy (alias Humphrey Bogart) unexpectedly called in to see me and was rather alarmed at all the uproar, but before he could escape was detailed to walk with Jean's father in the direction of the office just in case we really were on our way home.

At that precise moment they heard my key click in the lock and in I walked, all smiling and happy, until I saw their faces and thought someone must have died, or worse. Of course, Jean and I were sorry to have worried our parents so much, but this was mixed with a little resentment that, while we hadn't done anything actually bad, we were still in the wrong, and that rankled. However, we all simmered down after a while, the police search was called off, and we were forgiven for being thoughtless. I understand now how they must have felt but didn't entirely then, and it's far too late to say, 'Sorry, Mum.'

My mother was in the process of clearing Naughty Gran's house and found a small length of very thick and beautiful black satin. 'Aha!' she thought, 'I won't throw this away, Vená might like it.' I was seventeen at the time, and the day of the bikini was dawning, ousting the more conventional and sedate one-piece swim suit. My eyes must have lit up when Mum handed it to me because my brain had already manufactured it into the most gorgeous black bikini and had moulded it over my equally gorgeous vital statistics of 32-20-36. A bikini of black satin – Wow! That would make the boys stare and turn the girls' complexions to a delicate shade of green; two birds with one stone – Wow again!

The old Singer sewing machine was dragged forth from its lair in the cupboard under the stairs and with Mum's help very soon produced a minute and sophisticated two-piece. Mum even supplied some knicker elastic recycled from a pair of Naughty Gran's passion killers, for safety's sake. I think she had a few reservations about her daughter appearing in public dressed in such scanty wear, but she was wise enough to keep a still tongue and confine her misgivings to a doubtful glance when she thought I wasn't looking. We were both surprised by the transformation brought about by putting on the bikini. One minute Vená was stripping off rather ordinary under-garments and the next a glamorous stranger was slinkily showing off around the bedroom and amazing her mother. You will know by now that most of the time I am modest by nature, but I have to admit that Clark Gable would have had a hard time choosing between me and Rita Hayworth. All I needed now was a nice hot day so that I could round up all the friends within reach, especially my boy-friend Roy Bartlett, and go to the long sandy beach on Hayling Island. Eventually one did materialise at a week-end and we all set off on our bicycles, singing our fool heads off as we went. I allowed no slacking and chivvied the stragglers unmercifully. They must have wondered what on earth had got into me as I was usually the Tail-end Charlie in group activities. They were shortly to find out!

We arrived like a flock of starlings, swooping out of nowhere and filling the air with excited chatter and teenage laughter. I had decided to play it cool and allowed my female friends to expose themselves in ruched-elastic swim suits or that very serviceable and modest one-piece that also had a little skirt for the very shy. Now was my moment and I slowly removed my blouse and skirt for maximum effect. It was a sensation. Not that anyone actually said anything. All eyes were fastened on my hitherto discreetly covered form and I distinctly heard gasps of admiration (or it may have been amazement) while I was trying to give the impression that all this was pretty old hat to me and nothing out of the ordinary at all.

Perhaps I succeeded too well, because one of my girl friends (grr!) suggested that we go for a dip - probably to get me hidden as soon as possible. We dashed across the damp sands, splashing through warm pools left by the last high tide, and then flew into the lazily lapping and shallow sea. We had a wonderful time larking and swimming and jumping and then I remembered it was show off time again.

'I'm going in now to do some sun bathing,' I yelled, hoping everyone would admire and envy the rear view of my retreat, and added some wiggles for good measure. A sense of misgiving invaded my smug well-being as I heard giggling and then positive shrieks of laughter, and turning round I saw all my friends in various stages of collapse and all pointing at the lower half of my bikini. Admittedly it had felt a trifle odd as, swaggering and swaying, I emerged from the water with a weight that swayed of its own accord and seemed to be quite independent of the rest of me. What I hadn't realised was that the thickness of the satin and Naughty Gran's ferocious knicker elastic had trapped a goodly portion of sea water and I must have looked like a pregnant duck. What a comedown for Black Bikini Highflier! There was only one thing to do: nonchalantly pull it to one side and let about five gallons of water return to its natural habitat. I tried hard to continue a don't-care saunter and retain my dignity, but, Boy, it was difficult. One very important lesson was learned that afternoon, and that was that the B.S.B. was for sunbathing only in future!

Roy was due to be called up to do his National Service and had chosen the RAF. This was torture for both of us and we wondered how we were going to survive the next two years. This dire happening precipitated arrangements to get engaged and, to give us something to look forward to, we decided that the most suitable date would be during his first leave period which was due at Christmas.

Naturally I hadn't seen Roy in uniform and had sorrowfully waved goodbye to a rather thin and anxious young man in familiar clothes. And here I was at Christmas, waiting for him on the station platform with my stomach in knots and a heart that pounded, scanning the windows of the train as it pulled into the station. I couldn't see him anywhere and was beginning to feel sick when a door burst open, accompanied by a very loud 'Yahoo!' and suddenly there he was - a great butterball in Air Force blue. What a terrible transformation. I couldn't believe that this chubby fellow was the same person I'd waved goodbye to just a few months ago. What had they done to him? Exercised and fed him to twice his normal size, that's what they'd done. However, love conquers all, and we had a most touching reunion and the next day he bought my engagement ring. It cost £12 0s.0d. which, before you start to laugh, was roughly a month's salary. The engagement ceremony took place that afternoon in a café where, behind a teapot, Roy slipped this most precious emblem on the third finger of my left hand (much to the delight of two elderly ladies sitting at the next table).

To celebrate this momentous occasion we went dancing that evening and had to run the gauntlet of ribald remarks from our friends. Most of the comments were too rude to repeat, of course, but living on Cloud Nine is a wonderful experience and so we forgave them and put it all down to jealousy and showing off - a thing we'd never have dreamed of doing. Having been promoted to our new and important 'Engaged' status, we immediately made plans for our wedding which was to take place in two and a half years when Roy would be discharged from the RAF and we would both reach the grand old age of twenty-one. This gave us both an incentive to save as hard as we could, and God knows we had little enough to spare, but in a strange way this added spice to our (nearly) continuous efforts to build our nest.

Roy took his bicycle back to camp with him so that he could telephone me from the nearest phone box, which was a good two miles from his quarters. One evening when Mum and I were busily sewing away a knock came at the front door. I answered it and found an elderly gentleman standing on the doorstep. He enquired politely:

'Are you Miss Godfrey?'

'Yes, that's right.'

He went on to explain that he had been walking past our nearest phone box and heard it ring. Curious, he picked up the receiver and a young man asked him if he would be kind enough to take a message to his fiancée.

'My dear,' he said, 'He would like you to ring him at 8.30 when he will be waiting at his phone box.'

I was touched by his kindness and thanked him profusely, while he raised his hat and, smiling, walked off into the winter gloom. 'Dear old chap,' I thought, and having lipsticked my cultivated pout, followed in his footsteps on winged feet to speak to my beloved. An elderly Cupid, would you think? I expect it was the 'winged feet' that prompted that pretty notion!

Despite our anguish at being parted initially and subsequently at the end of Roy's leave periods, those two and a half years passed very quickly and, almost before we knew it, he thankfully left the RAF and shortly after, on 30 June 1951, we were married.

CHAPTER 3

Naughty Gran must have had considerable charm in her youth as she was snapped up and married to a Naval officer, son of a very respectable family. In rapid succession they produced five children, two girls and three boys, with my mother, Norah, being the eldest. It is possible, I suppose, that Naughty Gran got fed up to the back teeth with all these pregnancies and inconveniences, because she packed a suitcase, plonked a hat on her head and walked out of the door, never to return. Complete consternation reigned because in those days wives didn't do things like that – well, not often, anyway. What to do with all these children was the first and obvious priority. Norah herself was still quite a child at this dramatic time, but with help from the paternal grandparents, managed somehow to keep the household intact. Initially the three boys had been taken by the Local Authority and installed in a boys' home at Hayling Island, but then my indignant and dear Great-Gran stepped in, demanding, successfully, the return of them to the motherless family. It has occurred to me that the whole of my mother's life was spent looking after various generations of her family, right from a tender age when she should have been able to enjoy her own childhood. But between them, Great-Gran and Norah brought up the four children well and, most important, with love.

When Norah reached the time judged ripe for employment, she joined the considerable workforce in the local corset factory that later also employed her sister Edna – at this time little more than a babe. Surprisingly, Naughty Gran reappeared and rented a house in the town. Was this good news or bad news? they wondered. A bit of both, really, because Norah was having accommodation problems and so, rather reluctantly, went to live with her mother for a while with little Edna, while the boys stayed with Great-Gran.

Norah had been saving hard to buy her first new dress for a special occasion and then joyfully brought it home and hung it carefully in her wardrobe. All day at work she counted the hours and minutes until she could put it on and be the belle of the ball that evening. At long last she was released and flew indoors, savouring the magic moment of seeing her new and beautiful dress awaiting her pleasure. What she found instead was an empty hanger from which dangled a pawn ticket. It is difficult to imagine

Norah's feelings at that moment, apart from the blinding realisation that Naughty Gran had struck again and that there were probably a couple of empty gin bottles on the mantlepiece by now, as she only ever laughed when recounting this tale to her family, and we laughed with her. Now I could cry for her – made worse by that soppy Peg sniffling and blowing her nose heartily when told this humorous tale! As a bitter afterthought, I discovered that Norah herself redeemed the dress, and that would have meant many more weeks of savings from her scanty pay packet.

One of Norah's uncles was a Naval officer and when she was nineteen he invited her to a dance at the Royal Naval Barracks. Judging from all the old photographs in the family album, she was a lovely young girl, so it was not surprising that she was in demand that evening by young unattached (and maybe attached, for all I know) Navy personnel. There was one in particular that she was drawn to and he couldn't take his eyes off her for a single moment. His name was Harold Godfrey and was a Physical Training instructor. These two didn't let the grass grow under their feet; they married a year later and the following year my brother Roy was born. That must have given them food for thought, as it was a further six years before Great-Gran and the midwife delivered me in the daffodil-filled bedroom.

Norah seems to have been at her happiest when surrounded by as many as possible of her family. Her three brothers regarded her and Harold's house as their second home (what a good job there was no poll tax), sure of a genuine welcome and a good meal. I fear Vená/Lavinia was spoiled to death and that all this male attention went to her silly little head, but, Oh, how I did enjoy it.

Norah survived the Second World War but Harold did not. She became a widow at the age of thirty-eight with a twelve-year-old daughter and an eighteen-year-old son to provide for. She was never quite the same ever again. Though she had a large family to keep her thoughts and fingers occupied, she had lost the love of her life and nothing can compensate for that.

She lived to see both children married and had four grandsons to cosset and spoil. She also continued to cosset my husband Roy and myself outrageously when we lived in her house in our early days of marriage. I was able to redress some of the balance when, almost twenty years later, she became so very ill and spent her last days in our home. Norah, dear Norah, I miss you still.

Naughty Gran's other daughter, Edna, was sixteen when I was born. She had obviously inherited some of her mother's eccentric ways but in compensation was loving, generous, and definitely full of fun. The only thing that Naughty Gran was full of was booze which brought on an urge to sing, and dance on pub tables.

Edna and my mother were very close and thoroughly enjoyed a girly get-together, but my father, who was slightly Victorian in his outlook, took a pretty dim view of this frivolous young girl and sometimes made his feelings known. It seems he was particularly concerned that if the small Vená spent too much time in her company she would turn into a 'painted hussy' and that would never do! In my childish eyes Edna was really beautiful with wide apart large eyes and a retroussé nose. If you can imagine a fair-haired Vivien Leigh with a cheeky expression instead of a soulful one, this is my memory of her youthful years. I would sit and watch her apply make-up, brush her corrugated waves into smooth swells, and make little kiss-curls along her forehead with tongs that had been heated in the old Albert Range fire. I was utterly fascinated by this exotic member of our family, despite my father's disapproval (or because of it), and would howl mournfully each time she departed after a week-end visit.

If Sunday mornings were fine she would take me in my push-chair to the Army Barracks to listen to the brass band and flirt with any and all of the young bandsmen who flocked around my push-chair after the performance. For a long time I thought it was me that they were interested in as I was plied with sweeties, but with the wisdom that comes with age, realise that this was just a cunning plan designed to entrap my beautiful aunt. She did, in fact, fall in love with one handsome young fellow and he with her, which meant that the main supply of sweeties dried up at source, which was a shame. However, for Edna it was a different story. She glowed and bloomed and they started saving for their marriage while my mother helped her compile her 'bottom drawer'.

Perhaps Edna was too exciting to be considered suitable as an addition to her lover's family as their disapproval was as strong as my father's and, it seems, he did not have the strength of mind to stand up to them and sweep Edna off her feet into a virtual runaway wedding. As reinforcement, the family had long ago selected another girl as an odds-on favourite in the marriage stakes, and as it was easier all round to comply with family pressures, he did just that, leaving a devastated Edna in their wake. She vowed that she would never marry, and so far as we know, has not.

Until the Second World War broke out, Edna was a machinist at the local corset factory, and though it took some time to recover her high spirits after her love affair had terminated so miserably, she presented a bright face to the outside world and did her crying at home. The war prompted her to move to London where she was employed in munitions. This was really the work of a man and involved extremely heavy machinery but she coped admirably, regaining her love of fun, and made many new friends. From all accounts she wasn't short of boy friends in the least but seems to have shied away from any serious encounter, preferring to be lighthearted with a group of friends rather than to risk further heartache. Like Naughty Gran she loved to dance and sing (though not on a table) and was a wow at dressing up and entertaining her colleagues during their short lunch breaks. Her favourite costume was two saucepan lids to cover her boobs, pyjama trousers, and a chiffon headsquare as a yaskmak, for her Harem Girl act. This sense of theatre must run in the family what with Naughty Gran, Aunt Edna, myself doing a pretty good imitation of Marlene Dietrich, and now one of my sons who tries his hand at any old thing.

One day there was a bad accident in the munition works and a large piece of metal flew across the workshop and became embedded in Edna's neck. I don't really know how badly she was injured, but certainly it was sufficient to warrant compensation. Anyone other than Edna - except the likes of me - would have been prudent and saved the money for a rainy day, but, being Edna, as soon as she felt better she blew the whole lot on new clothes and recovered very quickly as a result. It just goes to show that one man's meat is another woman's tonic, if you will forgive me.

Around this time she was visiting us at least every three weeks; Mum and I looked forward to her visits so much and drooped after her departure. There was so much laughter in our house, though my mother was rather shocked by her 'bad' language.

'Well!' she informed us, 'I work like a man, so I smoke, drink and bloody well swear like a man, why not?'

As my father had died some years before, his restraining influence was missing and so Edna behaved exactly as she wanted. Pure delight would flood my show-off little soul when Edna allowed me to wear some of her rather daring outfits and, on reflection, I must have looked rather like a mini lady of the night. I knew very well that my mother did not approve of this at all but went ahead anyway - more 'theatre' I expect.

Digs in London at that time were awful beyond description, according to Edna, and she moved at fairly regular intervals in an effort to find something that was even faintly habitable. She declined to return to her home town, nevertheless, as she had so many friends and ties in London by then that I imagine it would have felt tame and dull by comparison, even though we dangled the carrot of a comfortable home in front of her.

One day she had the great good fortune to be looking in a newsagent's window at the precise moment he was putting in a card that requested a lodger. She immediately applied and was accepted. Here her life changed beyond recognition and Edna became almost another person. She went to live with an elderly couple called Mary and Fred. Fred was huge and gentle and had once been a Grenadier Guard, but was now bent with age and probably snuff sniffing. Mary was very ill and required much nursing. It hadn't been suggested that Edna should undertake any obligations but she instantly loved them both and they loved her, and she spent her free time looking after Mary until her death. Fred, by this time, was getting frail himself and she took on the role of the daughter he had never had, sometimes bringing him to see us for a visit. Edna was still full of fun, as was Fred, and we enjoyed having them to stay with us.

After Fred's death Edna was permitted to take over the tenancy of the council house, where she has remained to this day. She doesn't visit us and has never encouraged us to visit her. We occasionally send letters but there is never a reply and even her Christmas card is now conspicuous by its absence. I fear she has grown into a lonely and strange old lady who has no wish to be reminded of her vivid youth and long gone beauty, and I feel sad for a moment until I remember something funny that she said or did and then I can't help smiling.

CHAPTER 4

The sun streaming through my bedroom window brought me rapidly from a deep sleep into a startled realisation that this was Saturday, 30 June 1951. Blinking in the strong light, my gaze was drawn to a long white veil with the head-dress of mother-of-pearl orange blossom attached in readiness. Alongside this filmy creation, and also hanging from the picture rail, was THE DRESS complete with small train, and my heart skipped a couple of beats. In my eyes, nothing in the world was as beautiful as THE DRESS which was made from figured satin and had a 'sweetheart' neckline and long sleeves – to say nothing of the hundreds of material-covered buttons that poor someone would have painstakingly to fiddle with to trap me inside. This was to be its second public appearance as I had bought it from a friend, earnestly hoping that I would look as mystically beautiful as she had on her wedding day.

Fully intending to be spoiled rotten all day, I sat in the garden and communed with nature while my mother fluttered around and ran my bath. Nature suddenly had to take care of herself as an avalanche of cards and letters poured through the letter box and required my urgent attention. It was quite amazing just how many friends, family and acquaintances were wishing Roy and me a happy life together. The next excitement was the arrival of my friends Mary and Jean who were to be my 'big' bridesmaids and we screamed with laughter at silly jokes until Mum reminded us that as the wedding was at 11.00 a.m., we didn't have a lot of time for nonsense. This gentle nudge precipitated the girls in the direction of Roy's house to collect the little Pauline who was to be my 'small' bridesmaid, while Mum and I set about the deadly serious business of trying to transform me into the most beautiful bride that ever walked up an aisle. That took quite a bit of doing and before we had quite accomplished this feat the girls returned with Pauline. They reported that Roy was tense and very red in the face and that his mother had just scorched his wedding shirt. Although that alarming information should have induced mild panic, all it did was to make us go into fits of laughter and I had to repair my recently applied make-up.

Pauline's hair had been subjected to curly-rags the previous evening and I daresay the poor child had spent an uncomfortable night, but when we had dressed her in the little Kate Greenaway dress the curly-rags were removed and with shiny thick ringlets formed round our fingers, carefully pulled down beneath her poke bonnet, she looked delightful. A bit too delightful, I thought, and likely to divert attention from the bride! To proclaim my virginity to the whole world we were all dressed in white, though I have never been able to convince my grown-up sons that I went to the altar in pristine and untried condition: disbelieving and cynical tykes that they are.

Lavinia probably had a hand in the choice of flowers for the bouquet, as I fancied gardenias and set the florist tutting rather, because they would have to be sent from London and then it wasn't certain that any could be found. However, when the taxi arrived with the back seat awash with flowers and twiddly bits, there they were, amid sweet peas and lily-of-the-valley, and proves conclusively that it does no harm to aim high if you can afford it – which I couldn't; perhaps that was why the bridesmaids had to make do with posies of sweet peas which, I hasten to add, looked extremely pretty.

Well, at last it was time to climb carefully into the car and, accompanied by my brother Roy who was gratefully giving me away, I drove serenely away to take part in a ceremony that would alter my life. The church, which many people in this city think should have been chosen to be the cathedral, is magnificent and has an aisle long enough to satisfy even me. And you can bet your bottom dollar that I made the most of every stately step! At what seemed miles away I could see Roy standing and waiting for me, which was a considerable relief to the approaching bride and quickened my steps in case he felt like making a run for it. Fortunately he had no such notion and turned and smiled at me. He looked quite unlike my usual gipsy lad, now resplendent in the new eighteen-guinea suit (an absolute fortune) and no sign of a scorch on his shirt, thank God.

Throughout all the preparations prior to 'The Day', there had been only one niggling worry and that was because Naughty Gran had been tracked down and had consented to be a guest. The family rallied round to keep her off gin and found slightly more respectable looking clothes for her to wear. She behaved very nicely in church and we all fervently hoped it would continue at the reception but didn't have a lot of faith in this, what with all the sherry, etc., that was bound to come her way. My dear mother had saved so hard to be able to give us a reception that we would never forget and had chosen a rather grand restaurant. The last thing she wanted was for Naughty Gran to climb on a table to dance and show off her drawers. Consequently my mother was frequently heard hissing to the male members of this merry gathering:

'Keep an eye on her and don't give her another drink, whatever you do!'

Actually, apart from tucking into the ham salad before the soup had arrived, she didn't put a foot wrong, and I have a feeling that she was probably among the better behaved section of the party. All wedding receptions get noisier and - polite way of putting it - less inhibited as they progress, and this one was no exception. A friend of Roy and his mother had a small band (a Group in today's language) and they entertained us with jolly numbers throughout the wedding breakfast and then the bride, bridegroom and the best man mounted the stage and sang, 'There ain't nobody here but us chickens' to a surprised audience, after which decorum sort of deteriorated, rather. Mind you, the restaurant staff seemed really to enjoy this function; I imagine it was quite a nice change from their usual bookings. We certainly enjoyed it and I can still hear my dear Mum's slightly tearful voice requesting, 'Please play "Good luck, good health, God bless you",' amongst the more ribald suggestions and I can't remember if it ever did get played. I hope so.

My mother had arranged for the restaurant to be decorated with plants and flowers and at the end of the reception our family and friends piled them into taxis and followed Roy and me to the Station. Our honeymoon plan was to stay overnight in a hotel in Salisbury before travelling on to Cornwall the following day, so when the Salisbury train drew in they hastily transferred the foliage and flowers into a carriage, daubed the window with suitable messages, pelted us with confetti, and off we went. We had booked into a lovely old inn and were delighted to see dishes of cockles displayed on the bar counter. Boy, were they good! I suppose we were hungry after all that food, drink, wedding cake, etc., to say nothing of all the excitement, and it was just to keep us going until dinner was served.

In 1951 and in my state of virginity, my married and/or experienced friends had warned me to cover the sheets with bath towels and be prepared for 'it' to hurt. I began to feel very nervous and suspect that Roy did also and apart from 'it' looming over us, there was no lock on our bedroom door, which did nothing to put us at ease. Matters, however, were taken out of our hands when we became conscious of a lot of racket going on outside in the corridor and, taking a peep through the door, discovered that boisterous members of a cycling club were taking up residence next door. They didn't settle down so neither did we, and off we went to Fowey next morning still virgins and pure as the driven snow!

Here our luck changed rapidly. We stayed on a farm near Fowey and the lady of the house told us that the bed in our room was two hundred years old and Roy said that was how old he felt when getting out of it the next morning. Also, we were lighthearted because we'd found out that there isn't too much to get worried about concerning 'it' and after the practice run, it's a doddle. It was a beautiful honeymoon, spent walking, swimming, and trying not to go to bed before everyone else as we were keeping our new marital status a secret. I'm not quite sure where we went wrong, but on our last evening a lovely home-baked cake was presented to us with good wishes from all for a very happy life together. And two tarnished but glowing newly-weds returned home with heads buzzing with happiness.

Then, as now, it was a near impossibility to start married life in a home of your very own, even though the prices of yesterday sound ludicrously cheap. It was all relative really, as wages were so low that many young couples were compelled to live with their families. We were no exception and my dear mother gladly let us have two rooms for ourselves. In return for our kindness in accepting her generous offer, she did our washing and shopping, and had a lovely cooked meal ready and waiting for us when we returned from work. No wonder Roy and I were so content with our lot, it was the life of Riley, and believe it or not, Mum was happy. We were very proud of our first furniture, even if the bedroom suite did have Utility marks stamped on it. Truly, it is not a case of sour grapes, but it does seem to me that the newly-weds today start marriage practically fully furnished, complete with electronic twiddly-boos and don't know the real thrill of saving hard and then getting whatever it is, and in a way it's a shame. Maybe distance has lent enchantment to the view, who can tell?

My mother was rather puzzled one morning when she went into our bedroom and found my side of the bed neatly made and Roy's generous half looking like a haystack that had been struck by lightning. 'What on earth . . .' she wondered, and buttonholed me as I came through the front door after work. I have a slightly mercurial nature and had completely forgotten taking revenge upon Roy for being so mean to me and picking a row earlier in the day, so that I couldn't think what she was talking about.

'Come with me,' she commanded. 'I've never seen such a mess.'

Together we mounted the stairs while I wondered what the matter was. The moment she flung open our bedroom door memory couldn't but help come flooding back and the extraordinary sight had us laughing helplessly and clutching our sides. Hastily we made the bed properly so that Roy would never know how silly I'd been. He did, of course, as Mum and I snorted once or twice when trying to repress giggles and he demanded to know what the joke was. Fortunately he laughed with us.

After a while and much saving up we bought a scooter and are given to believe that we were the very first to own a Lambretta in the district and obviously set a trend, as before long we encountered more and more. This being so, we helped to form a club called 'The Jolly Rogers' and thereby entered a whole new and exciting time. We made many new friends and had lots of fun at rallies, picnics and the like, and as it was all things Italian at that time, I rode side-saddle on the passenger seat and tried hard to look like Gina or Sophia. I can't think I succeeded very well as these goddesses were very sophisticated and even my best friend would have to admit that I could never be described thus. The trouble is that I quickly dissolve into paroxysms of laughter and rend the air rather noisily and I simply can't imagine Sophia or Gina having to mop up tears of mirth; perhaps I'm wrong and they are only showing off.

In 1956 we became the proud (and cocky) owners of a sports model Lambretta and decided to make our way to Italy via France and Switzerland. My mother thought we were mad, especially when we were ready to leave, and I must admit we must have looked a fearsome sight - two daffy people, duffle bag strapped on the running board, two panniers and a rucksack at the back, all topped with a Union Jack fluttering bravely above our heads. Scooterised gypsies thoroughly enjoying themselves. It was all surprisingly easy and we made our way through France on my schoolgirl French and through Switzerland on schoolgirl English, stopping nightly at modest accommodation and picnicking on huge chunks of local bread and cheese.

We had started our adventure on a hot, steamy and stormy day, and this was the way it continued, except that the further south we got the more scorching and humid it became. The RAC had provided us with a route that took us through flat and monotonous French countryside and then precipitated us definitely upwards and downwards in Switzerland. I was petrified with fright when Roy was negotiating the Simplon Pass with its horrendous sheer drops and got shouted at for leaning at an angle of 45° into the road side and, hopefully, away from the abyss and eternity. Occasionally we were caught in tremendous thunderstorms where there was no shelter, which meant that we were soaked literally to the skin. As it was so hot our clothes didn't take long to dry but Roy's shoes stubbornly refused to stop squelching and dripping until we found out that the remedy was to hang them by the laces and let them flap in the breeze as we drove along. Our over-loaded scooter went like a dream, but we did get stared at (in disbelief, no doubt) by the village and small town inhabitants as we roared by surrounded by packages with Roy's dangling shoes and bare feet. We exchanged cheery waves and greetings, so we couldn't have been too bad an advertisement for the barmy British!

Our first-born was conceived on this holiday. Quite naturally we were the butt of many good natured quips from our friends when they discovered this amazing fact, and blamed the spaghetti, the vino and the sultry nights. Actually, it happened on the one day we didn't travel owing to a ferocious storm and had seemed a good way to pass the time until it stopped raining. A very fertile storm, that!

Nature has a way of deciding events. We had been married nearly six years and were thinking that perhaps it was time seriously to consider increasing the world's population by one or two, and now all the shilly-shallying was stopped and we were being pitchforked into parenthood. We were delighted, my dear mother was over the moon, and the rest of our families were mighty pleased and slapping themselves on the back. As an aunt of Roy said, 'A reproduction of Roy and Vená would be wonderful.'

I wouldn't go so far as that, but he's not bad, as it turns out! During pregnancy I grew enormous and was fit, happy and never sick.

'How lucky you are,' said my mother. 'Keep thinking happy thoughts and when the time comes just do everything they tell you.'

This homely advice worked pretty well and Robert Bruce was born on 8 May 1957 with no fuss whatsoever.

So another vital change in my life took place. Most of it sounds very boring but, as a brand new mother, I was engrossed, besotted and absolutely sickening. We attended baby clinics every Tuesday afternoon, strolled around our lovely small lake to give young Robert some fresh air and met friends similarly occupied. Our offspring was a fat little porker with Roy's dark hair and merry grin, and we thought he was probably the best baby in the world. My mother knitted so many clothes for him that there was no possibility of him ever wearing them out and, as we had gone mad and bought the most gorgeous high pram, we felt we owned the best looking, best dressed and best prammed baby in the town - which we did, of course.

It was necessary for financial reasons that I returned to work part time, which further delighted my mother as in one fell swoop she got rid of me for part of the day and gained a whole baby. When Robert was 2½ years old we had another lovely son, named David Godfrey, this time without the assistance of a thunderstorm, and he was even heavier than the first: placid and happy, and so were we.

Shortly after David was born, I was to experience one of the saddest times of my life. The first dreadful happening was the death of a very close friend who was killed in a car accident in Spain, and within weeks we lost yet another very dear friend in childbirth. As if this wasn't enough suffering, Fate had another sword up her sleeve and we were devastated when my wonderful little mother died after months of awful suffering. With a lively toddler and a new baby to contend with it was obviously physically very difficult to nurse her at home, but we managed somehow and I am everlastingly grateful that she spent her last days at home with her beloved family. The extreme pain of losing her seeped through the relief that her anguish was at an end and was difficult to bear. Throughout my entire life she had succoured and supported me with so much love that, at first, it was inconceivable that she wouldn't be with Roy and me to watch our children grow and, equally painful, they wouldn't really remember her. I was forced to grow up fast at this time and learn to live without her; missing her kind and gentle presence has not really diminished, even after all these years.

CHAPTER 5

'Mum - why don't you have another baby?'
We were all in bed one Sunday morning, little boys bouncing on the end of the bed, Roy reading the Sunday paper, while I was just lying there admiring our small sons.

'I've already explained, Robert. We can't afford another baby.'

'But you said it doesn't cost anything to have a baby - you know, when you told us how babies are made.'

'Yes, but it costs money to buy another pram, another cot, and all the clothes and things.'

A long, long pause, and then:

'Well, I think it's because Dad is too embarrassed to do it.'

The Sunday paper shook slightly and a quiet voice said:

'Oh no. He's embarrassed if he doesn't do it!'

This, of course, is what happens when one has tried hard to be open and frank with the children and then have to go around with crossed fingers in case they say something outrageous and not suitable for public ears. Even I have been guilty of causing two faces to turn scarlet, of all places, on the top of a bus.

I was three years old and had obviously been listening to the adults' conversation at home when Aunty Lilly had a boy friend, now known as Uncle Ern. They both thought it would be nice to take dear little Vená for a ride on top of a bus and dear little Vená thought so too. I must have found the conversation lacking in oomph because I suddenly announced in a very shrill pipe:

'Uncle Ern's got his new teef in!'

Chortles circulated the top deck (and probably the lower one as well) to the discomfiture of the lovers and I found myself bundled off at the next bus stop none too gently with my small hand gripped tightly by Uncle Ern's big hurty one. I am happy to disclose that their tender romance survived in spite of my assistance, but I was never asked to accompany them again - ever!

On the other hand, these two lads have supplied us with many a good laugh. For instance, David, home after his very first day at school, pounced upon by me, anxious to know if all had gone well, answered my string of questions with:

'Well, Mummy, there was a salvation lying on the crinc-cronc under the miranda.'

His older brother translated:

'He means an Alsatian dog lying on the concrete under the veranda!'

I honestly prefer the former; it's so picturesque.

It was David also that was overheard asking for a box of 'stand-up fireworks' in our local small shop and who on another occasion told a sort of joke and then finished it off with 'Every one's a Jim!'

Being virtuous, Roy and I have always encouraged the boys to indulge in sporty activities, but there was one afternoon when we bitterly regretted our devotion to duty. We, plus a largish group of friends, organised a game of friendly football in a field at Selsey. The female contingent of the party watched from the side lines while the males, dads and sons, amazed us with their energy (I can't say skill) charging about after the blow-up football. All was going well until one of the dads crashed to the ground and gave an agonised yell. We rushed to the scene of the accident and found that he was quite badly injured as his foot was now at right angles to his ankle with a piece of bone sticking out. His wife and I sped a good half mile to the nearest phone box to call an ambulance and then, at a slightly slower pace, made our way back to the impromptu football pitch. The ambulance arrived at more or less the same time as ourselves and we saw the poor injured footballer being carefully stowed inside and then he and the ambulance disappeared in a cloud of dust.

Naturally we were all looking white and a bit sick and had decided to blow the whistle on this ill-fated game when, to our intense horror, a second scream rang out from where our son Robert was standing. Fearing the worst, we flew to his side.

'Whatever's the matter, Robert?' I screamed in fright.

'Oh! Mummeeee,' he wailed with great tears running down his cheeks, 'Now the rotten football's gone down.'

He escaped sudden death by a whisker and tremendous self-control.

I have to confess that their parents are slightly less than perfect and an incident that occurred prior to the enlargement of our family illustrates this well. I expect you will remember the famous 'Cod War' of some years ago; well, we had a slightly shorter one called 'The War of the Winkles'.

Saturday tea times were always special and we celebrated the week-end by having either winkles or cockles with lots of new crusty bread and butter. This weekly event was usually good humoured and much enjoyed, but on this particular occasion one or both of us must have been out of sorts. Everything prepared, I took a very large dish of winkles into the sitting room and carolled, 'Tea time, Roy.'

'Where's the pin?' asked my dear husband, one eye on the television.

'I'm just getting you one, you lazy toad,' I replied, sweetly.

I rummaged around looking for a large one unsuccessfully and settled for a small one that had just pricked my finger.

'Here you are.'

'What do you call that?' indignantly from Roy.

I considered it from all angles and then said, 'A pin.'

'It's not long enough.'

'Oh! Is that so? Get one yourself then.' Bad temper is very contagious.

This last retort galvanised Roy into a quite unwarranted rage and he picked up the coffee table and hurled it down with such force that the dish and winkles went high in the air and showered over the room with a terrible rattle. Even after the majority had landed, there continued the odd 'plink' and 'plonk' as some rolled off furniture to join their friends on the floor. Stunned silence ensued for a moment or two and then Roy said, 'I suppose I'd better pick them up,' in a very meek voice, and spent the next hour crawling around on hands and knees, sniffing out his tea. As with all our spats, we burst out laughing, found longer pins and then settled down to a slightly dusty but delicious supper, as it was a bit too late to call it tea.

Sundays were also nice, as well as rather busy for both of us, and on one particular Sunday morning the boys were playing happily in the garden, Roy had his head under the bonnet of the car trying to find out why it wouldn't go, and I had been engaged in the kitchen cooking the lunch and doing some washing – at the same time, isn't that clever? Having got as far as rinsing and spinning the sheets, I risked putting them on the garden clothes line despite a high wind that was threatening to turn into a gale. This accomplished, I was just about to baste the roasting joint when a huge gust of wind whipped one of the sheets off my line, turned it into a spinnaker as it sailed over the fence and deposited it, quite neatly, on to my neighbour's clothes line. It was amazing. Then I rushed out to tell Roy who absentmindedly withdrew his head from the bowels of the car, said 'Oh?' vaguely, and disappeared from view once more.

My reaction was just as unreasonable as Roy's winkle war. 'Ho!' I thought angrily, and stormed back into the kitchen, switched the oven off, put my coat on, and walked out. Having taken this extreme step I had no real option but to carry on. After all, how silly I would look tippy-toeing up the garden path, hoping Roy's head would be firmly jammed in between the valves or whatever it was, and besides, I was still furious, but not sure why. So I stomped crossly along cold and windy roads, muttering, 'The rotten sod!' and 'He doesn't care about me, the rat!' until I felt very sorry for myself indeed. In fact, I'd worked myself up into such a paddy that any stray sane thought was quickly suppressed and replaced by more acrimony. However, after a long while, when chilled to the marrow and with legs aching from miles of jerky walking, the angry fire ceased smouldering within my breast and I wanted to go home.

Meanwhile, back at the homestead, no-one had missed me until sensing that it must be near lunchtime and wondering why the usual Sunday call, 'Five minutes, boys, to wash your hands. Hurry up!' hadn't been heard and – even worse – why no roast beef aroma was wafting down the path. There was no sign of me in the kitchen, nor anywhere in the house, and they were just beginning to wonder if I had been spirited away when I came in the back door. Utterly bemused by these strange events, we all stared at one another, speechless and embarrassed. To ease the situation I rattled pans about and switched the oven on again and told Roy I would explain later, after lunch. It was a rather quiet meal and every time I looked up I found one or the other looking at me guardedly and we were terribly polite all the while, most unnerving.

Frankly, I didn't have any idea of what I was going to say to Roy, so I started off by saying:

'I say, Roy, do you remember the time when you threw all those winkles up in . . .' and was interrupted by:

'Good God! You didn't walk out because of the winkles, did you? That was years ago.'

This struck me as being so funny that I felt the laughter welling up, couldn't control it, and we ended up guffawing madly and clutching our sides. As for the kids, well, they already knew they'd got some daft parents, so they joined in, politely at first, and then wholeheartedly, for the sheer joy of everyone being happy together.

There was also the time when Roy left home. This happened in the early days of our wedded bliss when we were still enjoying dear Mum's hospitality because we were too poor to do otherwise. He and I were having a fierce disagreement and it must have been pretty heated because he crashed his fist on the table and yelled:

'That's it, I've had enough. I'm leaving!'

Stony-faced, I heard him thunder up the stairs, crash about while throwing things into a travelling bag, re-thunder down the stairs and slam the front door behind him. Mum just about had time to say:

'Great Heavens, shouldn't you . . .' before we heard his key in the lock and his face peered round the door.

'I haven't got any money,' he announced. 'Will you lend me some?'

'No, I won't!!' I replied through prune-shaped lips.

'Oh, well, then,' he said (looking rather relieved), 'I can't go,' and that was the end of the matter, except for a good laugh, of course!

Way back in 1962, Civil Defence was taking on a new lease of life and, as I had been a member when Roy had been taken away from me so cruelly to do his National Service, I was obviously still on the membership list. I say 'obviously', because I was totally surprised to receive a visit from a Major who invited my family and me to take part in a Civil Defence Exercise in a small country town called Bishop's Waltham.

In view of the fact that it would be an exciting day out with a free lunch, we accepted his kind invitation and looked forward to it. The Major explained that upon arrival at the designated site we should become a 'distressed family' owing to being bombed and, therefore, homeless and not happy. A considerable understatement, I should think!

Anyway, off we set with our two small boys and found a most realistic mock-up of a bombed area. Wobbly half-buildings, smouldering fires, rubble everywhere, and even craters caused our eyes to pop a little from their moorings. Following directions, we reported to the First Aid Post and suffered nurses to make us look grimy and stick bits of plaster on various visible parts of our anatomies. Lucky old Roy was given a starring role and had (supposedly) fallen down what was left of our staircase and broken his arm. I still think Lavinia should have had this coveted part, especially as I was the only bona fide member and much better at acting than my husband, and besides, I would have enjoyed groaning and moaning with my arm in a sling.

The idea was that we should wander around this scene of devastation in a state of bomb shock, and perhaps Roy – and I have to admit he was pretty good – and I played our parts too enthusiastically, as poor little David's eyes filled with tears and his powerful lungs with air for a great bellow. We knew from past experience that he could keep up a penetrating protest for a long time and he didn't disappoint us. Still, it did add realism to the gruesome scene and, I'm sorry to say, a few glowers from other distressed families who weren't taking the exercise as seriously as they should have been.

Staggering around, we saw firemen saving lives, demolition workers saving lives, nurses saving lives and doctors saving lives. It was most impressive and ersatz blood flowed in great quantities over everything while, of course, David yelled even louder, if that were possible. Through the drifting smoke we caught a glimpse of the Major who galloped towards us and shouted over David's cries:

'Well, hello, Mrs Bartlett. How nice to see you . . .'

He stopped short at this point and then said in a voice full of concern:

'My goodness, Mr Bartlett, what have you been up to?'

Roy, who was obviously a better actor than I had given him credit for, replied:

'Oh, I fell down the stairs and broke my arm.'

The Major tutted commiseratingly.

'I am so sorry to hear that, Mr Bartlett. How good of you to still attend our exercise. Well, I must dash - lots to do. Nice to have seen you,' and disappeared in a puff of smoke.

Once he was out of earshot I just couldn't help one of my hearty laughs escaping, and Roy, joining in, caused David's yells to subside and a watery smile quivered about his soggy little face. By the time Roy and I had ourselves under control, the two small boys were jumping about in a most 'undistressed family' way, having decided that, okay, if that's what Mum and Dad think of as a fun day, we'd better humour them.

A little later we heard the welcome sound of a spoon banging a saucepan which meant that lunch was ready. The WVS had womanfully cooked a substantial and very nice concoction on outdoor stoves and we thankfully repaired to the roofless church with laden tin plates. As there was no sign of the Major, Roy removed his slipping head bandage and sling and tucked in gratefully; it's surprising how hungry distressed families can get.

Roy and I fully expected to hear from the Civil Defence after that event; you know, will you re-join, or when can Roy come to collect his medal for gallantry for serving his country with a broken arm, but, no, not a word from anyone. Let me see, 1962, well, that's thirty years ago so I don't suppose we will now. It's a good job we weren't holding our breath.

Yet another contentious affair took place when the boys were quite small, and this one is indelibly etched on my memory and I'm sure will never fade.

'Well, it's about time you *could* swim,' said Roy, in reply to my efforts to be excused from an excursion to the beach. 'Come on, lads - let's take Mum to the sea and teach her to swim,' knowing full well that if the boys were involved I wouldn't be able to wriggle out of it, the swine!

'Oh, goody, yes!' chorused the two very small boys, sensing yet another adventure with their daft mother.

'I've got just the thing in the shed that will help Mum,' Robert squeaked in excitement. 'Come on, David, let's find that black lorry tyre we saved from Cub Camp.'

Son No. 2 was getting equally fired up at the thought of a possibly interesting afternoon at my expense.

'Ooh, yes!' he agreed, and then rather hurtfully, 'That should be about the right size for Mum.' I could have killed him quite easily but, to my credit, resisted the temptation, though heaven knows why.

Picnic packed, beach gear bundled up (including the big black tyre), boys shoved into the back seat, and we were ready, if not all of us willing, to set forth for trial by water. 'Waggons roll,' screeched the younger members of the family from the back seat, incidentally causing GBH to the eardrums of their elders and betters in the front.

A long line of sea anglers stretched along the beach and we cleverly deduced that a competition was in progress and that we should have to stay well clear of the lines. Sea anglers take these occasions very seriously and have been known to get quite ratty if someone lights a fag and then has a nice clearing cough, in case it frightens the fish away, let alone if a family with strange black gear plonks itself right in the middle of the proceedings. We more or less tippy-toed through and around the 'Men-versus-Tiddler' gladiators and eventually found a largish and empty piece of beach on which to rest our weary bodies. But not for long, owing to restless and eager offspring. Reluctantly I donned my swimsuit and poked an exploratory toe into the Solent.

'My God!' (in a scream), 'It's icy and I can't possibly put my whole body in it - I shall die from hyperwhatsit.'

'Oh, come on, Mum,' from the two wet and rather blue younger generation, hopping about in the waves. 'We'll show you what to do and it's nice and warm when you get used to it.' I had grave doubts about the truthfulness of this statement but let it pass without comment.

'Look - put this tyre round your middle and we've tied a thick piece of rope to it and Dad will hold it on the beach and if he thinks you might be drowning he will pull you in.' All in one breath through chattering teeth and terribly unconvincing. However, in for a penny . . .

It was more than a little difficult to manoeuvre myself as the centre of a big black doughnut on the end of a piece of rope through the boisterous waves to deeper water, but at last my frozen feet paddled frantically to find the bottom and couldn't. Roy later recounted that, as far as he could see, all the anglers' heads were turned in my direction in open-mouthed amazement. I wasn't in the least surprised; I was open-mouthed in amazement myself at being talked into performing such a damfool caper; moreover, they and their lines seemed to be rather closer than when I first humped my way out to sea. It was unlikely that they were moving towards me, I reasoned, so I must be drifting down on the current. There was no need to panic; here I was, secure in the knowledge that I hadn't the least idea of how to swim yet, well out of my depth and encased precariously in a huge and wobbling black snake that had a mind of its own, and (best of all) my fate was in the hands of unreliable relatives. Also lurking at the back of my mind was the fear that should I accidentally foul the lines of the competitors, there would probably be a queue waiting for the chance to murder me.

A combination of waves and the bucking black snake altered my centre of gravity and precipitated my head smack into the next wave. Surfacing, I screamed as loudly as I could, convinced that I was about to drown, and my faraway husband started pulling the rope. From the shore came this comforting message:

'You're all right, Mum – just lie still.'

In a pig's eye! There is only one way to panic and that is not by lying still. I screamed when I could spit enough Solent out to do so and gurgled when I couldn't. Across the water floated another message: 'We'll help you, Dad. HANG ON, MUM!'

Unceremoniously I was heaved and pulled (still screaming when possible) until grounded and safe at last. Unfortunately, my dear family didn't leave it at that and come rushing down to their beached next of kin. Oh, no! I suppose the most charitable explanation is that they had forgotten I wasn't a dinghy and were making sure I was out of reach of the next high tide. The one that appeals to me more is that they are all as thick as two short planks, and is probably the correct one.

After a little floundering I managed to discard my extraordinary encumbrance and shakily got to my feet. Blood trickled down my arms and legs and mingled with bits of seaweed and that nasty sharp grit found on shingle beaches. I was suffering from an overdose of salty sea, shock, and (most likely) hyperwhatsit for good measure, but did I receive any sympathy or commendation for my bravery? Oh, no, again. In response to my very mild criticism of the way in which I had been treated, Roy positively yelled:

'Well, it's your own fault – fancy acting so stupid and making such a scene – and look at all the anglers laughing their heads off.'

Quite frankly, that was the very last thing I wanted to look at and consoled myself with an unspoken threat that went: 'Just you wait till we get home, Roy Bartlett, Robert Bartlett and David Bartlett!', and whose idea was it anyway that I should learn to swim – certainly not mine. As always, my thunder was stolen by a whine from Robert:

'Oh, Mum! You've gone and split my tyre!' and for the very life of me I couldn't help laughing.

CHAPTER 6

It is difficult to pinpoint when one phase of a lifetime ends and another takes its place; a kind of merging happens and before you know where you are, the little tykes have become big ones (but just as much trouble), Roy and I have become slightly more substantial weight-wise, and some dear ones have left us and others have joined. I tend to identify periods of time with different jobs, and the happiest time of my working career was undoubtedly the twelve years spent in the laboratory of our local hospital. There I made many friends, one of whom is Peg.

Just prior to joining the hospital staff, I was recovering from a very traumatic period of my life and decided that a change of employment would perk me up and make life bearable for Roy again - it certainly did that! It just happened that, taking my flagging courage in both hands, I tottered to the main office of the hospital to see if there were any vacancies going and a voice I knew well accosted me with:

'Oi! Vená! What are you doing here?'

I turned to the giver of this gracious greeting and, beholding a friend from our youthful days when we both belonged to the Young Wives Club, replied:

'Oh, Betty - how lovely to see you. I'm looking for a job.'

'Well I'm blowed!' (she's not so suave as me), 'There's a vacancy in the office where I work.' It must have been fate because the following Monday found me quaking slightly at a tatty old desk, learning the many complications of hospital routine.

After two years of very hard work and lots of laughs, a young lady joined the team. She was outstandingly beautiful and seventeen years of age. Enter Carly, and it was no wonder she was the successful candidate for the post because, apart from having lots of rotten qualifications, she was such a pleasure to gaze upon, and it would have been downright foolish not to have snapped her up before someone else did. The strange thing was that Carly was convinced that she was rather plain and she was certainly very shy - until I took her in hand, that is! As the rest of her colleagues ranged from 'Oh! My God!' to 'Not too bad', this was a bit incomprehensible to us, and we were constantly reassuring her that she wasn't quite as ugly as she feared, and that her inferiority complex wasn't a complex at all and it wasn't her fault that she was simply inferior. As for the male members of the department, well, they were all bowled over and (unheard of previously) became very gallant and considerate. Naturally, under all this kind and tender care, Carly blossomed and became even more lovely. If I were writing this description of anyone other than her, I should promptly be sick, but her sunny temperament precluded an upset stomach, and the wretched child had a keen sense of humour, and so with this finishing touch, we (reluctantly) conceded defeat and put up with her.

Despite the large age gap, Carly and I appeared to be kindred spirits and almost immediately became firm friends. Lunch-times usually coincided with a male colleague calling:

'Coming to the pub, Carly? Oh, bring Vená if you like.'

Somehow it reminded me of the Barbara/Vená relationship all those years ago. Oh, well, at least I know my station in life and I can't deny that a great deal of fun can be obtained from being second fiddle.

One of Carly's favourite stories concerns an incident when I was employed as the receptionist/typist in the blood taking clinic, known in the trade as 'Vená's Dracula Department'. We were never short of customers who waited more or less patiently to be deprived of their life's force for analysis and, being possessed of a kindly nature, I made a habit of trying to make our patients feel relaxed and loved. It was unfortunate on one particular day that a very sick and frightfully obese lady attended Vená's D.D. for a blood test and with great difficulty eased her way through the main door and then took her place in the seated queue. 'Hmm,' I thought. 'She's never going to squeeze all that and the walking frame through the smaller door into the nurse's room, I'd better help.' Brave words indeed. Gradually the line of patients diminished until at last it was my time to do my Angel of Mercy act. 'Come along, Mrs Hawker-Parker,' I said brightly. 'Leave your frame by your chair and just put all your weight on me - I'll take you in, don't worry.'

Trustingly, the dear soul did just that and we immediately landed in a truly massive heap on the floor. It was chaotic for a while with men patients struggling to get poor Mrs Hawker-Parker upright and rescue me from suffocation, but at last it was achieved and I was able to fill my starved lungs with a great gasp of air. Until this moment my concern had been solely for my charge's wellbeing but now I was in a more or less fit state to assess my own predicament. The first thing I noticed was that my white hospital coat was tucked up around the bosom area along with my dress, which meant, I reasoned, that my Aertex knickers and stocking tops would be on view to all and sundry. Carly was so proud of me. She thought it was marvellous that I didn't panic but just lay there laughing my silly head off. Little does she know that it was hysteria, and I shan't tell her. After a while I regained as much control as I could muster under the circumstances while a kindly gentleman approached me, saying:

'My dear, are you all right?'

This very nearly set me off again, as I had visions of my glamorous drawers and chubby legs inflaming his baser urges enough to make him chat me up. A little flight of fancy, you understand. I am given to understand this sorry story is passed on to new members of staff as a Terrible Warning not to over-estimate one's capabilities – especially where heavy patients are concerned.

I am Carly's senior by thirty years, and as you might imagine, I was very flattered to be invited to the many shindigs that the younger people had at, seemingly, the drop of a hat. I also have to confess that the usual method of invitation went thus:

'Carly, will you come to the party at (wherever it was) tonight (or whenever)? Oh, yes, you can bring Vená if you like.'

My long suffering husband invariably declined owing, no doubt, to a previous engagement, and regarded the laboratory staff as another species entirely. Generously, he always bade me to go and enjoy myself, which I did with great gusto and didn't mind his bossiness one little bit.

The most memorable party was our own. Roy and I decided to hold a thank-you party for the numerous invitations I'd received from my young colleagues and, full of Lavinia type enthusiasm, swept into the 'Plan' mode. As it fortuitously happened, two young lady technicians had just embarked on a Catering for Private Functions project, and, having completed a comprehensive catering course, were delighted to practise on our unsuspecting guests.

Seventy-five invitations were sent out and all were accepted. Roy and I had recently moved to a bungalow with, fortunately, a very large garden, and we decided to combine this bash with a house-warming. It had rained steadily and stormily throughout the day and we prayed that the weather would relent before evening time. It did – the storm clouds grew less and disappeared over the horizon and a full moon shone brightly on seventy-five guests, family, gatecrashers and our elder son's Rock Group complete with roadies. It was a bit of a squeeze but got very friendly; so that didn't matter. The food was superb and displayed very beautifully for about five minutes and then it was a matter of chance (if you had a long enough arm) what one's clutching little hand could grab through the ravening horde. Roy and I had provided a barrel of the most renowned and feared beer in Hampshire and guests had been asked to bring a bottle, so that what with all that food and about a hundred bottles of this and that, we looked set for a rare old evening. I had bought a special outfit for the occasion which was much admired, and I must admit I felt the admiration was completely warranted. Roy had been a little sniffy over my choice but soon came round when he heard the envious oohs and ahs and a treasured comment, 'Vená! How original.'

Robert's Group was set up on the patio and they were commanded not to play too loudly. Fifteen minutes later a policeman pounded on the door.

'Excuse me, Madam,' he said, eyeing my khaki combat shirt and warlike beret with some slight surprise. 'We have received a complaint from one of your neighbours. They say there is a very noisy teenage party going on at No. 11 and think the parents must be away.'

'Absolute nonsense!' I replied, hoping he wouldn't notice that I was having to shout. 'We are all respectable middle-aged ladies and gentlemen employed by the Health Authority, and my son's Group is playing a little background music.'

As the amplified reverberations came crashing from the patio via the front door, his expression changed from bewilderment to amusement.

He said, 'I see, Madam. Sorry to have bothered you. I'm off duty at 10.30 - all right to pop back?'

'Of course, officer, and do bring some friends,' accompanied by a beery kiss on his cheek and then a friendly goodbye wave.

I shall never know if he did or not, but we had no more official visits from the police that evening - at least, we didn't hear any!

It seemed to me that every time I turned round I tripped over a group of at least three doting males clustered around the vivacious Carly and thought, 'That girl will come to a bad end, I'd better do something to distract them - other than chucking a bucket of water over them.' A brilliant idea flashed through my befuddled head like a comet; of course, I will do my famous impression of Marlene Dietrich! Having at last attracted Robert's attention and been given the microphone, the patio stage was mine, after a louder than usual blast from the Group to announce my solo performance. I expect it went down well; I, at least, enjoyed it very much, quite forgetting that I wasn't wearing a slinky skirt and high heels. I don't really remember too much about it, to be honest. Roy, devastatingly hurtful with the truth, said later that he thought I looked more like Michael Heseltine out on a jolly in a tank than my idol Marlene.

The next morning as I was making my way groggily to the bus stop, I trod on a large jacket potato and wondered what on earth it was doing on the pavement and what a wicked waste of good food. And then I saw another, and another, and lots of bread rolls with unidentifiable bits attached. The horrid truth dawned slowly and I forced my aching eyes to confirm that this loathsome trail started at our own front gate and seemed to stretch on into infinity. Oh Lord, I thought tearfully, I'd hate to live next door to me. I shall have to apologise to all the neighbours and hope they forgive us.

As for the gruesome food trail, my young bleary-eyed colleagues were astonished that I hadn't been aware that a 'friendly' war game had taken place in the road. I took a very dim view of this behaviour because, after all, I was the one that was wearing combat gear, it was our bread and potatoes, and no-one had seen fit to invite me. I imagine that wretched Carly had declined to take part and so Vená wasn't asked!

Carly has grown into a beautiful young wife and mother who wouldn't dream of going to such parties now, I'm sure. Even though we dissolve into fits of laughter over the crazy times we shared, I really am finding it difficult to resurrect the flirtatious, silly, and chubby-legged young girl who inadvertently made such an impact on my social life. I suppose it is a case of goodbye Carly, and hello to the beautiful and competent Carole. They both have a special place in my heart.

CHAPTER 7

Floral Art is not so much a hobby as a raging passion and definitely Lavinia's territory. For many years I enjoyed fiddling about with flowers and trying, not entirely successfully, to create a complete picture and this, basically, is the difference between Floral Art and Flower Arranging. While employed at our local hospital laboratory I bulldozed a good friend and colleague to join me in enrolling for a course in this fascinating subject and we were privileged to be tutored by a very gifted lady.

The classes started in September and by October we were champing at the bit to compete in the Novices section in the Autumn Show at our Guildhall, knowing full well that this was a little ambitious, to say the least. We received a lot of help and encouragement from our tutor, who was kind enough to say she thought we stood a good chance of getting some sort of recognition from the Judge. Come to think, she may have meant 'Could do better – must try harder'! At last the great day arrived and I was in a fine old ferment and, most likely, rather hard to live with. However, from the moment I entered the hall where dozens of middle-aged ladies were purposefully dashing about and looking horribly capable, I was absolutely smitten. The atmosphere was electric with excitement; the smell of fresh flowers mingled with the sharper aroma of foliage, husbands hovered gingerly trying not to get in the way of their competing spouses (whose faces were getting rather flushed): all combined to lift me up on a great wave of euphoria.

'Oh! Ecstasy,' said Lavinia.

'Shut up and let's get on with it,' said Vená.

Our combined talents, or on this occasion lack of, resulted in no sort of recognition at all from the Judge, and while this was a little disappointing, it in no way detracted from the glamour of the competition. In fact, it spurred me on to consider entering the prestigious Southsea Show.

Our tutor commiserated with our lack of success but thought that a little salutary treatment at the outset wasn't a bad thing as nobody loves a cocky-ass, or words to that effect. The weeks passed pleasantly and every Tuesday the hospital gardens received a good but surreptitious pruning for the evening class and I responded to the excellent tuition like a daisy in the sunshine.

'Now,' said our tutor one Tuesday evening, 'How many of you ladies are interested in entering for the Southsea Show?'

No hand shot up faster than mine.

'Right. From now on we shall be practising hard.'

I might have complained bitterly if this had been work, but as it was all so interesting and satisfying, nobody noticed just how hard she was working on us. This is a little tip that I have copied since my student days and it works a treat!

The Southsea Show lasts for three days and is considered one of the finest and most popular events along the south coast. It also means that the floral creation has to withstand heat or cold, maybe wind, and the inevitable proddings from curious fingers, for a very long time. A bit of a challenge really, but despite a few butterflies in the tummy, I felt reasonably confident that I wouldn't disgrace my teacher, and Roy and I set off in an overloaded car to Southsea Common the evening before the Show opened. Roy had received so many instructions that he said he felt dizzy and might be sick.

'Nonsense!' said Lavinia briskly. 'Put your head between your knees for three seconds and then fill the flasks with tea.'

His reply was bordering on the pithy and both Lavinia and I have noticed that in times of stress he can be very vulgar.

Never shall I forget that evening. The Floral Marquee smelt so delicious as we entered, laden like two pack horses. It was akin to the Guildhall Show, but it was more pronounced and laced with tea and perfumed ladies. But there was no time for standing and sniffing; we were embroiled in the formalities, thankfully dumped a great mountain of greenery, carefully gave the flowers a long drink in buckets and soaked the Oasis. That accomplished, Lavinia and I took a deep breath, rolled our sleeves up, and set about creating a few masterpieces. Even though I was so absorbed, I became conscious that something was going on and raised my head to a listening position to find out what it was. Sniggering was going on, and, being a novice, my first thought was that my fellow competitors didn't think much of my work but then realised that it wasn't me at all that was causing rather snide amusement. From the corner of my eye I followed the general direction of their glances and pinpointed a rather nice looking lady busily engaged with her entry, and from the whispered remarks gathered that she was working in the wrong section. According to the rules of the competition this would have disqualified her with no arguments. I was further incensed to overhear that they weren't going to tell her about her mistake, and pointedly ignoring those mean spirited harpies among us, strode over and put the matter right. She was so grateful to be informed but, of course, it meant that she had to start from scratch as well as cart all the paraphernalia to her proper section, which didn't leave very much time to complete her entry. There were a couple of spin-offs from this nasty little situation, namely that I went back to my work spot feeling virtuous, which is good for the soul as well as the fingers, and that I was pleased to note that the culprits had the good grace to look embarrassed and ashamed. And so they should.

I hardly dared re-enter the marquee after the judging but a large shove in the middle of my back from Roy propelled my entrance rather more quickly than I would have wished. Together we made our way to my section – and I nearly fainted. Not one, not two, but *three* prizes, one of which bore the coveted white card with a red sticker that means a 'First'. For once both Lavinia and I were speechless and full of bliss. Roy and I hugged each other in our delight and we laughed like two silly children. Apart from the sheer joy of having won First Prize, this also meant that I was no longer a novice and could quite legitimately call myself a flower arranger, and that was even more blissful. It suddenly occurred to me to wonder how the wrong section lady had fared and we made our way through the excited (and some disappointed) contestants to her section. I recognised her arrangement and was delighted to see that she, too, had won a prize.

'Yah boo sucks!' said that vulgar Lavinia, while Vená fervently hoped that the would-be saboteurs did very badly. What a satisfying day!

I was rather curious to know why Roy was hovering around my arrangements for such a long time and it transpired that he had been listening to the comments of people viewing the exhibits, confessing that he was jolly proud of me. Knowing how difficult it is for Roy actually to spell out a compliment, I was immensely touched, realising that this was the highest possible praise. He was even more cock-a-hoop when several of his colleagues commented favourably at work and was obviously thrilled for me. I've discovered over the years that Roy is a funny old toughie with soft spots. So many of our friends and acquaintances were pleased with this amazing result that Lavinia began to get ideas above my station and accepted all sorts of commissions to do arrangements and, consequently, the hospital gardens became even more denuded of greenery. Naturally my friends at the laboratory were agog to hear about all the dramas and excitements that seemed to happen so frequently with my new preoccupation and I sensed a real interest to be involved. One or two said they would dearly love to have a go as it sounded so absorbing and funny – I may have exaggerated very slightly – but found the conventional times of Floral Art classes an impossibility.

'Vená,' said nice friend Katie, 'Why don't you take a class here if it can be arranged?'

Lavinia surfaced, brim full of enthusiasm, and in a short space of time had a gaggle of eager students and permission to use the canteen once a week immediately after work. I had put a notice on the board advertising the 'Floral Art' classes and some wag who should have had a smack round the ear added an 'F' in front of Art. This looked so funny that having had a good laugh, I decided to leave it as it lent a certain air and I would probably have the distinction of being the only Floral Fart tutor in the land.

I look back on those classes in the canteen with great affection. We had so much fun and despite all the time spent laughing, or maybe because of it, the girls were quick to learn and latent talent came bursting forth most satisfactorily. That is not to say that we didn't manage to have an occasional disaster, but that served the purpose of learning from mistakes and was always taken in good humour. At the end of each term I held a competition and was impressed by the high standard achieved. One of the nice things about this contest was that the entries were put on display for all the staff to see, which was appreciated and enjoyed. It is actually rather surprising just how many people are keenly interested in Floral Art (with or without an added 'F') and our class appeared to become quite famous in the hospital.

Approaching Christmas one year, we were asked if we would decorate the canteen and this little project was undertaken with such enthusiasm that Lavinia had to curb her crew as there was real danger than no-one would be able to get in the door, let alone have a meal. The hospital gardens suddenly looked bald while the canteen looked like the hospital gardens did before we started flower arranging. Still, after a bit of compromise and a distribution of greenery around the waiting rooms, etc., we were all satisfied it was perfect. Such a flurry of holly, candles, cones, pine branches, and anything we could get our hands on, it had been, and spiced with good friendship and shrieks of laughter. Best of all was that everyone loved it.

The canteen was also to be the venue for the Christmas party and we had been asked to provide half a dozen buxom wenches to serve the food. Lavinia reckoned that Vená was definitely buxom enough to qualify, so that left just five to be found. Not that there was a shortage of curvaceous ladies, it was just that some were more suited to becoming wenches than others. It's all in the mind, you know. Some, like that Peg, get all silly and shy, but anyway, she didn't score on either count. Before long, though, five volunteers were found to be suitable and we set about acquiring, loosely speaking, a sort of uniform. This was to be a white mob cap, a very low cut blouse, a long skirt, and a white pinny. I thought we all looked beautiful, especially those who could manage an impressive cleavage surrounded by upthrust bosom. Generally speaking, we were quite successful judging by the appreciative whistles and comments when we made our entrance, each carrying a tray of mince pies immediately beneath our heaving bosomage, and the party deteriorated from that moment on.

Suddenly there was consternation. One of my young ladies was missing and all that remained of her was her mob cap. And that, I am sad to relate, was floating forlornly in beer slops. It was a pitiful sight; one minute it had been pristine white and perky, beautifully designed and stitched by her poor mother, and the next it lay drowning in stale beer, stained and dishonoured. But where was its owner? Were we to be involved in a murder mystery, and if so, where was her battered and bloody body? These charming thoughts were bandied about in semi-alcoholic concern by those sober enough to think as clearly as this, until someone reported that she had last been seen disappearing into a caravan used by technicians when 'On Call'. At this point the proverbial veil will be drawn.

One other major project that Christmas was the enormous nativity scene on show at the laboratory for both patients and staff. Although many funny things happened during its construction the end result was rather beautiful, even if one or two angels were a little unconventional. It was indeed a proud moment for me when all was completed and a tape recorder was balanced (rather precariously) on a step-ladder behind drapes and belted out Christmas carols to one and all. A slight snag had manifested itself in the shape of the Baby Jesus. The angels had taken up so much of the white material that none was left for the poor baby who, unfortunately, ended up lying peacefully in his manger with a puce coloured face. Now I've encountered many a puce coloured babe in my time, but this one (being who He was) rather upset our Boss who relayed a message that, in his opinion, the Infant was too highly coloured and could we make Him paler? There was only one thing for it, one of the angels had to make do with a slightly shorter skirt but as she was tucked away at the back of the scene it didn't notice too much. The Baby Jesus from then on lay even more peacefully with a deathly white complexion and a rather holy smirk, and everyone was happy, including the Boss. I have made and supervised many nativity scenes since, especially during my years with the Education Department, but never have I enjoyed one as much as this, nor have I had to clutch my sides when laughter caused pain. Come to think, we don't usually go and look at a Crib to have a good laugh, do we?

In the flat period that strikes immediately after Christmas and the New Year, I cast around for ideas and came up with Bridal Flower Arranging. As this is intricate, demanding and fiddly, it more than filled the winter evenings with interest and a little swearing as well as the pure joy of getting the hang of it occasionally. Naturally my friends and colleagues received a daily bulletin and one tentatively offered the information that one of her young friends was getting married and couldn't afford the understandably high charges of a florist's shop. I (or Lavinia) jumped at this chance and excitedly said I would do them for the price of the flowers if the bride was prepared to take just the tiniest of chances. It must have been Lavinia shouting her mouth off, as Vená would never have dared! The bride-to-be was delighted and grateful and I was panic- and horror-struck. What had I done? I might very well ruin the great day in her life and she would never forgive me. Oh, God! As Vená had wilted into a quivering heap, the onus was now upon Lavinia and she can't always be trusted. However, we pulled ourself together and tried to look business-like and efficient to instil confidence and faith in our first non-paying client.

The night before the wedding I didn't go to bed. I sat and looked at the rose buds, daring them to open, drank lots of tea, and wished I were dead. As dawn broke I said a short prayer and, with fingers that trembled, manipulated rose wires and rose heads, stub wires, ribbons and gutta. I suddenly realised that I was humming a little song and that my hands were steady and I was enjoying myself.

'There you are!' said Lavinia. 'I knew I could do it - a piece of cake!'

A long time later the fruits of my night of agony lay on the table before me, dainty and bridal, and I thought perhaps I should take up praying professionally as it had worked so well.

Meanwhile, back in our bedroom, Roy, having enjoyed a good night's sleep and snore (the swine), tumbled drowsily out of bed and staggered downstairs to see how I was getting on. He was astonished to see that the kitchen table was awash with the bouquet, posies and button-holes, and that I was packing up all the gear required for this sort of caper.

'Good God!' he said kindly. 'You look awful, what's the matter?'

There's not a lot a lady can reply to a daft question like that, so I stumbled upstairs to splash my face with cold water. That revived me enough to be able to make the journey back to the kitchen and get the breakfast. Now that my initiation seemed to be successful I was able to relax and fussed about supervising the packing and loading of the flowers carefully in the car. I could tell that Roy was rather impressed by the sheer volume of the work as well as the (I have to admit it) beautiful end product. As soon as we had finished breakfast Roy was despatched to the bride's home with the flowers and I repaired to the bathroom to sooth away the night's ravages. This accomplished, I found I had time for a quick cup of coffee before setting off to the church, hoping the caffeine would serve to keep my eyelids apart. I arrived in good time to say a prayer - regretfully not for the bride and groom - that Roy had obeyed all my instructions to ensure that the flowers were received in good condition and that the bride's bouquet wouldn't fall to bits as she walked up the aisle. That nightmarish thought was just starting to make its mark when rustling and music announced her arrival. Scarcely daring to look, I swivelled my head and beheld a bridal vision carrying a gorgeous bouquet. I simply couldn't believe that I had actually created something so lovely in all that panic, but there it was for everyone to see. It was one of the proudest moments of my life and made my eyes go misty for a moment, but then, all women sniffle at weddings, don't they? I seemed to hear a chortle and Lavinia said:

'I don't. Didn't do badly, did I? Said it was a piece of cake – hope we get some!'

It never fails to amaze me how fast news travels in this town of ours. In no time at all I was inundated with orders for wedding flowers, having suddenly acquired the reputation of being 'jolly good and ever so cheap', which meant that, okay, I liked being described as jolly good but wasn't quite so keen on being categorised as cheap! Nevertheless, I was enjoying my newly found fame and took great pleasure in watching starry-eyed brides gasp when they saw my efforts and if I didn't make my fortune, so what? The trouble is that I never seem to do things by half and I was foolish enough to accept two orders per Saturday (if the times of the ceremonies permitted), which was really more than flesh and blood could stand as I would have to stumble out of bed at 3.00 a.m. to start the first one. I was on the point of thinking, blow this for a lark, when rescue came in the shape of a dear little bride-to-be asking if she might have her bouquet made of those new silk flowers. Crikey, I should say she could! Why hadn't I thought of this? From then on my orders could be made well in advance of the wedding day and I didn't have to get up in the middle of the night – it was wonderful. I did all the family wedding flowers, the very last one being for our younger son David and his bride Tina, and a very fitting swan song, I thought, while hanging up my hat.

A few months later, when Lavinia was getting restless, I noticed an advertisement in our local paper where the Further Education Department was begging for Floral Art tutors to take classes. She and I held a brief conference and decided to apply. I was engaged and did two terms, and while I enjoyed these sessions, somehow the zing had gone out of teaching because my students were rather serious and (quite rightly) intent upon learning as much as possible without the frivolous waste of time caused by a funny anecdote and a good old laugh. It takes all sorts, as they say, and showed me it was time to hang up my *chapeau* again.

This year, 1990, I had an urge to compete in the Southsea Show once more after thirteen years of absence from the scene. I was surprised how little things had changed: the heady atmosphere, smell of fresh flowers and, it seemed, the very same pink-faced 'Club' ladies bustling and creating beautiful arrangements, and it was like coming home. I hadn't quite lost my touch as I won three prizes – no First this time – and glowed with pleasure. I had also entered one of my orchids which won a Second and that was rather like having one's offspring win in a Baby Show.

Lavinia and I are wondering what to embark upon next. How do you fancy Bonsai, Vená? That's a good idea, Lavinia. Roy! Will you take me to the garden centre?

CHAPTER 8

'While you're down in Bovey Tracy, why don't you call in at the Orchid Greenhouses in Newton Abbot?' This advice came from my employer, the head teacher, and sparked off a new and exciting hobby, opening my eyes to the delights of being an Orchid Keeper.

It was bucketing with rain when Roy and I arrived at the greenhouses – which was why we were there – and, I must confess the premises didn't look in the least inviting. To get there we had trundled down a wet and muddy private road with the car wheels crunching into rain-filled potholes occasionally, turned in through a rickety gate and beheld some old and unkempt greenhouses, dripping in the torrent and lashed by a fierce wind. A sad and soggy sight, I sighed. Before I go any further, I must add that the owners were in the process of moving to a new venue and the existing one was going hang, so to speak.

Opening the door we stepped into a warm and quiet environment and shortly afterwards a man appeared to greet and welcome us into his own little world. He explained that this was the coolest area and that as we moved along the greenhouses the hotter and more humid it would become. I surveyed the many rows of pots that held small ugly things with twisted leaves that sprouted tentacles reaching out in all directions and thought, 'Yuk! They're weally howwible' (quoting one of our grandsons), but said, as politely as I could in my disappointment, to their guardian:

'Ah, yes. They are not quite as I imagined orchids.'

He must have been well used to this response because he smiled and said:

'See if you think so in half an hour's time. I think you will be pleasantly surprised.' He was right, of course, and I felt Lavinia itching to get her hands on one (at least) of his incredibly beautiful and mystical plant-beings. Two hours later we emerged; I was clutching two heavily protected pots and Roy was clutching an empty pocket. Well, it was his own fault, really. I distinctly remember him saying, 'You might just as well have two while you are here,' though that was before he knew how much they cost. He will jump first and look later, but usually to my benefit.

For the rest of our holiday the new orchids lived on the window-sill of our bathroom in the hotel and thrived, to my immense satisfaction. Shortly after our return home someone happened to mention that a local DIY store had orchids for sale. 'What?' I shrieked, and tore off to investigate. It was true, they did; they also had them displayed on a table standing in a howling draught, and if there is one thing that orchids detest above all else, it is a cold wind blowing around their little feelers. 'Poor little things,' I thought, 'I'd better rescue a couple of them,' and that made a grand total of four in my collection.

At this point I decided I'd better consult the library and really find out what I should be doing for my new family. Somehow I can't think of orchids as plants, it sounds much too mundane. There was masses of material for me to get my teeth into and I was astonished to discover that there are over 30,000 species, all with very strange and hard to pronounce names. I then sent for literature and ordered a monthly magazine to be sent which, I realised, was edited by the owners of the Orchid Greenhouses in Newton Abbot. Lavinia was besotted and became a terrible bore, rattling on *ad nauseum* about the blooming things. It wasn't long before boxes marked 'GREAT CARE - EXPENSIVE ORCHIDS' began arriving, making me feel as if I were a knowledgeable and famous specimen collector. The strange delight of carefully unwrapping the packaging layer by layer to behold a peculiar looking something is beyond words . . .

Pretty soon there became an acute shortage of space with warmth for my pampered darlings and I was just about to suggest to Roy that we move to a bigger house when hooray! (no offence, David), our younger son asked Tina to make an honest man of him, was accepted, and left a whole vacant room behind him. Funnily enough, it was Roy who suggested using it as an Orchid Room, and no sooner were the words out of his mouth, when every piece of furniture was distributed around the rest of the house and the stage was set for transformation. Modestly at first, with two tables holding large trays standing close to the window. Then the weather turned chilly and heating had to be installed in the form of an electric thermostatically controlled fan heater, which droned away happily using up lots of electricity.

'This room is not humid enough,' I announced authoritatively, as I was now the proud owner of a humidity gauge. 'We shall have to do something about that.'

'Well, I don't see what we can do,' Roy answered. 'And I'm certainly not going to stay in here all day breathing to make it wetter for your blasted plants!' He can be so silly at times.

'I have no wish to have you loafing about all day breathing,' I informed him coldly, and added, as another brilliant idea struck me for further verbal punishment, 'Go and get the children's paddling pool from the shed.'

He glowered and then moved off muttering, 'My God! Why do I have to be the only poor sod in the street with a potty wife?'

'I heard that!' I yelled after him, trying hard not to giggle.

It was while he was gone that I thought maybe the pool was a good idea and would solve the problem. It was small and solid and the grandchildren had outgrown it, so if it didn't leak, it would appear to be the perfect solution.

I suspect it was Lavinia who greeted Roy on his return, red in the face and puffing with exertion, struggling with the wayward pool. Anyway, the po-faced Vená had been transformed into an eager, enthusiastic and loving person, delighted to see him (and the pool) and make amends. With Roy's ruffled feathers smoothed, we were soon engaged in harmonious team work, laying heavy duty black polythene sheets over the fitted carpet in the corner of the bedroom and draping another artistically over the blue pool, forming a most interesting miniature pond. The next stage was filling it with water and we trudged back and forth from the bathroom with buckets until a reasonable level had been reached. We stood back and surveyed our creation with critical eyes.

'Hmmmmm,' I observed, not quite satisfied. 'It shouldn't do, but it looks boring.'

'I think,' said Roy reflectively, 'it isn't right with still water. It should have movement. Little ripples on the surface, or something like that.'

'Roy! You are clever; it's a water pump we need,' I flattered him, and before my dear and innocent husband had time to demur, he was on his way to the pet shop with the cheque book. It took very little time to fit and I truly think that Roy was as interested in the pool project as I was, because he immediately asked if I would prefer a fountain shaped water splash or an umbrella shape. I chose the latter and he disappeared once more with the depleting cheque book and a big grin. Later, when we were watching, starry-eyed, the water tumbling over the black polythene sheeting and listening to the liquid splashing sounds, it became obvious that we needed quite a lot of growing plants to cover the sheeting. Of course, more orchids! Our more interesting house plants and curious pieces of driftwood gradually found their way upstairs, along with a toad made of soapstone who peeped coyly out from under the leaves at the edge of the pool.

'There is still something missing,' I insisted. Lavinia tacitly suggested fish.

Roy thought for a while. 'Fish!' he said suddenly, 'Give it a bit of life.'

Yet again he departed for the pet shop and returned with three goldfish. They were colourful and lively and were soon darting and frolicking under the watery umbrella. At long last all three of us were satisfied. It looked pretty damn good.

Shortly after the arrival of the goldfish, Roy and I went on one of our walks along the harbour foreshore. I usually get footsore long before Roy shows signs of tiring and made my way back to the car to do a bit of knitting and wiggle my aching feet about. Scarcely had I achieved a wiggle and a stitch, when I heard an excited shout:

'Vená! Vená! Come quickly, there's a lovely piece of wood on the beach.'

I was interested but weary, so replied:

'Well, why didn't you bring it back with you, you silly bugger?'

'You won't say that when you see it – it's *enormous*. Come and have a look.'

Definitely interested now, I struggled to put my shoes on and followed him along the beach. I couldn't believe my eyes; it looked like a whole small tree, stripped of all bark and weathered to perfection. It was gnarled and knotted and, most exciting of all, curved sharply at the centre to accommodate two sides of our pool.

My laughter affliction overtook me when we tried to pick it up and the more I tried to stop the louder it became. Roy gets very cross with me at these times and now was no exception. 'Will you shut up and lift your end,' he bellowed. This, I fear, did not help and he had to lay his end down until the spasm passed and I could attend to the business in hand. Somehow or other we carried and dragged it back to the car. It was a pity that the tide was low, otherwise we could have floated it along with the aid of a piece of rope. Never mind, we got there in the end, but then the problem of getting it on to the roof of the car had to be overcome. Neither of us is very tall and our new acquisition weighed about half a ton. A passing fisherman informed us that we'd got a 'knotty problem there', but didn't stop to help. Eventually it was secured with lots of rope and, exhausted, we made our way home very slowly and carefully.

It wasn't until we were trying to angle it through the front door that we realised just how huge it was and how we had rather over-estimated our capabilities. Nonetheless, having got as far as the front door, we weren't going to give up at this stage! Aeons later we stood panting and limp but triumphant, with the tree looking as if it had been there all its life, or rather since its death, as it was driftwood.

Now we were really getting somewhere and news of our 'tropical forest' spread like a forest fire, enticing friends and orchid fanciers to our door, begging for admission. There was one awful drawback to this, though: it meant I had to try and keep the house looking clean all the time and I do hate cleaning up. But it is no good having one room as a jewel if the setting is mucky, as it usually is! So much praise was heaped upon my worthy head that it was turned a little and I wondered what else I could do to impress the population. Lavinia whispered in my ear, 'What about some suspended orchids?' 'Good idea,' I whispered back (in case Roy was listening) and promptly sent away for two. The small matter of having something to suspend them from I left to Roy. He is no carpenter but came up trumps with a contraption fastened to the chimney breast that jutted out into the room and then attached bamboo hooks on it to dangle the pots. At the very top we placed a fern that clapped its little fronds together in delight at such a heaven in which to live. In fact, it loved its new home so much that it grew to amazing proportions and cascaded like a dainty waterfall, making an even more forest-like environment for the main occupants, the orchids.

I hate to admit this, but I became that awful bore, known mostly as an 'Orchid Snob'. At the drop of a hat I would airily refer to such tongue twisting names as Zygopetilum, Paphiopedilum, Phaelenopsis, and even Odontoglossum, enjoying the glazed eyes and open mouths of my audience. It seems to me that more men are interested in orchids than women, as our visitors were usually enthusiastic husbands accompanied by tepid wives. I did receive a lot of earnest attention from the aforementioned and positive dislike sometimes from their ladies. Perhaps they felt excluded, as it does sound rather like a foreign language at times and the strange and mysterious orchid isn't everyone's cup of tea. One afternoon a couple arrived asking if they (or rather he) would be allowed to take a peep at my collection and the lady opted to wait downstairs while her husband accompanied me to the jungle. He was bowled over when I opened the door and ushered him inside and, naturally, I closed it behind us to preserve the heat and humidity. Twin souls with a common theme are quite capable of losing track of time, which we obviously did, because the door suddenly flew open and there stood his wife with a very funny look on her face. To this day I am convinced that she thought the Orchid Room had reverted to a bedroom. Poor man, he was most embarrassed and he'd only been interested in my Zygopetilum!

It was most extraordinary - this room took on its own personality and, I swear, grew of its own accord and became a tropical rainforest. Everything flourished so heartily that Roy and I began to wonder if it would decide to take over our bedroom as well and maybe even follow us downstairs. I was now growing orchids from minute seedlings which are sold in glass phials and would not produce flowers for five or six years. Even I was learning the art of being patient, though I will never get Roy to agree. One method of producing baby orchids is called 'merrystemming' and I think that is a delightful name to bandy about. Unfortunately this is a complicated system and laboratory conditions are really required. I had often wondered why so many doctors are orchid fanciers.

During this period of bliss, Lavinia was very firmly dominating our household but even she was slightly taken aback when someone from the Local Authority Adult Education Department contacted me to see if I would be interested in tutoring a Saturday Workshop. Lavinia accepted with glee and left Vená to worry about her lack of qualifications, proper, that is.

Lavinia argued that if you can create a successful Orchid Room and get hordes of people queuing up to see it as an amateur, surely a Saturday Workshop would be child's play. I took her word for it and she was right. Out of a class of fourteen, only one person knew anything at all about orchids and we all had a great deal of fun.

A turn of events in family affairs resulted in our decision to sell the house and repair to a new home some miles away, still by the sea but more rural. This meant that my glorious jungle would have to be dismantled and the room restored to being a third bedroom for selling purposes. I tried hard to close my mind as we gradually emptied the room, putting the orchids into the unheated greenhouse and feeling like a child murderer, and for the life of me was unable to control the odd tear that slid unbidden down my cheek. People are more important than plants, I told myself firmly, but it didn't help a lot.

We had chosen a perfectly ghastly time to try and sell a house and buy another. All prospective buyers and movers appeared to be in the same boat and eventually we all seemed to give up the notion of selling at the same time. So here we are today in the same old home which we love but minus the green magnet at the top of the stairs. The changes haven't been so drastic as I had feared; the orchids, mostly, have survived without heat and humidity, the fish are still frolicking but in the garden pond. The pond itself is made more beautiful by the addition of that superb piece of flotsam, the driftwood tree, with roses, fuchsias and pansies peeping through its twisted branches. The paddling pool has been passed on to two little boys in the next road and the dismantled contraption with the bamboo hooks is awaiting the next car boot sale. As for the room itself, it is now the Laura Ashley room full of dried flowers, straw hats, stone jars and a chintzy decor. It is also a multi-purpose room; a bedroom for the not infrequent visitors, it was great fun to design; it makes a very good hobbies room; and - quite important - I use it as an office. Since Peg and I decided to pool our various experiences, I write in it. In fact, I am scribbling away happily this very minute, reliving its recent exciting history and enjoying myself immensely. If I listen carefully I seem to hear splashings of goldfish and the umbrella fountain along with the gentle whirring of the heater that could be mistaken for tropical insects darting in amongst my wonderful orchids. All that was needed, you know, was a couple of bright parrots and a monkey. If I ever make another, I think I'll do that!

CHAPTER 9

In 1969 I had to go into our own hospital for a minor operation and of course this necessitated getting new nightie, dressing gown, slippers, etc., just for show (we all do it!). The 1960s was the decade of shockingly bright colours and my new nightie was in the excruciating pink-to-livid range in see-through nylon. For modesty reasons the bosom had copious ruchings, dartboard shaped, and probably resembled Queen Boadicea's breast plate on a frosty morning – impossible to ignore. Anyway, I thought it was beautiful and looked forward to sitting up in bed and swanking in front of friends and family.

Came the time when my first visitors were due and I sat up with hair neatly combed, face scrubbed and probably glowing from reflected nightie glare, awaiting my friends from the laboratory. Eventually they arrived and bustled to my bedside with 'Hello Vená' expressions that quickly changed to ones of incredulity. Together and separately they burst out laughing so heartily that they had to hold each other up. I was stunned! Had I suddenly sprouted a pimple on the end of my nose? Had my hair fallen out? What a way to greet a sick colleague and how hurtful. My supervisor (and ex-friend) was the first to control herself somewhat and, with tears in her eyes, pointed at my chest area, indicating the zone causing so much mirth. I squinted downwards over the bulges and ruchings and saw to my horror two nipples sticking out and clearly visible to any passer-by because the rotten manufacturer had economised on material in exactly the wrong spots. And while I can have a good laugh at someone else's miscalculation, it didn't seem quite so funny to me as apparently it did to my friends. However, good humour returned when the offending points were hidden beneath a bed jacket and a kind colleague volunteered to nip round to my home and return with my good old sensible bed gear that would cover a multitude of sins. Later, when back at home, the shocking pink nipple-exposer was cut up and used to stuff soft toys for various charity stalls. And good riddance, I say.

1975 saw me back in the same hospital undergoing a more serious operation. Of course I remember very little of the preliminaries, but engraved upon my memory is waking up feeling extremely groggy, opening my eyes and looking up into the face of one of the dishy young male technicians that I worked with in the laboratory. He had come across to relieve some poor patient of a blood sample and had decided to pop into my ward to see if I was back in the land of the living.

'Oh, Dave,' I croaked feebly, 'How kind of you. Yes, I'm feeling much better, thank you.' Out of the corner of my eye I could see Sister bearing purposefully towards my bed with that 'I'm in charge here' look on her face. She said:

'Ah yes, Mrs Bartlett, have you passed wind yet?'

Well, honestly, as if I'd own up to passing wind in front of Dishy Dave! I can only suppose that she thought Dave, in his white coat, was a doctor and that here was a jolly good opportunity to impress him. She certainly did that and, hopefully, Dave would think that the blush spreading across my face and neck was post-operation temperature and not embarrassment!

Still in the same hospital but fit and well this time, I was returning from lunch with two of my friends across the car park when – wham! – an electrically controlled hospital van ran into my back and knocked me flat upon the tarmac. My friends screamed, the driver carried on regardless – after all, he worked in a hospital, didn't he? – and I stayed where I was gently wondering what was happening. Having sussed out the situation I started to laugh which caused my friend Cath to panic and say:

'Oh my God! She's hysterical. Vená, can't you get up? Oh dear, she must be injured.'

'No. I can't get up and I can't move,' I said, which alarmed Cath even more and made her shout for a doctor.

'No, Cath,' I gasped, 'You don't understand. I can't get up because I've wet my knickers!' Then none of us could stop laughing but eventually they helped me to an upright position and escorted me to the cloakroom to repair surface damage and wash my knickers. Feeling very free but slightly depraved, I made my way back to the laboratory where for the rest of the afternoon my soggy drawers resided on Cath's radiator, filling her office with steam, and I tried to keep out of draughts. It took a long time to live down this episode and I am sad to relate that my so-called friends henceforth referred to my nether-garments as Vená's Boiling Bags!

I'm told that I will do *anything* to get attention, and it may be true because yet again I was admitted as a patient and this time I was quite ill after an operation, spending the next few weeks in a haze of pain and with very little sleep. I must have become pretty exhausted because one night I fell into a very deep sleep (extremely rare in hospital as any patient will confirm) and then gradually awoke to a strange feeling all over my body. Was I dying? I had never felt anything like this before and feared I must be very seriously ill. My eyes opened with an effort and there by my side stood an old lady. My Guardian Angel, I suppose, I thought placidly. I noted that she was holding a fruit bowl and was placing fruit all over me. Must be some sort of ritual before I can pass through the gates of Heaven. How nice, here I am strewn with bananas, grapes, apples and oranges . . . and suddenly alarm bells tinkled in my mind. Whoever heard of going to Heaven covered with bananas . . . that's too silly for words . . .

Realising that I was still very much alive and not in the least likely to die, I became panic-stricken and rang the bedside bell for immediate assistance. My Guardian Angel just stood and stared at me in a most unnerving way until a nurse arrived panting in response to my prolonged call.

'Minnie!' she said, 'What are you doing to Mrs Bartlett? Why are you out of bed?'

'I want a bed pan,' came the reply.

'Yes, but Minnie dear, that isn't a bed pan, it's Mrs Bartlett's fruit bowl.'

Thank goodness I awoke when I did!

CHAPTER 10

Roy and I had planned to take our two youngest grandchildren, Lewis and Harry, to Selsey Beach for a picnic, swimming and games on the beach, and while I was packing the lunch the two small boys were hopping up and down with excitement. It was a beautiful day and at the sight of the curling white-topped waves dancing up the beach the lads quickly shed their clothes and donned titchy bathing drawers. It was a pretty sight and Roy and I gazed proudly at our descendants for a moment or two before dishing out mile long instructions about keeping close inshore and don't you dare go more than three yards away from Grandad and Grandma. Lewis, aged four, was quite a strong little swimmer, while Harry, one year younger, made up for his lack of swimming skills by ignoring advice and jumped into every wave that came his way. Roy and I decided not to swim as we had undertaken the role of warden, so Roy rolled his trousers up to his chubby knees and I hoisted my skirt as far as was decently possible, i.e., just past my shapely but equally substantial ditto.

All went swimmingly, if you will excuse me, until Harry, the stupid boy, was bowled over by a boisterous wave and disappeared. With a remarkably quick reaction, Roy fished Harry out of the sea but in doing so tripped and fell backwards, also performing a disappearing act, except for his arms which succeeded in keeping Harry aloft. With a little help from me we all ended up with our heads above water and repaired, dripping profusely, to base camp further up the beach. Roy was the wettest and when I'd managed to stop laughing, I said, 'It's no good Roy. You'll have to take off most of your clothes and dry out - you'll catch your death.'

He agreed and shivered his way through our picnic lunch while his extremely soggy clothes remained wet and collected gritty sand and the odd bit of seaweed. By mutual agreement we decided to return home after all the food had been demolished, and a very uncomfortable Roy drove us home dressed tastefully in a damp clinging shirt and damper underpants - which fascinated and cheered up the small fry no end!

I usually travel in the front passenger seat but on this occasion squeezed into the back to keep the two lively children from jumping up and down and distracting the already cross driver. We were almost home and just driving past some parked cars when I spotted an elderly lady stretched out on the side of the road, surrounded by groceries. Obviously more swift action had to be taken.

'Oh, Roy, stop!' I screamed, which he did with a squeal of brakes. 'We must go and help – I think she's passed out.'

My second scream rent the air as Roy opened his door and jumped out. Having driven quite a distance in his scanty attire, he hadn't noticed that all was not as it should have been and that his predicament was exposed in its entirety.

'Oh, my God!' he groaned after leaping back into the car at the rate of knots. 'I shall never live this down. Blasted kids!'

Naturally by this time the street was buzzing with kindly people rushing to the assistance of the prone lady and, luckily for Roy, all heads were turned in her direction – at least I think it must have been all as we haven't had any comments from friends and neighbours!

Skipping back a generation, when our own sons were very young, I was a member of our local church's Young Wives Club. It was a very active organisation and much enjoyed by those who wouldn't otherwise have had much opportunity to join in a mad social whirl because of young families, and it goes without saying that we were all looking forward to a barbeque planned to take place on Hayling Island beach, with permission to have a bonfire.

Young husbands were all invited because we needed them to transport us, children, and the enormous amount of prepared supper, and, as lots of food was in the offing, they were only too happy to oblige. It was a great success with not the slightest hint of drama – the children were kept at a safe distance from the splendid bonfire, stomachs stuffed to capacity, and a really jolly time was had by all.

Towards the end of the evening when it was time to gather up every scrap of rubbish and put the bonfire out, I thought it would be a good idea if I performed my famous Pied Piper act, thereby removing all the children at a stroke from the scene of activity. Or so I thought. 'Come along, children, and follow Aunty Venâ. We are going to have a Follow-my-Leader through the sand dunes.'

They needed no urging and off we set, singing noisily, through the tussocky dunes. We jumped and danced and did incredibly silly things in a long wiggly line, the Leader enjoying the entertainment just as much as the Followers. Eventually we all flagged and puffed so I directed our mini-human-snake on to the beach to head back to the cleaned up barbeque site. Having tired feet by this time, it was my misfortune to trip over a rock with considerable force. Now, I had been dying to spend a penny for much of the evening and this sudden jolt proved to be the last straw for my heavily overburdened bladder. It was the absolute classic 'good news, bad news' situation: blissful internal relief and dire external consequences.

Fortunately it was dark enough for the children not to notice (and then tell their parents) and I sent them scampering on ahead so that I could try and work out what on earth I should do. It was not a scrap of good trying to kid the assembled company that I had fallen into the sea and made my shorts so wet, as the children would be bound to pipe up and say, 'Oh, Aunty Vená, you weren't anywhere near the sea', the little sods. No, the only thing to do would be to mosey around the edge of the gathering until I could find Roy and confess all. His reaction was utterly predictable.

'What!' affronted and indignant, 'You aren't getting in my car like that. You'll have to take them off and wrap a tablecloth round you.'

That was quite brilliant of Roy. I was allowed in the car to take my shorts and knickers off (so long as I didn't sit on a seat), while he retrieved our tablecloth from the boot. It wasn't a very discreet one, in fact it was bright orange and white check, and made me look like a slightly chubby Dorothy Lamour. As the party was practically over, I decided to stay in the car and shout goodbyes through the window and just hope that no-one would be insensitive enough to comment on my change of costume. This hope was particularly pertinent regarding our two small sons. Not a chance of course!

'I say, Daddy! Why is Mummy wrapped up in our tablecloth?'

'Oh, is she? I hadn't noticed. Perhaps she's cold!'

Good old Roy.

Another Young Wives function was to present a pantomime to unsuspecting groups such as Cubs, Brownies, Scouts, the Mothers Union, Friends of the Church... and anyone, really, who would invite us. This was great fun and, cockily, we thought we were in great demand. I usually played a semi-important role. One year I was Miss Outer Space - Queen of the Stratosphere, and teetered on five-inch heels with a tunic that barely (carefully chosen description) covered my behind, tastefully finished off with a Dame Edna type blonde wig. I have photographs to prove this, in case anyone is in doubt. I was a tremendous success. On these occasions Young Husbands were detailed to build scenery and mind the children. In all fairness I must say that they were very willing, quite clever, and enjoyed many laughs and tipples together.

One winter it was decided that we should produce 'The Old Woman who lived in a Shoe', which, while it was a splendid idea, required much thought and skill given to the scenery, the focus of which was to be the shoe. Our friends Poppy and Dick undertook this mighty project and used hardboard, a real window rescued from someone's demolished shed, net curtains and so on. When this creation was complete, Roy and I were asked to assist Dick to hoist it on to his car roof, tie it securely, and then follow him in our car in case of emergencies. I still think we should have had a police escort. Perhaps not, we might have been arrested. Off went Dick and Poppy at about five miles per hour - it was an amazing sight - with Roy and me following at a safe distance to watch closely for any shifting of the load. We had completed about half of the 500-yard journey to the Church Hall when disaster struck. It all happened so quickly that we were actually running over the remains of the shoe before we realized it wasn't on top of Dick's car any more. Certainly our attention had been drawn to noises that went crunch, crack, shatter, chink-chink, but the quickness of the shoe had obviously deceived the eye.

Both cars stopped and Poppy and I jumped out, crashed into each other and fell in a heap on top of a mound of painted hardboard, empty window frame, glass, net curtains, plastic flowers, etc., stared at in disbelief by the men and kind lady who ran out with a broom. I think it was the latter that reduced Poppy and me to fits of laughter; we needed a bulldozer, really! However, we carefully salvaged and smoothed out practically all of the shoe, and a pretty neat repair job was effected in the Hall - though of course we all had to pretend there was glass in the window frame - and I am happy to report that this was one of our most successful productions and one that holds special memories for at least four people!

It may have been Lavinia that had the sudden urge to become an Earth Mother and keep chickens in the garden; it sounds more like her than Vená. Well, whichever it was experienced an overwhelming desire and that, of course, involved Roy. I don't think he has ever quite forgiven her or me. Anyway, this is what happened.

Having listened to me chuntering on for some months about how lovely it would be to have our own fresh eggs, with maybe some for our family and a few friends, and how interesting it would be to have them installed in a beautiful chicken house and run that he would be building, he finally bowed to wifely pressure and agreed to give it a go.

'After all,' he muttered, 'If we don't like 'em, we can always eat 'em.'

I was shocked. My mind hadn't reached that stage; I was still in the fluffy feathered pets that kindly laid eggs as a bonus scenario.

'Oh Roy! How could you?' I could almost feel tears in my eyes at the very thought.

The next stage was a plan of campaign. We'd better build the accommodation first, I decided, and then find out where we could purchase six feathery little darlings. The first part of the campaign went smoothly enough with just a few grumbles issuing forth from Roy's workshop, but suddenly a most desirable hen residence with all mod. cons. appeared (like a mushroom) at the bottom of the garden, surmounted by a beaming and interested face with a beard.

'That's wonderful, Roy, and aren't you clever?' I flattered, and then dashed indoors to find the Yellow Pages to skip through the C section for Chickens, or as a last resort, P for Poultry. It was surprisingly scarce on chicken suppliers and we seemed to be left with a choice of a huge dairy concern that also dealt with poultry, or nothing. I opted for the former and a few minutes later Roy was on his way while I stayed at home to add homely little touches to the chicken ranch to make the new occupants feel at home.

Meanwhile, back at the farm, Roy drove up with a swish outside a very large reception sort of place and was greeted by a gentleman who enquired if he could help him.

'Thank you, yes. I'm after six chickens, please.'

'Certainly, Sir. Will you come this way?' (This was most encouraging.)

Roy followed obediently and they both stopped by a massive deep freezer where, much to Roy's surprise, the man opened the door and started removing frozen birds. Roy was terribly embarrassed and said:

'Oh, I'm sorry. You've misunderstood me, I mean live chickens with feathers on.'

His companion also seemed embarrassed.

'I beg your pardon, Sir. It's our other farm you need for live birds. This is how you get there.'

Roy thanked him and set off on the chicken trail for the second time. When at last he found it, he reported to the farm office where a very pretty girl invited him to step into the manager's office.

'He won't be long, Mr Bartlett, he's just coming.'

Shortly afterwards the door opened and a man clad in a hacking jacket, jodhpurs, and leather gaiters strode in - a perfect country gentleman who frightened Roy nearly to death.

'Oh, good morning, Mr Bartlett. I believe you wish to buy some chicks.'

'Yes, please,' said Roy, 'I'd like six.'

'Certainly, Mr Bartlett. Would that be six hundred or six thousand?'

Roy started to panic. I think he was visualising a large lorry full of day-old chicks pulling up outside our little town house and was wondering how he could stop this whole ghastly mess.

'No! No! I only want six.'

'We only deal with bulk orders here, Sir.'

'Oh, sorry. I'll have to try somewhere else then.'

'Yes, Sir.'

That was the end of the conversation and as Roy stumbled across the office he couldn't be sure if it was a smile or a sneer upon those aristocratic features. My guess is that it was a smile. What a story to tell his friends at the dinner table! You see, there was this poor guy from a town who wanted six . . . And what's more I wouldn't begrudge him a good laugh; we've convulsed most of our friends with our side of the story and his is even funnier.

There is a happy ending. By pure chance we knew someone who wanted to find a home for four beautiful and rather rare hens and, of course, we jumped at the opportunity. They settled down and laid eggs galore for years and *then* we ate them.

Our son David and his nice girl friend called in to see us and ask if we'd like to accompany them to a garden centre that was holding a camping exhibition. Of course we would and did and I shall never forget it!

Camping has become a very sophisticated leisure activity these days, and we were amazed at all the refinements on sale for the simple holiday-minded family. Tents ranged from little tiddlers to massive affairs with lounges, bedrooms, kitchens, and one was practically a canvas mansion. One or two things puzzled me though, and I queried innocently:

'What's this little cupboard bit for, David?'

'Oh Mum, don't be daft - that's a little room for the loo.'

'Good Lord! I don't believe it. But what about all the toilet noises, everyone would hear everything!' Despite belief to the contrary, I am shy about some things.

David laughed. 'You wouldn't hear all that much, Mum. Hang on, I'll demonstrate.'

With this he disappeared and zipped himself inside the minuscule flapping room. I was a little worried about his 'demonstration', I must say, but then dismissed the thought that even daffy David would take it to extremes. A muffled voice called out:

'Now listen carefully and see how much you can hear.'

At this time we were the only ones viewing the tent and we were subjected to a series of explosive raspberries, and what sounded like a herd of hissing snakes and then he was pretending to be violently sick. It was a marvellous performance and reduced us to tears and near hysterics. Even Roy was grinning from ear to ear while trying hard to contain unseemly mirth.

In the midst of David's horrendous concert entered a family - Gran, Grandad, Mum, Dad and two children. Their faces assumed expressions that varied from deep shock to amusement and we decided that we didn't know the Phantom Raspberry Blower inside the bulging cupboard and beat a hasty retreat to the more rarefied outside air.

'Shouldn't we tell David?' asked his kind girlfriend in between splutters.

'Certainly not,' I replied, 'It serves him right for being so cocky.'

Roy said, 'I can't wait to see David's face when he unzips himself.'

That was a jolly good idea of Roy's, and we crowded round the tent opening and peered in just in time to see David's smiling face emerge from his little sanctuary, fully expecting a round of applause from his loved ones. What he saw instead was a row of stunned strangers with their mouths open, obviously unable to believe the evidence of their own ears! Scarlet-faced, he said, 'Oh! Excuse me, I . . .' and made a dash for the door. He found his original audience rolling on the ground in helpless laughter and, bless his heart, joined in the general mayhem. We have not visited this particular garden centre since, just in case someone might recognise us!

Not so long ago I spent two very happy years working in a Roman Catholic School, loving the rather intense and exciting atmosphere that Catholics seem to generate. By the way, this is Lavinia speaking. Christmas approaching heightened the children's glackity behaviour until they were appalled to hear that Santa was unable to come to the Christmas Fête. The head teacher issued an urgent plea for a substitute and in a mad moment I volunteered my unsuspecting Roy, who was snapped up with so much gratitude that I couldn't let him wriggle out of it. Still, he does admit that life is rarely dull in our family because he never knows what is going to happen next, but I don't think he will ever forget this particular caper.

Naturally he sulked and grumbled for a bit and then capitulated and tried on Santa's gear to see if any alterations were necessary. They weren't, so it was all systems go and all we had to do was to wait for the great day. He did seem to get touchy as time went by but, having assured him that he would make a perfect Santa, he cheered up sufficiently to bare his teeth in what was supposed to be a welcoming smile.

Down in the Grotto all was in readiness for Santa's appearance. A tree stood in the corner, dripping with lollipops and sweets, and at the base stood a big sack of small gifts for His Christmasness to hand out to the little darlings. A chair was installed for him and the whole place was festooned with fairy lights, so that the atmosphere was very festive. When Roy had donned his costume and adjusted the beard so that it didn't tickle his nose and make him sneeze, the children lined up and listened to his 'Ho, ho ho's' while they were waiting for admission. With practice, the Ho's got louder and quite frightening, so that babes in arms started yelling and the older members of the up and coming generation made comments like, 'Go on! It's only Mrs Bartlett's husband,' or, more rudely, 'Cor! What a wally he looks!'

Things got worse rather rapidly. A toddler peed on Santa and a half-sucked lollipop somehow got stuck to his beard, much to the annoyance of its small and very vocal owner. Santa's head started to ache and throb and then he realised that he needed a pee as well as that blasted toddler. When he

Vená's Interesting Part – According to Lavinia

couldn't wait any longer the Grotto was closed for five minutes while he made a quick dash to the loo. Much relieved he returned, entered the Grotto and stopped short in horror. Vandals had struck during his short absence; the tree lay on its side and bereft of its sticky crop, fairy lights had been pulled down, and, worst of all, the sack had disappeared. That was enough for poor Santa and, in a rage, he handed in his costume and beard and demanded his cards. I can't repeat his actual comments, for decency's sake. Just let it suffice to say that his colleagues in HM Dockyard would have been amazed at his turn of phrase!

An enquiry was held the next day by the head teacher and eager little informers from all classes gave evidence (gleefully) that this terrible crime had been perpetrated by Old Boys who had come back for the Fête and mischief. This established, the culprits were summoned to appear before his august presence and immediate punishment was meted out.

Back at our home Lavinia was copping it hot and strong. As before, I can't actually repeat what he said, but in essence it boiled down to:

'Don't ever ask me to be Santa again, my nerves won't stand it.'

Not the slightest chance, dear Roy, because my nerves won't stand it, either.

CHAPTER 11

Roy sometimes complains that living with me is like being permanently attached to a roller coaster and I concede that on the odd occasion I have been known to be a little unpredictable. And as Lavinia and I have dominated these weird chronicles so far, we thought it was only fair that he should get a good crack of the whip, if only to stop him moaning. Naturally I have to make an appearance here and there as we have spent most of our lives together, but the next few pages are devoted to my one and only love, and I hope he appreciates it. Right, off we go.

Unlike me, Roy was not evacuated during hostilities and had the doubtful honour of witnessing the very first air raid upon our town. As his mother was on a shopping expedition, he and his close cousin, Ken, were left in the care of their grandmothers, who were sisters. He remembers them as being elderly ladies, both dressed in those cotton wrap-over pinny garments and fur-edged slippers, so that they would have looked like sisters even if they weren't!

History was made that day – for the very first time the air raid siren sounded. The Granny-sisters thought hard for a while and then came to the conclusion that the boys should repair to the air raid shelter that lurked, doorless, in the back garden. This duty accomplished, for some unfathomable reason they went back indoors, climbed the stairs, and kept an eye on the lads from the back bedroom window. If you think this is strange, read on! They later reported to Roy's mother that the lads had danced up and down, clapped their hands and sung 'The Germans are coming, the bombs are dropping. Hooray, Ha Ha, Hooray!' War games have to be learned before one can play them properly, obviously. However, he is still proud that he can remember the very first air raid here.

This early naivety and ignorance soon evaporated when grim reality forced itself upon the youngsters. Roy badly wanted to go to a Saturday matinee at a local cinema and had been forbidden by his mother because she thought the danger was too great and so he stayed at home feeling hard done by and sulky. During the afternoon the air raid siren wailed its warning and Roy was directed to the shelter. Standing in the doorway he saw planes sweeping in from the coast and then dive and drop bombs very close to where he stood transfixed and very frightened. He remembers particularly the terrible and ear-splitting noise of this raid and there certainly wasn't any 'Hooray, Ha Ha, Hooray' this time.

Later, when the all-clear had sounded and he had recovered from his fright – kids are very resilient – he explored the streets to see what had happened and to pick up any shrapnel that might be around. Dust still hung dense and he suddenly realised that the cinema wasn't a cinema any more, just a huge pile of smoking rubble, made even more gruesome by dead bodies being carried out of where the foyer had been and put into a Council dust cart. A cold shiver has just traversed my spine as I once again mentally thank Roy's mother for having the good common sense actively to prevent him from going to the ill-fated Saturday matinee. He would most likely have been killed and the lovely life we have had together wouldn't have happened.

Bombing and fire bomb blitzes became more frequent; our beautiful Guildhall was burned to a pathetic shell, and Roy's mother decided it was time to join her sister at a lovely small waterside village in Chichester harbour. His father was serving in the Army by this time so that decisions had to be made by her alone regarding the welfare of her family. Thus it was that he, his mother and one of the Gran-sisters went to join his aunt in the large bungalow at Itchenor for the next two years.

He was accepted into the little village school where he did well, despite a three-mile walk which made him perpetually hungry. It was here that he met his friend Denny, who was the son of a smallholder and also had three sisters. They were a real old fashioned country family and Roy enjoyed their company immensely, particularly so when he was invited to eat at their huge table which was groaning with good food, served from large tureens. Despite frequent meals at Denny's house and, of course, at home, they were both usually pretty peckish and would augment their diet with wild birds' eggs, cooked over a wood fire in an old tin can. Little sods! I can understand it though; I was never quite full at Clarendon Park even if I did polish off everything that was going and which I could get away with.

During the long school holidays he and Denny had an ideal childhood. Very little in the way of restrictions impeded their play, especially on the many luxury boats that were stored and cocooned for the duration by their wealthy owners. It was a good job they couldn't see the boys being pirates, or Nelson and Hardy; they probably would have had a fit. There were many aircraft shot down in the area and they, too, had to be explored, presumably after dangerous items had been stripped. It was surprising that access to the shores of Chichester Harbour was easy and the boys could swim on hot days, though in my experience the waters there are rather muddy and they probably came out dirtier than when they went in. Not that they would care about that, of course. I was slightly puzzled when Roy told me that he and Denny used to smother their hair in thick soap, push the resultant mess into deep waves and bake it in hot sunshine.

'Why?' I asked.

'Don't really know,' said Roy, 'I think we just wanted to look handsome!'

There's no answer to that, really.

It must have been quite a nasty shock when the family returned home and all that marvellous freedom and country atmosphere disappeared, and again I understand, having experienced the same loss upon my return from beautiful surroundings. However, it must have been shortly after his return that I used to pretend that I hadn't noticed his wolf whistle and then, later, I fell in love with him in the pin table room when he was wearing that heart-stopping outfit topped with the trilby. Both Lavinia and I are firm believers in fate!

'Vená,' said Roy, 'Sid is going up the ladder to cut your clematis away from his telephone wires. You really shouldn't let it grow as high as that.'

'Point taken,' I replied. 'And you shouldn't let Sid go up the ladder at his age – you should be doing it.' (I always like to have the last word.)

He heaved a great sigh and disappeared. In fact he disappeared for such a long time that I thought I'd be wise to do a little investigating. As I reached the front door I heard chuckles and then, very clearly, 'For goodness sake don't tell Vená,' followed by more merriment. 'Aha,' I thought and opened the door to find a very red faced Roy and a slightly hysterical Sid.

'What's going on?' I demanded.

'Well,' explained Roy rather sheepishly, 'I didn't have my glasses on and when I got up the ladder I mistook a telephone wire for a clematis stem and cut it. That's all.'

'*That's all?*' I know very well that I sounded like a teacher at the end of a very bad day, but couldn't help it.

'That's marvellous! Now we've got to get Telecom to come and repair it. You are a fool Roy. May I use your phone, please, Sid?'

They both started laughing again and then Sid said, 'It's my wire he's cut!'

I said, 'Oh Roy, and you were in Bomb Disposal in the RAF,' and we all three laughed a lot more at the very idea and had to recover with a cup of tea.

Yes, in 1948 Roy had his call-up papers for National Service in the RAF. He first went to Wilmslow to learn how to bash a square and other nasty things and after six weeks when they couldn't stand him any longer, he came home on leave. It was on this leave that we trothed our plight and became an engaged couple. Not only did he catch me, he also caught chicken pox and then somehow or other made me spotty in very short order. Actually, we were both delighted because it meant we could be home together and neither of us were more than indisposed, just pretty to look at. Roy was extremely careful trying to preserve the horrid scabby spots, even to the extent of not washing in case they fell off and ruined his plan to stay home as long as humanly possible. It had to end though; his callous doctor tried an experimental flick, and that was that. Pronounced more than fit, he was forced to return to the tender arms of the RAF to try and catch something else that wasn't painful, just very, very infectious and/or contagious.

Because of his extended leave, the group he had trained with had passed out (not literally, though some might have) and moved elsewhere. It only needs one awkward new airman to muck up the whole system, as the RAF obviously weren't geared up to simply forwarding Roy as a latecomer of the group and absorbing him into something or other, and it seems that a lot of head scratching went on before a useful job was discovered for him. This new temporary post made Roy the envy of all the new airmen, though he had to put up with a great deal of ribbing. He was now the official (though temporary) locker painter in the WAAF's new-entry quarters and I have my suspicions that he enjoyed it very much. Not that he was without instructions from me at long range and, of course, I trust him mostly, but it did seem to me that it was a bit like putting a sweet-toothed child in charge of a sweet shop. Fortunately for my peace of mind, the locker painting job lasted a mere three weeks before his proper posting came through. It told him tersely to report to B.D. Wing.

'What's B.D. Wing?' he enquired from somebody that knew about things like that.

'Why, that's Bomb Disposal Wing – you'll love it there, but do be careful!' and chuckling, he disappeared through the Mess door where I believe you can buy beer. I rather think that Roy's new job came as a bit of a shock but, having done quite well in his training and now knowing how to 'steam out' a bomb, perhaps they thought he was a natural. Time would tell.

At the conclusion of the bomb steaming course (I can only imagine a bomb that looks like a Christmas pudding bubbling away, but it's probably not so) Roy was transferred to a bombing range on the Lincolnshire coast. On one dramatic occasion a bomb had to be collected and taken under police escort to a deserted beach. Along the entire route the police warned villagers through a megaphone to open windows and take cover in case of an explosion. It was pretty exciting stuff, this, and when they eventually reached the designated spot the bomb was covered by sandbags very gently and the men ordered to retire to a safe distance and keep their heads down. This accomplished, the bomb was detonated by wire and plunger. With hearts in their mouths, clammy hands and sweat trickling down their faces, the intrepid team waited . . . and waited. And then it blew up with a muted 'poof' of roughly the same noise level as a reluctant Christmas cracker and was a terrible anti-climax. Not so the next incident which might have had disastrous results.

A Polish Squadron came to Britain to practise firing at targets and where did they go for experience? Why, to Roy's bombing range in Lincolnshire, of course! The procedure was to tow targets made of canvas with tanks painted on them and propped up with tubular steel across the desolate stretches of sand at low tide, and then beat a hasty retreat before the Squadron swooped in with all guns blazing. There were six of these targets and Nos. 1 to 5 were trundled to their prearranged target spots by a Jeep, all according to plan. The trouble started when No. 6 target was waddling carefully along to its position - with the help of the Jeep - and the Squadron prematurely screamed across the sky firing cannon shells at Target No. 1. This was entirely out of order and it was obvious that the pilots hadn't seen the men with Target No. 6 in the danger area. There was only one thing to do and that was to run like hell before the planes completed a circuit to line up for Target No. 2, and try to contact them by radio. The whole team made it safely to the radio vehicle (it is surprising how fast one can move when being shot at with cannon shells) but as none of the pilots could speak or understand any English, there was no response. Happily, apart from severe shock, there were no casualties that day, but that was no thanks to the organisation of the bombing run, just to the speed that men under threat can attain when necessary. I squinted a look at Roy's little short legs while penning this episode and wondered how he did it. My God! How they must have twinkled as he flew across the wet Lincolnshire sands!

Pay parade happened each Thursday and all the airmen were required to line up on the stairs leading to the Officer's Room and await their names being called. Then they had to step smartly forward and receive the hard earned (or so they believed) pay. On a particular Thursday the Sergeant was doing his stuff by bawling out names at regular intervals when out of the blue some poor unfortunate on the stairs accidentally let forth a very rude noise. In no time at all the orderly airmen disintegrated in unseemly mirth, which didn't please the Sergeant one little bit. He appeared at the top of the stairs and demanded to know who had committed this diabolical act: own up immediately or there would be TROUBLE! Of course no-one dared and so they were ordered to assemble in the Games Room, 'Who ripped one off at the Officer?' barked the Sergeant, with a steely glint in his eye. This caused a further wave of half-suppressed laughter and he viewed the shaking shoulders and handkerchiefs stuffed in mouths with much disfavour. The culprit remained anonymous. 'Have it your own way, then! I'll soon wipe the grins off your silly faces.' The Sergeant never made a joke - a worth-while one, that is - and not the slightest vestige of a smile was seen for quite a while. Everyone was confined to barracks and all week-end leave was cancelled. In addition, they were detailed to scrub floors, clean windows, and polish everything to a frazzle that didn't move.

When poor Airman G. could stand it no longer he reported to the Sergeant and confessed that he was the guilty party. This belated but brave act released the men on Sunday, but they still felt like naughty schoolboys behind the bike shed instead of grown men. Isn't it strange how a 'ripped one' accidentally producing a deplorable noise causes such uncontrollable mirth? For my sins I know this only too well to be a fact!

A large leap in time to 1979 saw Roy, along with seven of his fellow workers, foolishly volunteering to undertake A VERY IMPORTANT MISSION, then cloaked in secrecy, on one of those incredible circular Forts that guard the entrance to the Solent. They are also nicknamed 'Palmerston's Follies', very unkindly, as it wasn't his fault that Britain didn't have to use them in anger against Napoleon and his reluctant forces. The Forts are built where fresh water springs are close to the surface of the sea bed - a left-over from the prehistoric River Solent - thereby ensuring that the soldiers of long ago could, if necessary, survive indefinitely under siege on the high seas. The walls of these magnificent monuments are immensely thick, made of granite blocks with a central sandwich of teak and iron. Consequently they are forbidding and virtually invulnerable structures, cold and damp and, even worse, home to thousands of pigeons. Not exactly homely and why Roy ever put his name forward for the project is a mystery; perhaps Lavinia had been getting on his nerves and this seemed to be a better place than most to escape to. However, the die was cast when a notice appeared on the board in his department, bearing the following extraordinary message:

APPEARING ON HORSE SANDS FORT
SNOW WHITE AND THE SEVEN DWARFS

CAST

Snow White	Knocker
Doc	Bob
Happy	Tom
Sneezy	Bill
Grumpy	Roy (!)
Bashful	Bill
Sleepy	Pip
Dopey	Chris

The work to be done on the Fort was such that it was necessary to live there for three weeks without any contact with the shore, apart from a ship-to-shore radio used to contact HM Dockyard in cases of emergency only. The only other concession was to be a water boat calling each day with fresh water and other supplies.

As these intrepid lads were required to embark on the bastion in September, which can be extremely chilly in the Solent if the weather is in a perverse mood, warm clothing was high on the priority list. By the time I had gathered everything that looked substantial and (hopefully) waterproof, the heap looked rather as if Roy was setting forth on an expedition to the North Pole instead of just a few miles south of our home. Better safe than sorry, I told him primly, when he looked askance at my efforts and protested that he wasn't strong enough to pick up that load, let alone carry it anywhere. I ignored this silliness and concentrated on food supplies.

A degree of ingenuity was required here. A three days' supply of fresh meat was all that was allowed to be taken as it was considered to be a risk after this time, and obviously the Dwarfs' wives would collectively have to rack their brains to provide interesting and nutritious meals for the little chaps.

'What about bread and milk?' we asked.

'No,' came the firm reply. 'It will have to be tins and packets. And don't forget the tin opener!'

The next couple of weeks found me baking cakes that would keep (if left alone), stocking up with tins of soup, corned beef and ham. I bought dozens of packets of cream crackers to substitute for bread and what seemed about half a ton of potatoes. My most important task was to teach Grumpy how to make suet dumplings heartily flavoured with mustard and, I was told after the event, they were relished by the team but did seem to cause rather a lot of wind in the Solent. Immediately prior to the start of the great expedition we purchased the three days' supply of fresh meat and lots of fruit. It was an unbelievable sight when the provisions were stacked and ready to go, piled alongside a portable TV, radios, fishing rods, magazines, books, binoculars, a stove, sweeties and sleeping equipment. Grumpy's wife was completely exhausted and a quivering wreck but Grumpy himself, she noted sourly, looked bright eyed and bushy tailed and quivering with excitement, not wreckage. Both Peg and I have noted that life is not altogether fair for most of the time.

It was nearing the end of September when Snow White and her brave band boarded the Dockyard work boat and headed eastwards, bathed in rich golden sunshine and caressed with a warm and balmy breeze. Rather like a fairy story, I thought sentimentally. Much to their surprise the Fort resembled a miniature hamlet. Even a little post office had been installed during the last war, not in use now, of course, and street lamps lined the little road. There had once been a fresh water well – now blocked off – which went down through the sea bed to the springs, and the team marvelled at the engineering and construction problems that had been overcome in harsh and dangerous conditions during Napoleonic times. However, one can only do so much marvelling at a time and the party set out to find the most comfortable section in which to set up their sleeping quarters, kitchen, lounge and bathroom. Bunk beds, bedding, a large trestle table and eight chairs had been provided by the Ministry of Defence and soon a fire was crackling in the little stone fireplace. Steak and sausages sizzled on the stove, wafting mouth-watering aromas around the Fort, the TV was rigged up, and it began to feel a little bit like home.

Snow White and her team worked normal Dockyard hours and during their lunch breaks would fish or explore the bowels of their new home. It was really rather spooky, especially as they had been given to understand that the Fort was haunted by at least thirteen ghosts. One is reported to be an elderly man with a beard and the remaining twelve are all young men. During the three-week stay none of the apparitions revealed themselves, which must have been a great relief. Chief Reporter Grumpy later supplied me with the information that the Fort is built honeycomb fashion, full of tunnels and archways and all littered with the skeletons of sea birds and pigeons that had found their way in but not out again. How sad. In the evenings after their meal the men walked around the top section and looked longingly across to the shore where their families were safe and cosy.

After three days had gone by I was missing my dear Grumpy and worried that he had by now demolished all the fresh food and was probably chomping his way through dry biscuits and rock hard cake. Lavinia whispered in my ear and we both jumped for joy at her great flash of brilliance. We have a dinghy parked in our garage and a dinghy is a water vehicle, I reasoned, and could easily reach Roy's prison if it were a calm day. With mounting excitement I mentally detailed our son David and best friend Tony as rescue crew, delivering fresh meat, etc., and then bringing Roy back to the shore for a brief reunion. There is no time like the present for striking a hot iron, so I immediately contacted the rescue team and outlined my highly illegal and cunning plan. To my intense delight they thought it was a great idea and 'Operation Cockleshell Heroes II' swung into action.

'Now,' I thought, 'I can't send food to Roy only. I shall have to (gulp) treat them all the same.' The following day appeared to be a good bet for Op.C.H.II, according to the weather forecast, which meant that I had to nip out smartly to purchase the following: eight steaks, eight pounds of sausages, two pounds of bacon, two dozen eggs, several loaves, and quite a lot of beer. The sum total of this little lot nearly broke the bank and the weight my back, but what the hell; it was all too thrilling for words and I couldn't wait for tomorrow to come. I packed the food, beer, and a letter to Snow White and Co., and then went to bed praying that all would go well and that we wouldn't be found out. A bit like Churchill must have felt on the eve of great battles. I didn't fancy going to prison but if the worst came to the worst, I should just have to pretend to be a nun in a nunnery during my incarceration.

'Hang it all!' snapped Lavinia. 'It's all arranged and now up to our fellow conspirators, David and Tony, so shut up and let's get some sleep.'

This telling-off worked wonders as my next conscious thought was, 'Oh, my God! It's tomorrow already,' and I shot out of bed.

Tony had decided on a certain time and exact spot on the beach for me to coincide with their return with - if all went well - dear old Grumpy on board for a quick kiss, hello and (sob) goodbye and, following his instructions faithfully, I could see our small boat bravely making its way towards the shore. As it got closer I realised that I saw two heads only and was bitterly disappointed. Obviously everything had gone wrong and I fully expected to hear a police siren heralding our imminent arrest and disgrace. However, when the boat was closer to the shore I realised that David and Tony were wearing enormous grins and the reason for them suddenly popped up, letting forth a wild 'YAHOO!' Just a minute - shouldn't that have been Hi Ho, Hi Ho?

You will have to imagine the soaring violin music for this magic moment. The dinghy slithered on to the beach and Roy and I rushed into each other's arms. 'From Here to Eternity' seemed incredibly second rate compared with this real live dramatic love scene. Well, that is how it is in my memory; I have since been informed that what actually happened was a rapid hug and kiss, followed by, 'Can't stop . . . not supposed to be here . . . thanks for all the grub . . . 'bye!', a photograph taken by Tony to record the tender moment, and they pushed off (literally) to return the runaway as quickly as possible. I waved until the boat became a dot and, anyway, tears blurred my vision, so there was nothing for it but to trudge homewards. A sense of anticlimax set in after all the excitement and activity, like Christmas after the frenetic build up, and an unaccountable feeling of foreboding gripped me.

Just one week after the romantic beach scene my strange feelings were horribly justified. We were never to see the photograph that our dear Tony took of our reunion. Similar to the proverbial bolt from the blue, he suffered a massive heart attack and was dead before he crumpled on to his kitchen floor. He was just thirty-nine years of age and his loss affected many people. We remember his kindness and the fun he brought with him, and it is really true to say that a light went out of our lives. Roy, in particular, was devastated and treasures the memory of that illicit boat trip and also how Tony rescued a baby pigeon in trouble at the Fort.

A second shock was waiting for me. At this highly inconvenient time I was due to go into hospital for a major operation and, of course, the dreaded letter arrived while Roy was stranded in the Solent. Hoping (in vain) for some good advice and sympathy from a neighbour, I said:
'I do hope Roy is home before I have to go in.'
'Well,' she said, rather shortly, 'You'll just have to leave him a note, won't you?'
Grinding my teeth, I conjured up what I might possibly write in this note, probably left propped up against the tea-pot on the kitchen table, and came up with:

Dear Roy,
Just popped into hospital for a quick major op. See you soon,
Love Vená.

Honestly, some people are no help at all!
Roy looks back at the Fort adventure with fond memories that are tinged with sadness because of the death of Tony. He was asked if he would scatter his friend's ashes at sea by Tony's widow, Barbara, and felt most honoured to do so. As both Roy and Tony loved the sea in general and the Solent in particular, it was arranged that the ceremony should take place as close to the Fort as possible. And so the boat carrying Barbara, Tony's brother, our son David and Roy set forth to perform its sad duty.
Who knows, perhaps the spirit of Tony thought the occasion was a bit too sad and solemn because as the boat was coming in to the beach, Roy said to Barbara:
'Don't get out, I'll lift you. I've got my wet suit on.'
Barbara was most grateful for this courtesy until Roy stepped over the side of the boat - and disappeared. That is to say, he disappeared right up to his knitted hat, which remained just above the surface of the sea. After a few moments of stupefaction, Barbara started to giggle and then shrieked with laughter, almost falling over the side herself in controllable mirth. Roy's soggy hat, followed by his soggy head, emerged from the deep and, having expelled a pint or two of salty Solent, joined in the merriment. It seems that instead of landing on the flattish sea bed as expected, he had picked a spot immediately above a deep hole (probably dug out by some rotter hunting for bait) and had subsided rather further than intended. Which just goes to show how dangerous glackity bait digging can be. However, this humorous little episode had its uses. It relieved a very emotional moment and suddenly everyone was saying how much Tony would have enjoyed it, and for all we know, perhaps he did.
Barbara could not bring herself to have the film in Tony's camera

developed, understandably, and so the only record of the two events is in our hearts and will not be lost. As for the Fort caper, Roy, alias Grumpy, has plenty of pictures. He and his companions do not bear much resemblance to Snow White and her little friends; they look more like a bunch of brigands or pirates, with evil, unshaven and grinning countenances. A thoroughly disreputable looking bunch, I thought. A local expression sums it up quite nicely – a pretty deedy lot and no mistake!

We now take another quantum leap forward in time and Roy has just reached his fifty-eighth birthday and made the momentous decision to retire when he reached the age of sixty. If he reached sixty, he would mutter darkly on a bad day. We knew that money would be tight but as we don't go to many wild parties these days and our idea of going abroad is a trip to the Isle of Wight, we thought we could manage (just!) and the idea of all that free time was irresistible. The next two years flew by on leaden wings while we planned all sorts of cheaply wonderful treats and outings and indulged in cost-cutting exercises that were immediately offset by some mad extravagance or other.

Nevertheless, it came as a sudden jolt when we were counting his 'clock cards' and he was asked what he would like for a retirement present. The leaden wings became feathered and by some queer sort of magic, The Day was tomorrow!

I said to Roy, 'Don't argue about anything I might say tomorrow.'
He said, 'Why?'
I said, 'You'll see!'
End of cryptic conversation.
He awoke on 29 June 1990 with his usual 'early morning rats' made worse by me singing 'Happy Birthday to Youoooo' powerfully, if not tunefully. Unlike Roy I am at my very best early in the morning and full of beans, which affects him profoundly, even on this very important day.

'Don't get your car out of the garage today – you won't need it,' I remarked, over our second cup of tea.

'Oh, Vená, no! You've gone and messed up all my arrangements, haven't you?' he growled unkindly.

'Just eat your breakfast and get ready for work.'
'But I don't want George to pick me up. I've made other arrangements,' plaintively.

'JUST GET READY...'
At 7.00 a.m. I said, 'Your lift is here.' By this time Roy was emerging from the E.M. Rats and was a little happier and full of breakfast – there is nothing like it, I always say – and he managed a little grin and opened the front door. The little grin widened until it threatened to split his face in two when

he beheld his 'lift'. Standing outside his own garden gate stood someone else's magnificent white Silver Lady Rolls Royce, no less, complete with a uniformed chauffeur. Arthur, the chauffeur, might have just stepped straight out from one of the soaps and looked more used to ferrying someone like Joan Collins about than my homely (but lovely) husband. Before Roy had time to get his breath back, a reporter from our local newspaper hopped out from another car and took pictures of Roy and the Rolls, Roy and Arthur, and Roy and Vená. Yet another vehicle arrived upon the scene, though this time it was a humble bike carrying my friend Pamela, also armed with a camera. Both ends of the spectrum, you might say, as no-one arrived on a skateboard.

When the VIP had been interviewed and photographed from every conceivable angle, Arthur coughed discreetly and said:

'If you are ready, Sir, I think we should proceed as you may be late for work.'

And off they rolled in the Roller, not to a City bank or wealthy developer's high rise suite, but to the Heavy Plate Shop in the Naval Base. As they turned the corner, Roy gave a dignified, almost royal, wave and disappeared from view. Arthur drove Roy by the longest route he could find, passing many of his colleagues trundling along on lowly bikes. Both Roy and Arthur encouraged them on their way with the former kindly giving them a regal salute and the latter a friendly toot. Wasn't that kind?

Four policemen were on duty at the Base entrance and as the Rolls drew up, Roy let the window down to show his ID and pass, informing them:

'Mr Bartlett, reporting for duty in the Heavy Plate Shop.' Pause for a wave of his (now) autocratic hand. 'Drive on, Arthur.'

Stunned silence greeted his arrival and as he turned to give them a further treat by way of an encore with his aristocratic podgy little hand, he noted that four mouths were hanging open. A regular Rolls owner could never have enjoyed travelling to work as much as Roy did on that last day! Arthur parked the stately limousine right outside the Plate Shop so that his passenger wouldn't have far to walk to clock in, and then stood to attention on the pavement when Roy re-entered the Rolls to watch the fun. It wasn't long coming. His friends looked back over their shoulders and tried to peer through the windows to see who on earth was visiting in a Rolls at 7.30 a.m. One poor chap parked his more humble car at the rear of the Rolls, so Roy let the window down once more and hailed him with:

'I say, fellow, how long will you be there? My man will not be able to turn the Rolls.'

Roy's colleague stooped down, looking apologetic and embarrassed, and peered in through the window. 'Oh! it's you, you silly bugger!' he said and couldn't stop laughing.

Later that morning Roy came home by taxi to collect me for the party at lunch-time. There were approximately 150 men and three ladies. One of the ladies, called Jean, had prepared all the wonderful food and some of Roy's pals pretended to be barmen. It was a really super party which we will never forget and suspect that some of his colleagues won't be able to remember! The foreman made a touching speech, mostly about how they were going to manage without the man who was small enough to crawl into awkward spots to do the welding, and then presented him with a model Spitfire in a glass dome and a watch, and for me, a carriage clock and a gorgeous basket of flowers. Lots of photos, fun, food and drink, and just the slightest hint of moisture in my eyes.

Such a send off, too! We were escorted to a trolley that had two seats covered by a Union Jack, handed in, and then towed by a little motor truck all around the shop floor. The men banged on the benches, hooters hooted, and one man blew a horn. It was deafening, lovely, and we enjoyed every moment.

While we were having lunch, one of Roy's friends rushed to get the early edition of our local paper, and much to everyone's delight, there was Roy on the front page, grinning from ear to ear, in front of the Rolls, holding a packet of sandwiches. I wonder what happened to them. He probably left them in the Rolls and Arthur had them for his lunch! Our daughter-in-law, Tina, who was also invited to Roy's party, managed to procure a vendor's placard which read, 'Docky's Stylish Send Off' - and that is a *really* stylish souvenir.

The next day we set off for our retirement holiday in the Isle of Wight. Being a newly retired couple we naturally booked the Honeymoon Suite with a four-poster bed, spa bath, balcony overlooking wonderful scenery, and (what else for a Honeymoon Suite?) Laura Ashley decor. And just as a finishing touch, the most beautiful bouquet from Tina and David lying on the bed. Our mugs over-raneth.

Five months after Roy's hectic and memorable send off from the Naval Base, he received a very important communication informing him that he had been recommended for the Imperial Service Medal. Anyone else would have gasped 'Gosh!' and gone all pink with pride and pleasure, but not my silly stiff-necked Roy, oh no! His immediate response was, 'Oh, my God! (large groan) What did they want to go and do that for, the silly sods!' Beneath all the protestations that went on for at least ten minutes I seemed to detect a slight excitement and, not to put too fine a point on it, a smidgen of smugness creeping around his bearded features. I may have been wrong - it's hard to tell what's going on under all that hirsute foliage - but a gut feeling told me that he was as pleased as Punch to have been selected for his honour and I wouldn't have to work on him at all hard to attend the

Ceremony. I now admit to a smidgen of smugness flitting across my own features because, having only half opened my mouth and long before I could utter a single syllable, he capitulated.

'Oh, all right. But I'm only doing it for your sake!'

'Oh, thank you, Roy,' I said, being the sweet little wifie. 'I really am so proud of you, and God knows you deserve it.'

He looked at me a bit doubtfully, as if wondering if I was taking the mickey. I truly wasn't; I was very proud of him and he certainly did deserve it. It was so nice that someone else had thought so and given the magic recommendation.

In due course a splendid invitation card to attend the Presentation Ceremony arrived, and was greeted with heavily disguised pleasure by Roy and the sort that shows by me. The Presentation was to take place at the end of November in the Rear Admiral's Residence and included any members of our family we chose to ask. As it turned out, every one of them that we would have chosen was heavily engaged elsewhere, and so on a damp and misty morning it was simply Roy and I setting off together. Naturally there was nowhere to park in the vicinity of the Admiral's house and we ended up a good quarter of a mile away. While panicking that we should be late, I missed my footing and slipped on the wet pavement, very nearly falling flat on my face in the process and, incidentally, giving my ankle the fright of its life. After a few hobbles ankle decided it wasn't quite broken and we might be able to get there after all. Perhaps my unladylike curses spurred its recovery for we arrived at the Admiral's door with five minutes to spare. Phew! Much later we discovered that we should have simply bowled up to the door in VIP fashion and all would have been taken care of. The trouble is, we have so little experience of being required to act in VIP fashion that we carry on in our usual humble style which results in parking miles away from the occasion, near-broken ankles and faces red from the unaccustomed exertion. We shall know better next time, if there is one!

Waiting in the porch to greet us were two Navy ratings (one of which was a very smart Wren) who having 'Good morninged' us and taken our top coats, ushered us into a beautiful lounge which seemed to be packed solid with people.

'Ye Gods!' from Roy, 'This medal can't be much good if everyone's going to get one. I needn't have come, they could have sent it in the post.'

A dig in the ribs and a hearty 'Shhh' shut him up, luckily, as I had spotted a very smart man heading towards us and looking most purposeful, and I didn't want us to get chucked out at this stage after all I'd been through getting here! He introduced himself as the Rear Admiral's secretary and then handed us over (like packages) to the lady acting as hostess for this distinguished gathering. Very quickly she put us entirely at ease and we chatted about mutual interests: common ground indeed as far as I was concerned, as we both adored flower arranging, orchids, and anything to do with gardens. I fear that Roy was compelled to hover in the background while our conversation got more and more animated, but he grinned nevertheless, even if it was supposed to be his big day. This lovely lady is the wife of a retired Admiral and performs the role of hostess at ceremonies as a sort of semi-profession. So caught up in our favourite subjects were we, that she had to pull herself together and get down to business, as it were. There was just time for her to tell us that two other recipients of the award were here and make hasty introductions before the Captain and Flag Officer arrived. This was to herald the imminent arrival of the Admiral (and reduce the chat level so that he could be heard) and we accordingly settled down to await his entrance.

Quite a lot of research must have gone into the new medal holders' background and interests, for the Admiral had so many facts and snippets at his finger tips that Roy learned things about himself he'd either forgotten or didn't know. The Admiral made much of the men's intentions as to how they were going to keep themselves amused in retirement and what with the many active pursuits, such as diving, that are part and parcel of Roy's life, he made him sound a little like Action Man on a very busy day. I felt the familiar urge to collapse with laughter and only with the greatest difficulty controlled it by breathing deeply and not catching Roy's eye. I felt my cheeks burn with the effort and thought, 'I bet they all think I'm having a hot flush' - it certainly felt like one!

It was all so cosy and cheerful in this beautiful room; an inviting coal and log fire glowed and snapped in the impressive fireplace, chintzy chairs and settees abounded with little antique tables to accommodate coffee cups and cakes, and there were marvellous long casement windows and a pushed back grand piano. The Admiral circulated among all the families and was particularly interested in the children. It was a pity that we hadn't any of ours to show off, but one can't have everything. It was while chatting to the children that the Admiral discovered that one little lad was terribly worried because his best friend (!) didn't believe that his Grandad was about to receive a medal from an Admiral, no less. He resolved this knotty problem by arranging to have his photograph taken holding hands with the little boy on one side and an even smaller sister on the other. I could imagine the conversation a few days hence:

'I say, Stinker. You know you didn't believe my Grandad was getting a medal?'

'Nah! Prove it then,' with a sneer.

'Okay, Buster - what about this then?' Produces photograph with a flourish and a sneer.

'Cor! Blimey!' and other expressions of amazement.

'Yah boo sucks, ya boo sucks . . .'

It gladdens the heart just to think about it; well, it does mine!

Later, when all the photographs had been taken, refreshments served and enjoyed and the children no longer over-awed and getting a bit too relaxed, the ceremony was suddenly at an end and we found ourselves back in the damp, drizzly November weather, plodding back to the car. I said to Roy:

'Wasn't that wonderful and aren't you glad you came? And how about that nice little sailor calling me Ma'am - that made my day. I felt like the Queen.'

Roy laughed and took me out to lunch.

CHAPTER 12

'I'd love to run an antiques stall, Vená,' wheedled Lavinia, and Roy overheard.

'Oh NO, NO, NO!' plus a large groan. His only contact with antique dealers had been an occasion when that silly Lavinia had inadvertently given a rag & bone man one of his sports jackets, complete with Dockyard pass, wallet, driving licence, etc., with the resultant dust-up trying to get his possessions back.

Vená thought she'd better take over as Lavinia is not always predictable and would be quite likely to say something tactless at this delicate stage of negotiations.

'Well, I've been watching carefully when we've been to antique fairs and I don't think there's much to it at all. In fact, it looks a doddle to me.'

'And what do you propose to sell, may I ask?'

'You may. I've got masses of Mum's things that we never use and I can buy bits and pieces and re-sell them.'

'Humph!' (or something similar).

Roy retreated behind his newspaper, which meant that he was either sulking and not speaking to me or mulling over my latest idea. I very much hoped it was the latter.

Strike while the iron is cold, has always been my motto and I visited every junk shop I could think of for spotting a valuable antique, price a tanner, and came home with amazing collections. My next motto is, the dirtier it is the older it looks and someone (like me!) will buy it on the off-chance. Much sooner than expected I had accumulated ample stocks of peculiar things and reckoned it was time to try my hand at being an antiques dealer. By this time, of course, Roy had recovered from his sulks and was curious enough to want to see what would happen. We were both surprised on our first stall by the speed at which our goods changed hands for money and I had this pretty vision of becoming a millionaire in about a fortnight.

The more I sold the more I had to trundle around second hand shops and the more Roy's help was enlisted. As we were fortunately making a profit of sorts he didn't complain, but I didn't get the impression that his heart was really in it – at least not to the extent of Lavinia's! However, a milestone was shortly to be reached that made his eyes boggle, as well as mine. The occasion was one of the big D-Day anniversaries and a show was held on our Common. Many Americans came to our city for this event and most of them seemed to be eager to buy from our stall. My nephew had had T-shirts printed with a D-Day commemoration design and I tastefully intermingled a heap of them with my valuable antiques. Being British and jolly well proud of it, I wore one and stood behind my stall with tanks, guns and soldiers emblazoned across my ample bosomage. I must have looked pretty damn good because they sold like hot cakes, especially to our trans-Atlantic friends and, hooray!, so did my older wares. In fact we were overwhelmed with custom and had to answer questions like:

'Gee, Ma'am, is this a genuine English antique clock?'

I could truthfully answer 'Yes', because it was old and dusty, so it must have been and if it wasn't, well, anyone can make a mistake. I expect it was lovingly restored when he got it home and might have been worth a fortune; it's all in the lap of the gods. My friend had been allocated a small space at the end of our stall and she sold the 'Tiggy-Winkle' stuff, which also vanished with speed. At the end of that busy day we were astonished to discover that between us we had made almost £400. This was quite a few years ago and represented a great deal of money.

After this staggering success Roy was more than happy to let me manage a stall but though he rubbed his eager little hands together gleefully, we didn't ever achieve again the dizzy heights of the D-Day show. Anyway, he is more of your outdoors type of fella and disliked the smoky and musty atmosphere that accompanies us antique dealers. Lavinia was also losing the first flush of enthusiasm, so between the two of them the stall-holding sessions got fewer and eventually petered out altogether. The curious thing is that we are no richer than we were before, even though we made a profit every time. I wonder where it went; no doubt Lavinia spent it on something exciting at the time. I have picked up many interesting bibelots during the quest for bargains, most of which I have kept and believe some of them may be of value. Perhaps one day I'll have another antiques stall and find out. I would like to be able to report that Roy greeted this proposition with enthusiasm but I fear that wasn't so. In so many words, he indicated that enough is more than enough!

The car boot sale has taken over now and many happy hours can be spent off-loading rubbish – I mean unwanted goods – that have been cluttering up the kitchen, garden and garage for years. The best time to take part in one of these is just before spring-cleaning time, because there isn't so much to clean and put back to get grubby until the spring bash. The part I like best is maybe half an hour before the end of the sale when I take a deep breath and holler:

'Come along, ladies and gentlemen. Every item here is going for 10p!'

It is fascinating to watch people's expressions change and charge in my direction. Things that were spurned at 50p are grabbed up as if they were Ming vases (which I don't think was ever the case – I hope not); it clears the decks and we don't have to take junk home – unless we've bought someone else's, of course! It is a lot of fun, really, and as Lavinia says:

'If you haven't had a car boot sale, you haven't lived.'

And just for once I agree entirely.

That Lavinia has been at it again – this time in my garden – and what happened was . . .

'My God, Lavinia!' I said, 'You've gone too far this time.'

I was squinting through our conservatory window whilst screeching this message. She has been known to be totally deaf and blind when reason should have prevailed so that the Vená part of me has to raise the decibel level more than somewhat in order to restore order, if you see what I mean.

Before me lay the mighty garden expanse of 28' x 28' and I was taking stock of the contents by peering through orchids, geraniums, begonias, a couple of ferns and sundry cacti, hence the squint. Not that any of these plants in the conservatory were giving me cause to cry out in alarm, it was the garden. Lavinia had gone mad! Let me explain. We are a two-patio family (sounds grander than it is), one at each end of the garden, and both are covered with tubs, pots, troughs, window boxes and hanging baskets on the enclosing walls and . . . the Eiffel Tower.

Now Lavinia is not wholly responsible for the addition of the Eiffel Tower – it was Roy's idea. He is a welder born and bred and has only to glimpse a piece of metal loafing about to wonder immediately what he can turn it into, sometimes with amazing results. E.T. had started out in life as a pedestal used in churches for those huge and droopy flower arrangements and had been very useful while Lavinia was starry-eyed during the Floral (F)Art period, but was now in dusty and forgotten retirement in Roy's capacious garage. He discovered it while poking about for something else; it fell on his foot and then clattered on to the floor. Naturally his eyes lit up in eager anticipation, just in case Lavinia would agree to part with this erstwhile treasured possession, and nipped smartly into the kitchen to find out. Preoccupied with other matters I gave the required permission and continued the important business of cake making. After a while I happened to glance through the window and espied the love of my life standing with his head on one side, surveying the prone pedestal thoughtfully. He then picked it up, held it sideways, then aloft, laid it on the ground again, and turned it upside down. Another screech from me made him jump.

'Roy!' I gasped, completely forgetting the half-made cake, 'I can see it now. Whoopee!'

In a matter of minutes the welding gear was set up in his workshop and protective clothing and headgear donned. Unfortunately, as he positively scampered towards the workshop he yelled over his shoulder for all the world to hear:

'Don't come in here, you'll get a flash.'

Of course I knew he meant a welder's flash, but heaven knows what the neighbours must have thought! Pretty soon there were blue flashes of lighting from the welding storm and a fair bit of thunder to go with it; but in just under an hour, there it stood – the Eiffel Tower in all its glory. Lavinia was thrilled to the marrow and was already mentally hanging six baskets from the curly brackets and standing potted plants around its upsidedown base and, best of all, she thought, I can put it wherever the fancy takes me.

'Wherever the fancy takes me' . . . h'mm. Now we get to the reason for yelling at Lavinia for going over the top. She has, in this small garden, the following: a rockery, pond with fish, garden seat, cherry tree, apple tree, water butt, thirty-six roses, three clematis, two honeysuckles, a dozen or so assorted shrubs, wisteria, a bird table, a bird nesting box, a sink garden, five Bonsai trees, several thousand bedding and container plants (and what seems several thousand containers), hostas, pinks, astilbes, campanula, antirrhinums, pansies, fuchsias, petunias, lavender, foxgloves, columbines, forget-me-nots, candytuft, and probably many other things I can't remember. You can see that we really needed an E.T., especially as it is now bedecked and glorious with baskets of lobelia, petunias, geraniums and fuchsias, and takes up quite a lot of space. In order to accommodate E.T. I was forced to shuffle the wrought iron penny-farthing bicycle (also made by that clever Roy) to one side because with its sproutings of potted plants it also takes up a lot of room, and instruct Roy to put the wrought iron wheelbarrow (also ditto by Roy), loaded to capacity, on the garage roof.

I said, more quietly, to Lavinia:

'Do you think it is possible that you have overdone things just for once?'

'Nah! It looks great. I could get a lot more in if I tried.'

What am I to do with Lavinia? She invariably has the last word. Perhaps she should be writing about our experiences instead of me; on second thoughts, that won't do, it has to be done by someone who is sensible and that leaves just me.

Oh, by the way, I forgot to mention the driftwood tree draped around the fish pond.

CHAPTER 13

Peg has trouble with a malignant force she calls 'Old Sod' and I think of as Old Nick (or worse). Anyway, whatever one likes to call him, he certainly put the mockers on yours truly, as illustrated in this rueful account.

'Vená!' a friend carolled over the phone, 'Do you fancy a day out at Kew?'

I should say so. Further details revealed that a trip by coach had been arranged by a local branch of a near-National institution that I didn't belong to, and someone had dropped out at the last minute, hence the vacant seat.

'Oh, great. Yes, please.'

Instructions were received and understood and I then dashed frantically around the kitchen so that Roy would at least get fed upon his return and (if he put his glasses on) understand the reason for his wife's absence from my hastily scrawled note. A quick tidy up in front of the mirror, grotty household clothes changed to something a little more respectable, front door slammed, followed by a dash up the road to catch the coach, with a good two seconds to spare.

It was an extremely hot morning and when the coach door opened an even hotter blast of air nearly knocked me back on to the pavement. I could feel my already moistly pink face blossom into scarlet as I struggled through the rows of polite strangers and, thankfully, spotting my friend, sank into the seat with relief. Despite the heat we chattered away happily, anticipating the delights of Kew Gardens and planned our programme.

It was somewhere past Guildford that a lightning bolt of pain shot through my jaw, teeth, ear, eye and nose, and practically levitated me to the roof. My friend eyed me with alarm, probably thinking I was having a fit.

'Oh, my God!' she cried agitatedly, 'Whatever's the matter, Vená?'

For a few minutes I was literally unable to speak, the pain was so intense, keeping her in suspense while she waited with concern and anxiety. I was coming to the conclusion that I must have suddenly developed an enormous abscess under a tooth and that was very bad news indeed. You see, I have this phobic dread of the dentist's chair and will not under any circumstances darken their doors. I would sooner put my naked hand into a jar full of tarantulas, though I hope never to have to prove it.

The further we got away from home the more desperate I felt and it was with great difficulty that I managed to persuade my unhappy friend that I was able to continue with our planned day out. My fingers were firmly crossed while making this rash statement, but it did seem a shame that, through an act of kindness to me, her long awaited day out at Kew should be ruined. When we finally arrived and I stumbled off the coach it was into air so hot and humid that it would have curdled the milk at fifty paces, and made me think longingly of the baking coach which now seemed quite cool in comparison with the London temperature. Fortunately there are many huge and shady trees in these beautiful grounds and I wandered in a daze until I found one that had slightly more than standing room only in its shelter, and sank gratefully on to the grass. Perhaps, I thought, if I had the strength to admire nature, a kind of peace might descend upon my unworthy head, followed by a refreshing sleep that would magically remove this present purgatory. So I tried that and it didn't work. In fact it didn't work so much that a further and unconnected pain assaulted my already racked body. From past experience I recognised it at once: the dreaded cystitis. Ask any woman to name one of the worst hefty ailments and I bet she will reply 'cystitis' without having to think about it. The Gods seemed to be enjoying a 'Let's hate Vená' day and I couldn't think of anything extra wicked that I'd done for at least a week to deserve such retribution. My poor friend remarked that I had turned a funny colour, 'Like,' she said, 'pale in a reddish-yellowish way.' I didn't care a jot.

The afternoon passed slowly and painfully but at long last it was time to reboard the coach and point our noses homeward. I must have dozed for some of the journey because my befuddled brain suddenly registered that we were passing dear and familiar landmarks and buildings that meant that home was almost within my grasp. Tears of joy and relief swam in my eyes and I promised the Gods that I would be as good as gold in future and never, ever, put a foot wrong again.

Catching sight of me creeping carefully along the garden path changed Roy's cheery welcoming grin into firstly amazement and then extreme worry in case I should die before I made it indoors. He obviously bit back questions while helping me upstairs and into bed and it wasn't until I was as comfortable as could be expected, as they say in hospitals, that he asked me if it had been a very bad accident. It took a moment or two to understand this strange question until I realised that I probably looked as if I had been in one.

'Pass me the mirror,' I croaked through swollen tongue and stiff jaw and was duly shocked to see a hideous stranger peering back at me. My face is round at the best of times but now it had grown much larger on the afflicted side, pulling the eyelid sideways and downwards. As for half of my cherubic lips – there was so much extra face to cope with that there was real danger they would split under the strain. Aghast, I studied the appalling features that seemed to be studying me in return and decided to have a good cry. Try as I might and despite the thin despairing wail I did manage, not a tear would come to my assistance. For no reason that I can think of, this struck me as being very comical and so I laughed instead. Not very loudly, you understand, but it did wonders in releasing some of the terrible tension I had been under. A wayward thought trickled through my mind that perhaps I had Chinese ancestors somewhere or other along the line! After all, I looked like half a mad Chinese lady and now I was laughing in adversity instead of crying; it all fitted.

Meanwhile, back at my bedside, Roy was making noises about summoning our doctor to save my life, which was the very last thing I wanted. I badly needed some fluid followed swiftly by deep and merciful sleep. Having swallowed with difficulty a glass of water, I persuaded Roy to make me some tea and not phone the doctor while my back was turned and, in turn, promised to see the doctor in the morning should the need arise. I made no mention of visiting the dentist; we should have to see what happened. Tea seemed to settle and restore me a little and I was vaguely aware of Roy gently pulling the sheet over my shoulders and quietly closing the door. Some years later, or it might have been hours, anyway, it was middle-of-the-night dark, I roused to a strange and nasty taste but wasn't unduly worried because all felt so peaceful and nice. The next time I opened my eyes it was to bright sunshine and dear Roy caught in the act of putting a cup of tea on my bedside table.

'Hello, love,' he whispered, 'How are you feeling? Shall I ring for the doctor?'

Oh, yes, I remembered, I'm at death's door, and promptly discovered that I was pain-free all over. How incredible! I moved about gingerly in the bed just in case some pain or other was lurking dagger-like to stab at something vital, but, no, all seemed to be very well indeed. I recalled the awful taste in my mouth in the small hours and concluded that the abscess had burst of its own accord without the help of a dentist and that, in some miraculous fashion, the cystitis had decided not to bother after all. It was as if I had died and gone to heaven after dreadful goings-on. No, that wasn't it, because Roy was here with a cup of tea and, in any case, pretty soon I should have to pop to the loo and I didn't imagine one would be called upon to do that in heaven.

'Quick, Roy!' in a nearly normal voice, 'Pass me the mirror, please.'

Last night's gargoyle (Chinese style) was replaced with a paler version of my usual reflection and had slightly bloodshot eyes, but apart from that looked much the same as always. I was nearly delirious with joy and was able, at long last, to give Roy a detailed account of my day out at Kew. One of the very nice things about him is his ability to be calm, reliable and sympathetic when the occasion merits and every now and again he is worth his weight in orchids. He did confess to almost ringing the doctor but decided that it would be a shame to awaken me from such a deep sleep, having first ascertained that I was still breathing.

I will touch wood while saying this: just for the record, I still have the tooth that caused so much uproar, it gives no trouble, *and* I didn't go to see a dentist. That's the good bit; the bad bit is a niggling worry that perhaps Peg's dubious and malignant friend, Old Sod, might have been listening when my friend phoned and said, 'Vená! Do you fancy a day out at Kew?', and thought gleefully to himself of the golden opportunities for a little sport.

All my life I have been moderately conceited about my dainty and blemish-free feet - until now, that is. Until two years ago they were a delight to behold, and I have been known to flaunt them deliberately under the noses of foot fanciers, just in case a compliment was in the offing. Not only were they pretty, they were very serviceable and have carried me thousands of miles on the surface of this planet of ours without complaint. Not now; but I am complaining bitterly.

It all happened during that strange period of life called menopause, or 'change of life' as my mother would have called it, and started as an itch on the sole of my left foot and then almost immediately, my right foot. 'Well, here's a pretty kettle of soup,' I thought, 'What's going on?' Plenty was going on and it was fairly obvious that my dainty little plates would have to visit our doctor before long.

'Good gracious!' he said, looking terribly interested. 'Haven't seen anything like this before; I wonder what it is. I think we must send a bit to the laboratory and see what they make of it. Be about a month - come and see me then.'

That month seemed endless and the more I tried to ignore whatever it was, the more it itched. It was quite maddening and I nearly drove us all to drink. All the creatures I know about itch, and then they scratch, and that's an end of it. I only wish I was one of God's creatures because the reverse applied to me. Before the month came to an end my feet were raw, bleeding, and very loath to carry me anywhere. And I was as miserable as sin.

'Well, Vená,' reported our doctor, 'That test was not conclusive [a polite way of saying they haven't got a clue and not much chance of finding out!] so I'm arranging for you to see a skin specialist.'

Three months later I was sitting in the hospital waiting room with several other sufferers, trying very hard not to scratch in public – especially in the Skin Department – and a rather cross looking nurse bustled in.

'Is Vera [!] Bartlett here? Come this way, please, the doctor will see you now.'

The doctor was female, young, blonde, and obviously itchless, which made me look rather cross. If I have to itch I want everyone to itch, and particularly young, blonde and female doctors. She was reading my notes and said, without looking at my face or down at my feet:

'Oh, yes, you've got derma–' (I never did catch the itch's name), 'I'll give you some Derma– cream and see you in six months' time.'

I wasn't going to leave it there.

'But what have I got?'

'Oh, it's derma–.' And then, with a rather pitying look, she said:

'It's mostly women of your age that get it. I'm afraid it lasts from two to five years.'

'*Years?*' I repeated incredulously.

'Yes. I'll see you in six months to see how it's getting on.'

'How did you get on at the clinic?' asked my kind and considerate husband.

'Don't ask! She said it might last for five years.'

'*Bloody 'ell!*'

Despite dedicated applications of the Derma– cream and a valiant effort to stop scratching, whatever it was got worse and so did my health and temper. One day Roy found an advertisement in our local paper which read 'Help for Whatever-it-is Sufferers' and gave a help line telephone number.

'How about ringing this number and see what help they can offer?' he said.

I had nothing to lose except my sanity, so any port in a storm would do, including Mrs Blank on the help line.

'Hello, my dear, can I help you?'

'Oh, good morning. I have your number to ring for help for Whatever-it-is.'

'That's right, dear – now, tell me all your symptoms and any medication you are on.'

I had got as far as 'My feet are killing me . . .', when I heard her take a deep breath and then cut me off in my prime with:

'Oh, you don't have to tell me, dear. I've had Whatever-it-is for twenty-five years. I have it on my arms, legs, . . . and my doctor says . . .'

On and on she went and I tried to listen patiently to her tale of terrible woe and be sympathetic, but after about fifteen minutes thought I'd better terminate this expensive exercise in therapy, otherwise I might not able to afford the next tube of Derma– cream. A slight pause for breath on her part and I pounced like a hawk.

'Well, thank you for your help. Goodbye.'

I realised that listening to all her gruesome symptoms had made me itch more than ever and consequently had been scratching first one foot and then the other and a fat lot of help that was!

I am just entering my third year of this scourge and as yet haven't found a remedy. The nearest thing to blissful relief is a good old soak in salty water, preferably the sea, and a quick rub down with hydrous cream. To add to my present glamour, I wear cotton socks and floppy shoes with positively no foot flaunting in front of fanciers. Life can be very cruel. I am considering joining that sterling group of 'Help for Whatever-it-is Sufferers' and becoming a Mrs Blank. That way I can get relief by enthralling those who need assistance in coping with whatever-it-is with my symptoms and tribulations – and it won't cost me a penny!

CHAPTER 14

This is positively Vená and Lavinia's last ramblings, and we both thought it would be appropriate to finish off with snippets concerning the grandchildren (mostly), just before they finish us off! Roy and I are immensely proud of them, even if just occasionally a light clip round the ear wouldn't come amiss and seems rather tempting at the time. As they aren't our children, this temptation is firmly resisted and other more subtle means of restraint are substituted. It doesn't always work, of course, but is quite fun to operate, and we both have to admit that we forgive any misdemeanours simply because they are usually very funny. Take our day out at Brighton, for instance.

Arrangements had been made that Roy and I should meet son Robert with his two small boys, Lewis and Harry, on Brighton Pier at 11.00 a.m. Extra expense had recently been involved in the Bartlett household and it was imperative that we find the cheapest method of travel. After much research and head scratching, we discovered that bussing would be the most economical but took a mighty long time getting there. Oh well, one of us thought and the other agreed, if we ain't got much money we've got plenty of time and it might turn out to be an adventure. We should have guessed that it would!

I don't know if more people are moving about on Fridays, but certainly on this one we weren't short of interest watching the world and his wife hopping on, settling down for a bit and hopping off, and this made the journey pass quite quickly. Different towns and villages produced different kinds of travellers. There were comfortably-off looking ladies with shopping baskets for Chichester and Worthing, all ages and both sexes obviously going to work, and young mums struggling with push chairs and little ones, all along the coast. I saw no sign that the population of Britain is decreasing and suggest that the Government's Statistics Office goes back and checks its figures. Having pondered upon this weighty matter, I turned my attention to the middle-aged section and wondered if any of them were having a 'Brief Encounter' with a fellow passenger, but couldn't discern any likely candidates. Perhaps a bus terminus isn't so romantic as a railway station and not conducive to violins wailing tender music. Even so, one would have thought that out of a whole bus full of people there would have been at least one shifty-looking pair, but no luck. However, it is a matter for conjecture that perhaps someone on the bus had a daffy mind similar to my own and suspected Roy and me of having an illicit day out. True, we are middle-aged, and also true that we don't look all that randy, but we were excited at the thought of seeing our family at the end of the journey, and that might have been misconstrued – I know my brain would have leapt to a wild conclusion!

At last we trundled into Brighton, nicely in time to be able to grab a cup of tea at Fortes Tea Shop where we could do an efficient surveillance job for the arrival of Robert and the boys. For once Robert did something right by appearing with two bouncy youngsters at the precise moment we finished our tea, making their way across the road to the Pier. Preliminaries over (many hugs and kisses), we embarked on to the Pier and spent about a week's housekeeping in about ten minutes. Obviously we hadn't better linger here! Lunch was the next financial hurdle and we set off in search of tasty, nourishing food that was dirt cheap. Sadly, we discovered that our idea of dirt cheap is not Brighton's, with fish and chips at £2.50 per portion and an ice cream minimum of 50p.

'Can't be helped,' said Roy, 'We've got to eat.'

Gloomily I wondered if we'd be eating at all at the end of the week; it seemed to depend upon what was in the freezer and cupboard. But fish and chips, when beautifully cooked, have a marvellous tonic and satisfaction factor, and full of both and a sense of well-being, we rashly asked the boys if they would like a trip on the little train that runs along the sea front. Of course they did.

A board attached to the ticket office stated: 70p. Adults, 30p. Children, making it very advisable that Daddy and Grandad should walk, while Lewis, Harry and Grandma would travel the short distance in the comfort of the train. Out came my purse again and we went to the ticket office.

'Sorry, luv,' said the Ticket Man, 'She won't be going for a bit – the line is being repaired and it might take a little while.'

A mini-conference was held and by popular consensus we decided to buy tickets and wait on the train until the track was repaired. We waved 'Cheerio' to the men and climbed aboard. The tiny train was fairly full of holiday makers, a good percentage of which were children. We found one carriage that had a few vacant seats and, seated, examined our fellow travellers with interest. They were doing the same as us. A quick look at us and then a long look away, and we found that we were following the same pattern after a minute or two and it was getting rather embarrassing, as well as silly. I didn't dare laugh because I find it so difficult to stop and the boys would demand to know what was funny. Fortunately the other children caused a diversion by becoming restless and fidgety, while my two sat rather primly asking intelligent questions about the railway, the doors, the track, etc., making me feel like the grandmother of two brilliant and well behaved grandsons. Then having attracted everyone's attention, Lewis slouched in his seat and began what I thought was going to be another prissy question, in a very loud voice:

'Grandma! What's a blow off?'

'Yes!' chipped in Harry, helpfully, 'A blow off, a blow off!'

Faced with this difficulty, I hastily gathered them up and shovelled them off the still stationary train and we set off in pursuit of Roy and Robert. A light on the horizon gleamed for us though, because the train stubbornly remained *in situ* and our money was returned. Hooray!

It was a cloudy but extremely hot day and we were very thirsty. So we did what any sensible and thirsty grandparents would do, blew the whole of the refund on tea for the adults and orange juice for the boys, and then went on the beach. By this time we were all a bit jaded and my feet were throbbing like a disco. Thankfully lowering myself on to the shingle, I just had time to sigh with satisfaction before Lewis fell headlong into the sea, fully dressed. Scarcely had he been fished out and sort of dried off, than Harry yelled heartily and long as a result of a slapped hand for throwing stones. Roy and I looked at each other and decided it was definitely time to go and catch our bus home. We said fond farewells to the little boys, one with damp seaweedy hair and the other with a tear-stained face, and left them to the tender mercies of their father. This is the really lovely thing about grandchildren, you don't have to take them home with you when the going gets rough!

The homeward journey was curiously similar to the outgoing. I don't suppose they were really the same people but looked as if they were. Again, no 'Brief Encounter' candidates, just ordinary nice folk who probably went out to collect their pensions. A bit disappointing, but at least they won't have been asked in public, 'Grandma, what's a blow-off?'

Following an incident free (surprisingly), beautiful and touching wedding ceremony of son David and his lovely bride Tina, we all repaired to the wedding reception, relaxed and happy, and looking forward to a merry afternoon. Absolutely nothing to fault: wonderful breakfast, tons of drink, with both families and guests ensuring that the party went with a rather noisy swing. That is, until a worried-looking lady guest approached me with an extremely limp young Jimmy in her arms.

'Oh, Vená!' she cried agitatedly, 'Thank goodness I've found you. Your little grandson seems ill and can't stand up.'

Panic-struck, I grabbed him from her arms and, calling for Roy, rushed outside to fresher air and examined the paper white face and floppy body. It is no exaggeration to say that this was one of the worst moments of my life, as I thought he was dead.

Roy appeared, white and shaking, and, taking the youngster from me, cried:

'Jimmy, Jimmy! Speak to Grandad.'

Suddenly he stopped shouting and looked closely at the pathetic little scrap imitating a rag doll, bent down and sniffed. With disbelief in his voice he said:

'My God! The child's drunk!'

Fresh air and none too gentle tappings on his cheeks revived the four-year-old drunkard who, incredibly, resumed life after a few minutes as if nothing whatsoever had happened. He didn't even need a doctor as he seemed even fitter than before his binge, with little pink cheeks (probably from the tappings) and sparkling eyes.

'Oh God!' groaned his Grandad, 'I can't stand all these shocks. Come on, I need a drink.'

It was while we were supping a medicinal something that we learned that Jimmy had toddled from table to table, finishing off any dregs he found in empty glasses as he went. Really, I thought, people should be more careful and empty their glasses properly, sagely tipping my glass high to get the last drop.

Years ago, when we lived in our first dear old house, a very attractive couple of newly-weds took up residence next door and we all became fast friends very quickly. They soon produced an addition to the human race, to my delight, especially as it was a boy child and beautiful to boot. A few years later a second child was expected and we - the women - waited with bated breath to see if this one would be as perfect as the trial run child. It was, therefore, a shock to learn that Son No. 2 was a Down's Syndrome baby, and felt very sad for the whole family.

Named Richard, this child was an absolute darling of a baby and his parents and brother took his disability in their stride so completely that it was as if it didn't even exist. Pretty soon Richard was everyone's favourite baby in the whole neighbourhood and I was more than thrilled when Richard's mother awarded me the highest honour possible - Aunty Vená was to be the one to take him out in his pram for the very first time to the local shops. It was the equivalent of being asked to partake of a cucumber sandwich with Her Majesty the Queen. Even my own harum-scarum sons, aged six and eight, were smitten and I received a request to provide them with a baby brother exactly like Richard. Roy and I became his godparents and watched him grow and thrive, delighting in his happy and loving nature and the way in which all the children locally absorbed him so naturally into their lives.

One Christmas I was invited to attend Richard's Sunday School service with his mother, and the children sat in the front seats in classes, while proud mums and visitors took a back seat (literally) to watch their offspring being religious! At this time Richard was slightly deaf and queried 'Eh?' to practically everything that was said to him, but he sat there as good as gold and smiling while the Vicar started the service by asking the classes questions about the Nativity. Naturally all the mums and friends had lumps in their throats as the little ones shot their hands in the air and answered in clear piping voices, until . . . 'And what was Baby Jesus sleeping on in his crib?'

Richard's hand went up first. 'Eh?'

'Well done, Richard!' said the Vicar, 'That's quite right. Good boy.'

Aunty Vená had suddenly to leave the church to recover for a few minutes and upon return, didn't dare look at Richard's mother in case the urge to laugh heartily returned.

Over the years Richard has grown into a very nice and responsible young man, holding a position in his father's company. He has travelled the world with his parents and brother, is well adjusted and charming and, best of all, is just as delighted to see us now as he was when a small child. I have to admit it – he is one of the lights of my life!

Naturally we have to share our grandsons with their other grandparents, and at the time Harry was at the tender age of two and a half, there was one slight disadvantage for him when staying with his mother's parents. Unable to get his little tongue around 'Grandad', he settled for 'Pam-Pam' (which is rather nice, I think), and Pam-Pam has an overwhelming passion – he breeds huge tropical frogs. Now this pastime is fascinating to Pam-Pam but is utterly loathed by Harry, and during one of his visits to us, I asked:

'Oh, Harry, I forgot to ask – how are Pam-Pam's big frogs?'

Harry had been playing with gadgets on the floor in his usual rather serious fashion, and went rigid when the dreaded words 'big frogs' connected between his ears and brain. He got slowly up and came to stand about three inches away from me, his eyes as big as buckets. He shuddered a couple of times and the expression of extreme distaste was pretty to watch. 'Oh! Oh! *Gwandma!* They're *weally howwible* and they *pooh* on *people.*'

And having got that out of his system he turned round, went back to his project on the floor and made something extraordinary out of the gadgets. I thought it looked a little like a large frog!

His brother Lewis is also on the bright side, in addition to having been reared on a University campus, and when he was three years old came to stay with his dimmer grandparents, bringing his favourite soft toy to cuddle in bed.

'What a lovely bunny,' remarked his Aunty Tina brightly, 'What's his name?'

Lewis treated Aunty Tina to a long, hard look, and then said in a voice full of scorn, 'Rabbit.'

It was time for the adults to sneak away for a hearty laugh.

Then there was the time that son Robert brought three sons to stay in the caravan camp that is sited nearly within spitting distance from our house. I worried that our glackity son had let himself in for more than he realised and voiced my fears to Roy.

'Well, honestly, Roy, you know he never plans ahead in case of emergencies, or anything, come to that. And what about all the cooking and washing and plasters for scraped knees?'

Roy sighed in the long suffering way that never fails to let me know that I'm going over the top.

'I bet they're loving every minute. And you can bet your boots if he has any problems he'll be knocking on our door, so stop fussing, for heaven's sake.'

We had arranged to go to their caravan for a visit one morning and in order that Robert wouldn't think I didn't trust him while having sole charge of his own children, put it to Roy that we would be advised to turn up casually and a little late.

'Good idea,' said Roy. 'Let's take a flask of coffee on the beach first.'

Round about 11.00 a.m. we decided that now was casual enough in anyone's book, so wound our way up the beach and into the caravan camp. It was easy to see that no-one was at home so I poked a note through the window, demanding to know where the hell they'd been.

'Here, hang on a moment,' said Roy. 'Didn't Robert say he was going to take them for a swim this morning? Let's go and have a look on the beach.'

We climbed back up the shingle hillocks and there, coming towards us, was Robert accompanied by three wet little boys. Harry had no pants on and lifted up his long T-shirt to prove it, Lewis was sulking because he didn't agree with having to come out of the water to meet Grandma and Grandad, and Jimmy was fully clothed in Pompey colours kicking a football about. Robert appeared to be rather tired and, after a little probing, complained:

'They all want to do different things. Now we've got to go back to the camp to join in the blasted Scavenger Hunt. If they're not too late,' he added hopefully.

Actually the Hunt proved to be quite jolly. All participants were supplied with a list of things to collect from the beach and camp, and for the next forty-five minutes hordes of children scampered around combing the beach for interesting objects such as 'a feather', 'a cuttlefish bone', 'a lolly stick', and so on.

Our three were nowhere in the running as after about five minutes complaints came pouring in . . . 'Dad, we're bored' . . . 'We can't find anything' . . . 'Grandma, when's lunch?' . . . I suggested they all went to the refreshment bar for an orange juice or something, while I prepared a light lunch. This met with approval from the youngest generation, but Robert was very doubtful if this would work as the boys were at the picky stage and demanded different things to eat, with many arguments over what they liked and didn't like, and generally causing a quite unnecessary fuss. Lavinia was having none of this nonsense. It must have been rather a shock to the little horrors when they trooped in the caravan door, ready for skirmishes, to find softy Grandma missing and replaced with a determined looking lady with a steely glint in her eye.

'Have you all washed your hands? Right! Now sit properly at the table and I don't want to know who likes what - you will just eat what's put in front of you and no nonsense. There will be no ice cream afterwards until everything, I repeat, everything, is eaten. *Do you understand?*'

In amazement Robert watched everything disappear with no squeaks or moans. I explained to Robert later the simple psychology known universally as 'Mother's Blackmail', by picking a single dish that they all like and then disguising it as a carrot to dangle in front, or rather beyond, real or fancied dislikes. Works like a dream, every time. What I didn't mention to him was how he had almost ruined the entire operation by shrinking and joining the youngest generation during my harangue by inadvertently examining his own hands to see if they were acceptable at the table. Childhood training obviously sticks like glue (to my credit) but in the process very nearly convulsed me and had to be hidden under an extra fierce *Do you understand?*, to my further credit.

Robert told Roy and me how he had taken the children to the camp disco the previous evening and had spent most of the time mopping up tears of laughter. A chip off the old block! A special participation spot had been included and the compère had invited children who had a good joke to tell to come up on the stage and kill the rest of the audience.

Jimmy was the first of our three, and his contribution went thus:

'What plain crisps fly? Plane! Ooh!, sorry, I shouldn't have said "plain crisps", I should have said just "crisps"!'

An eerie audience silence greeted Jimmy's joke while they tried to work it out and then a few titters broke loose, followed by a couple of claps. So much for Jimmy's stage career!

Lewis toddled on stage next, eager to make matters worse.

'What crisps fly?' in a perfect show biz squeak. 'Salt and vinegar!'

The audience was getting the hang of things now and laughed heartily and even cheered a bit.

And now it was Harry's turn – the cherry on top of the cake!
Compère: 'Hello, little boy. What is your name?'
Harry: 'Four years.' (In his little squeaky voice.)
Compère: 'I see, and how old are you?'
Harry: 'Harry.'
He had everyone's attention riveted by now and there was much applause. The compère saw there was future in a few more minutes of this sort of repartee and made his little joke.

'Ladies and Gentlemen! As you can see, we have Royalty with us this evening [pause for effect] – will the Royal Parents please stand up?'

There was, naturally, no response to this request and the heads of the audience swivelled back and forth, not quite sure if this was a joke or not. Not even the most humbly born parents put in an appearance as Mum was miles away and Dad was propping up the bar in case it fell over! Hastily putting Plan 'B' into action, the compère turned to the little boy.

'Now, Harry. Tell all the nice people your joke.'

Harry wouldn't have recognised a wisecrack if it had jumped up and bitten him. Not that one would have guessed from his assured delivery.

'What did the tree say to the flower?'
'I don't know, what did the tree say to the flower?'
'Let's go for a walk!'
And that really brought the house down.

It will probably seem to you that my family spent most of their time doing silly things in tents and caravans. We didn't really; it's just that sillier things happen in tents and caravans than at home. Take the case of the missing towel, for instance.

'Grandma, Grandma! Come quick. Harry is waving his willy out of the caravan window.'

'What?' I screamed and flew into their tiny bedroom and did indeed find Harry shaking his half-inch long object with vigour through the open window. Not only that, he had a very interested audience of two little girls sitting on the next door caravan step, completely convulsed with mirth (or hysteria).

'What are you doing, Harry?' I demanded to know.

'Daddy said I was to take my wet bathers off and dry myself with the towel, but I can't find my towel so I'm drying myself out of the window.'

'But Harry, there are two little girls watching you.'

'Oh, is there? Do they know where my towel is?'

Dear innocent little four-year old!

Assisting Robert set up yet another camp for him and his offspring reminded me of a week-end that Roy and I had spent camping one glorious late spring – at least thirty years ago. We were accompanied by our friends, Poppy and Dick with their two little girls, and Roy's huge friend who rejoiced in the name of Buff and had recently become a widower. Buff and Roy very much shared the same interests, such as diving and spear fishing, apart from owning a small motor van that was handy for transporting a goodly chunk of the amazing amount of gear we obviously couldn't live without. Our destination was the geological wonder of the south coast, Durdle Dor in Dorset, and that Friday evening we were all in high spirits, bowling along in Buff's van and our car that had been converted from a van. A right parcel of gypsies, you might say, and you would be correct. All those years ago Durdle Dor was visited by very few people, very much sans the great acreage of car parks and caravan sites that sit like a silly hat on a magnificent head today. Of course it is still awesome with the evidence of Nature's wrath in the folded and twisted rock strata, but somehow it was much more so then with the utter quiet and peacefulness – at least until we arrived! It is funny how everyone completely disregards the amount of noise that they themselves make, while taking extreme umbrage at others' high decibel levels.

While the rest of the adults set up camp, willingly and unhelpfully helped by our two small sons and the two little girls, Buff prepared and cooked the supper. There is absolutely nothing so mouth watering and nostril titillating as sausages and bacon, etc., sizzling away in the open air on a still and beautifully warm evening, and that spurred us on to renewed efforts to get the camp complete before we died of hunger. It was a feast beyond compare and we congratulated ourselves on having the wit to kidnap Buff for the week-end. Replete and drowsy, we slouched on the turf and were fascinated by the hundreds of little lanterns provided by glow-worms in their mating season. Perhaps after a while they mesmerised us as well as their intended mates, as one after another we drooped, yawned, and somebody gave a snore that woke us all up and made the children giggle. Unanimously we decided it was time to call it a day and would repair to the one and only tent – ours. Why had we thought we could squeeze in four adults and four children in space intended for four persons is a mystery and will remain so for ever. Lavinia got tense and edgy as ever since she was shut in a cupboard for a jolly jape that went horribly wrong, she has become claustrophobic and there was no way she could be induced to enter that small tent full of those big bodies, and something would have to be substituted. Desperation sharpens brains (so I'm told) and a brilliant idea came forth. She could sleep quite happily on her own in the car, bearing in mind that it was a converted van and Roy could let the back seat down to make a kind of platform and would be long enough for her to stretch out, well, nearly. Roy agreed that this was a good idea and then I had another – good old mesmeric glow-worms!

'Hey, Roy!' I said, 'I think I'll put the lounger on it - that will be a lot more comfortable.'

'You'll be a bit close to the roof. Still, give it a try and see what happens.' He sounded rather doubtful about this second idea.

It worked very well because having the windows open eliminated that awful shut in feeling and very soon I drifted into a gentle limbo, still smiling to myself at the thought of all those bum-shaped bulges protruding from the sides of the tent. That was the good bit. The bad bit roared up in the shape of two very raucous motor bikes plus owners and passengers that matched their vehicles. In all that vast amount of space, they homed in our little patch and promptly lit a bonfire and turned on very loud music. Since the start of this diabolical intrusion, I had been pretending that I wasn't stretched out and helpless in our converted car, and I wondered how long it would be before Roy would blow his top and tackle the young tearaways. It seemed a long time, but I don't suppose it was, and then I observed the tent shaking and rolling from side to side. I could imagine the turmoil inside as Roy struggled to unzip the opening and not tread on innocent bodies at the same time, but at last he managed it and fell out on to the grass with a face distorted with rage. 'Oh, dear,' I thought, knowing how unpredictable his temper can be when really roused. 'Don't get too mad - they'll kill you.' Now free of his temporary home, he positively shot across to our unsociable neighbours and bellowed:

'What the hell do you think you're up to? We've got four children trying to sleep in here, SO PUT A SOCK IN IT.' The last part of the message nearly burst my ear drums.

'Woo! Woo! Up the Boy Scouts,' came the taunting reply, with appropriate gestures.

That did it! Roy gave a roar of anger and drew his fist back. I drew my breath in, terrified that they would all set upon my little and fiery husband, leaving me a widow with small children to bring up. I needn't have worried, for out of the gloaming stepped our Giant Buff, followed by Dick. The culprits wouldn't have known that Buff was the most gentle of men and would no more dream of striking his fellow beings than row across the Atlantic on a plank, and I could see that they didn't really believe the evidence of their own eyes. Awed, is the expression I will use, and suddenly scared. Buff laid a restraining hand on Roy's arm and said:

'Come on, Roy, simmer down. They're not worth it,' at the same time treating the bikers to a contemptuous and searching gaze.

In seconds there was dead silence and Buff and Dick returned Roy to the tent and shoved him through the flap. There were twitterings and murmurings from the overcrowded tent for a short while and blessed peace reigned once more. Much relieved, I took Buff's advice to Roy and simmered down into a deep sleep. The early morning sun in my eyes woke me up and with a start I remembered the dramatic events of the night. Like thieves in the night they had slipped away, leaving no forwarding address. The only reminder of the unwelcome visit was a few smouldering embers in what was left of the bonfire, and wisps of grey wood smoke. Poppy's voice through the window made me jump.

'Good gracious! When did she die?' and laughed her head off.

Later at breakfast – again cooked by that genius, Buff – we could talk of nothing except the night's adventures, and came to the conclusion it was no wonder they had sneaked off so quietly, pushing the bikes instead of roaring away. We suddenly saw the situation from the interlopers' point of view. All set for a bit of fun annoying towny-type campers, they see one small tent straining at the seams with live bodies, one small van and another not quite identifiable vehicle close by. Out of the tent struggles an extremely irate small man, followed by probably the largest person they've ever seen and a medium sized one. Added to that, various faces popped out of the tent flap, heightening the impression that at least twenty people were occupying it. All that is odd enough, but they might just have looked in our converted-van-car, which was black, and spotted a dead woman laid out tastefully on a lounger. It all fitted neatly together. They would have wondered why a dead woman in a small black hearse (on a lounger) was parked on the cliffs at Durdle Dor, and indeed, if the twenty occupants of the tent had murdered her and were looking for somewhere discreet to dispose of the body. More than enough to make anyone scarper before the nosy police came asking awkward questions!

That little mystery satisfactorily solved, plans for the morning were made. Roy and Dick decided to take the children down to the beach, dear Buff did the washing up and then went to tidy up his van, while Poppy and I had various chores to do in situ. Before Buff had finished the washing up, however, a screech came forth from the tent.

'Oh, no! Oh, Vená, I think I've come on.'

Poor Poppy; she obviously thought that Buff had gone to the beach with the rest of the party. In days gone by the most natural of bodily functions were never, ever, discussed in mixed company, and Buff's eyes inadvertently met mine and we both flamed into a pretty scarlet. Horrorstruck and unable to let Poppy know that we weren't just girls together, we heard the next thrilling instalment:

'Oh, it's okay. It's just the pattern on my knickers!'

Poor Buff stumbled away as hastily as he could, in case other girlish secrets were about to be divulged, while I started to laugh uncontrollably. Puzzled, Poppy poked her head out of the tent flap to see what all the commotion was about. It was minutes before I got myself together enough to acquaint her with her 'crime' and stopped laughing abruptly when I saw how upset she looked. It sounds little enough in the 1990s but not so then. To the best of my knowledge Poppy and Buff avoided all eye contact for the rest of the week-end.

The remainder of our camping expedition was marvellous with golden, warm, sunshine, clear, oh so clear, water, and the spectacular Dorset coastal scenery. The children were all well behaved (for once) and no-one tried to drown themselves. I couldn't help thinking how much Naughty Gran would have enjoyed this caper, especially the bikers episode. But then, she most likely would have joined them, dancing round their bonfire, swigging gin and showing off her drawers. There is one set of rules for the likes of her in life and an entirely different set for the Poppys of this world!

Coming more or less up to date again, Roy and I were driving along one day with Jimmy, Lewis and Harry stuffed in the back seat. My attention was drawn to their conversation when I heard Lewis say:

'I know where babies come from.'

'So what? Everyone knows that,' a bit cockily from Jimmy, five years Lewis's senior.

Not to be outdone, the baby of the bunch, young Harry, aged four, piped his contribution.

'I know where babies come from. And I can remember being borned out of my Mummy.'

'No, you can't,' contradicted Lewis.

'What did it feel like, then?' asked Jimmy scornfully.

Harry pondered with a screwed-up thoughtful face and then said:

'Like pink jelly and twinkles.'

Naturally his two brothers rolled around in the back seat in helpless laughter, but 'pink jelly and twinkles' set me thinking. As a matter of fact I was amazed at his description that seemed so apt and one I would have used myself when giving birth, had I thought of it. Do some very young children actually remember being born, I wondered. After all, science has discovered that pre-natal children have a nice little life of their own, sucking a thumb or giving poor old Mum a hefty kick in the ribs, so it is not beyond the realms of possibility that 'being borned out of Mummy' stays in the memory for a few infant years. The other possible explanation is that young Harry is a spin-off of that flashy Lavinia and was just showing off with a dramatic turn of phrase!

The very last proud Grandma story belongs to Jimmy, then aged five.

'Grandma! We had a story today at school about a big ship called the *Titanic* – you know, the one that bumped into an ice cube!'

And that, I think, takes a bit of whacking.

'Well, Lavvy, I can't think of anything else, can you?'

'You've got to be joking! What about the time that you . . .'

'Shh, you silly old fool! We daren't expose Peg's delicate earholes to that sort of thing. She'd probably walk off in a huff and refuse to do the typing – you know what she's like.'

'Yeah, I certainly do! I've had a lot of trouble with that one. Needs a bit more dash and flash, I reckon. Still, poor thing, she didn't have a Naughty Gran as an ancestor, did she?'

'You're right, Lavvy. But what a good job we didn't inherit any of her strange ways.'

'Amen to that. Over to you, our Peg. I'll help you with your boring bit, never fear. '

PART TWO

PEG'S BORING BIT - ACCORDING TO LAVINIA

CHAPTER 1

Wandering into our bathroom one afternoon very recently, I spotted a small grey-brown pellet nestling in the carpet adjoining the wash basin. In an instant my soul departed from these urban surroundings and lit gently upon a tussock covered with similar pellets in one of Liddon Farm's glorious meadows.

'How strange!' I mused, 'What on earth is a rabbit turd doing in our bathroom?'

I then remembered that my husband, Keith, had clumped indoors for lunch straight from a site visit in a semi-rural area on the outskirts of our town. Admittedly he had pounded the doormat heartily with rather muddy shoes, but as they are of the variety that unhelpfully provides bars and ridges across the soles, this little relic had survived all the way to the wash basin where it was deposited for a second time. It looked so natural on the grass-green carpet that my inner self was reluctant to return to its proper time and, along with my grandfather (known to all as the Guv'nor), strolled happily in the sunshine and listened to one of his dodgy racing stories. It was bound to have been one about the day that 'something or other' had beaten 'something or other else' and filled his pockets with £5 notes, as that was his favourite sort of tale, and I was surprised to find how sharply the childhood details came back to me. Then the ears in my memory picked up a crisp 'Sshh!' from him and made the phantom me automatically drop four paces behind while he raised his gun and shot a rabbit that has now been dead for half a century. This was a safety rule most strictly observed as the penalty was never to be allowed ever again to accompany the Guv'nor and his gun. A truly dreadful threat that must have been successful as none of us ever got shot, which was just as well as he would have been in terrible trouble with dear Gran, to say nothing of the Authorities.

The Guv'nor indicated the general direction of the kill with a jabbed forefinger and I scampered off to retrieve it without a second's hesitation. I sometimes think that he trained us to be deputy gun dogs. He was notorious for using anything that came to hand and if the dog didn't feel like following him for miles while he shot at innocent animals, then kids would do just as well. In fact, in some ways we were better even if we couldn't run as fast, as we didn't give the poor creature a good chew on the way back *and* we let all its fleas hop off first, which was more than the dopey dog did. Fleas know immediately when their host has kicked the bucket and desert the sunken ship in double quick time, but experience taught us that it was prudent to wait a minute or so to allow the slower ones to follow suit. Invariably these were big and fat, presumably tanked up on rabbit blood, and had probably been fast asleep in the warm, cosy fur. Also, they could bite ferociously, which could have been revenge for the dastardly deed. Not that we considered it was dastardly. Uppermost in our minds was the thought of the magnificent pie the rabbit would be part of within the next couple of days, and our mouths would water in anticipation. I suppose children are much closer to our pre-history forbears than society-blunted adults, as here and now I will go to extraordinary lengths to avoid killing anything at all and can easily grieve all day over the poor defenceless ant that met with a sudden squashed end because I didn't see it in time. The very thought of actually killing a rabbit now fills me with horror, but so long as someone else is responsible for despatching animals, I enjoy mightily the smell of cooking meat and later consuming it. Strangely, I relish still the golden days spent with the Guv'nor and his gun and feel no shame for my part in the proceedings.

There is no room for sentimentality on a farm, especially when there are many hungry mouths to be fed, and while all the domestic farmed animals were cossetted in comparison with today's gruesome methods and were regarded with affection, market day saw no tears when they were sent off for slaughter. Except for dear, sweet Gran, who hated to hear her beloved cows bellowing in anguish when deprived of their calves and maintained always that they cried real tears. I believe she was right, remembering how she spent her precious and few spare minutes stroking and talking to them. Perhaps they had their own means of communication because there was never any need to call. The mere sight of Gran appearing at the gate that separated the side garden from the orchard – so-called because it must have been so many years ago and had retained its name – was sufficient for pretty Jersey and Guernsey heads to jerk upwards from grazing and in moments she was surrounded by her 'beauties'. Everyone at the farm was considerate to the livestock as far as it goes, but Gran operated on a different wavelength with them in a realm unknown to the rest of us. And she enjoyed steak and kidney pie and roast chicken as much as anybody. Perhaps we are all a strange mixture of emotions, hard economics, the survival instinct and the love of meat, even Gran.

My family is closeknit but also on elastic, which is very nice. Of necessity, and sometimes choice, members of a family go their separate ways and probably don't see each other for long spells. This makes absolutely no difference as far as we are concerned, and the tenuous elastic will twang the family together at the slightest hint of trouble. I say 'family' in the widest sense as it includes friends who have become part of the clan over the years, initially through the ever-open doors of Liddon.

My grandparents bought Liddon Farm as newly weds and brought up a family of two girls and four boys. One small son died from the horrendous Spanish 'flu shortly after the First World War and a second succumbed with asthma when I was very small. My mother was the eldest child and so my little brother Ray and I were fortunate indeed to have two lively young uncles and an extremely pretty little aunt as companions. I realise now that they weren't much more than children themselves, but they seemed rather old and fusty to us at the time. Liddon is a farm of nearly four hundred acres and the farmhouse had developed from an Elizabethan centre cottage by growing large additions each end, one eighteenth century and the other nineteenth, and is situated in the most beautiful of countryside, now sadly diminished by modern farming techniques.

My mother fell in love with, and married, the personable young butler who worked for a charming elderly lady in a nearby large house. They lived at Liddon for a short while and then my father joined the Merchant Navy and batted back and forth across the Atlantic on the liner SS *Majestic*. This meant that my parents had to drag themselves away from Liddon to live in Southampton, as travelling from the farm to the docks was quite out of the question in those days. It must have been a strange transition for my mother who had lived in the depths of the Hampshire countryside all her young life, but I believe she settled down to town life very quickly and seems to have enjoyed it. Dad owned two bikes; one he took to New York for sightseeing and left leaning against any old thing on the pier head when returning to Southampton, and the other received similar treatment at Southampton for use at home. The Southampton bike was stolen once and had to be replaced, but the New York bike was always waiting for him, exactly where he had left it, for years.

Dad delighted in bringing wonderful American toys home for Ray and me which were the wonder and envy of all our small friends. One toy that I can vaguely remember covered the whole of the dining table and consisted of an engine, rather like an old-fashioned fairground chuffer, powered by burning methylated spirits. From this little power source ran a whole series of miniature roundabouts, things that tooted and whistled, and kept us wide-eyed and quiet for hours. Ray and I were never allowed to get near this amazing toy by ourselves and had to wait for Dad's return from New York. Eventually we realised that this was Dad's toy really and lost interest. I would love to see it once more, but, like so many childhood treasures, it disappeared.

What did disappear very quickly was a large teddy bear that travelled clear across the Atlantic with Dad, was given to me early one Sunday morning, and then went for walkies after breakfast. Or rather, Teddy was clutched in my arms and I was clutched in Dad's until we reached a small lake that was near our house. It may have been that I was sorry for Dad having to carry both of us and decided to make his burden easier, but I don't hold a lot of faith that this was so. Whatever the motive may have been, Teddy suddenly sailed through the air with the greatest of ease and then vanished with a large splash in the deep part of the lake and was seen no more. Naturally I yelled blue murder and implored passers-by to rescue him from his watery grave, but Dad thought they were giving him funny looks and it didn't seem wise to linger in case he was lynched for throwing his poor little daughter's favourite toy in the pond. What hurt him most, he told me in later years, was that having rushed home with this wretched screaming child, he got it in the neck from Mum for letting me throw it away.

'I'll never understand women,' he said 'Young or old.'

I recently lost my lovely father and have in my possession his 'Pig & Whistle' silver trophy, designed to be worn on a watch chain, which I now wear as a pendant. It bears the legend: 'Cribbage Tournament. SS *Majestic*. Voyage 184. Presented by G. Noblet. Won by L. Francis 1934.'

My brother Ray, small friend Penny, and I spent so much of our time at Liddon that my memories consist almost entirely of what happened there and very little of my proper home with my parents. I can see now just how ungrateful and unkind I must have been as I suffered agonies of homesickness for Liddon and acted like the horrid spoiled brat I undoubtedly was. When the dreaded time came to leave I am ashamed to say that I resisted with might and main, making it impossible to remove me from the steps because my weight had mysteriously increased ten-fold and my body had assumed the substance of a strawberry jelly out of its mould. I have no idea how I accomplished this, but until I was guaranteed a good hiding (an empty threat!), no-one could shift me. All that this fuss achieved was an extra ten minutes of tears and yells from me and a lot of upset for the adults.

Penny also suffered severely when wrenched away from our heaven. At least Ray and I went home locally in Hampshire, but she, poor girl, was forcibly removed to another part of the world entirely – all the way to London. In fact, Penny is still homesick for those childhood days and vows that her ashes will be scattered in the orchard. This, of course, depends upon the permission of the new owners. The worrying thing is, that just supposing they don't wish to have the remains of Penny scattered over their meadow, where will she go? I have a sneaky feeling that it will be a good move on their part if they comply with her wishes as I think there is a definite possibility of things going bump in the night if she's thwarted. She is a strong-minded woman.

My darling Gran was possibly the kindest person in the whole world. She was still pretty in middle age with long silver hair that she wore in a sort of shiny cow-pat arrangement on top of her head. Penny and I would fight over whose turn it was to brush the silver cascade while Gran patiently allowed us to make astonishing new hair styles and, inevitably and unfortunately, many knots. Always she wore black dresses that had little touches of white or silver here and there. When I gaze fondly at old photographs of her I see that she could be considered quite stylish, but to her brood of tearaways our description would have been 'cuddly'. How she put up with us with so much love I can't imagine. Even Gran admitted we weren't the best behaved children in the land, but I can see her still convulsed with laughter at our daft antics, so perhaps we weren't quite as bad as I now fear.

The Guv'nor was a locally well-known character and held in affection by most folk for his slightly eccentric ways. When researching into our family tree, my niece discovered that he had inherited £2,000, a pretty large sum of money at the beginning of this century, and a farm from his father. Now, that sort of capital should have ensured a very comfortable existence, except for one thing: he loved gambling in general and horses in particular. This coupled with the depression years of the twenties and early thirties depleted the family finances quite severely and so he sold Liddon to a very large estate and remained there as a successful tenant farmer.

He was an immensely kind man and would respond to our pleas to 'Make a face like a bulldog, Guv'nor' by pulling the most convincing imitation and growling ferociously. We were almost deliciously fooled into believing that he really had turned into a fearsome beast and would run, shrieking, while he chased us around the lawn. On the very odd occasion that he had a good day at the races he would fill his pockets with loose change and walk on his hands like an acrobat, while we children scrabbled madly to collect the loot.

Sometimes we had other children to befriend or be-enemy, depending upon our whim, as Gran had paying guests to augment the farm income, also family and friends, nearly all with offspring, so that Liddon was bursting at the seams and buzzing with activity. Naturally we didn't think there was anything extraordinary about the groaning table that Gran provided for her ravenous brood three times daily. Many times I have wondered how she accomplished this amazing feat using an old-fashioned wood and coal burning stove, an open fire and an oil burning oven. She made her own butter and cheese, jams, marmalade and wine, and turned home produced and wild meats into succulent dishes of delight. Now, I think I pour a gallon of work into a pint-sized day, but Super Gran was in a different league.

As a young wife she attended the Sparsholt Agricultural College to learn how to make cheese and butter. She passed all her examinations with flying colours and was awarded a copyright emblem to imprint her own butter pats. It is a cause for regret that no-one in the family can find any trace of her personal emblem and I haven't any idea even of what it looked like.

While Penny and I were recently indulging in a good old nostalgia session, she reminded me of the night that Gran and the Guv'nor suffered a disaster in the shape of a leaking hot water bottle. In those long gone days Liddon was not served with mod. cons. such as electricity, and the survival kit consisted of oil lamps, coal fires and those marvellous comforters called hot water bottles – unless they leak, of course. Keeping warm in a bitter winter was difficult. Not only were the beds laden with blankets, but we also snuggled down in a feather mattress and so long as there was an air vent sufficient to keep us supplied with oxygen, it was wonderful. We also wore very sensible night gear and the Guv'nor's sexy outfit was a large and voluminous nightshirt that looked as unyielding as the Rock of Gibraltar. So, when the bottle leaked it was some little time before the dreadful truth emerged, and when it did he leapt out of bed with a roar that almost frightened Gran to death. In the ensuing skirmish with the soggy bed, the tail of this cumbersome garment froze solid and even had tiny icicles hanging in a fringe from the hem. I do grumble just occasionally about the many modern drive-you-mad gadgets, but central heating is high on the list of things I do not wish to be without.

Penny and I shared a small room at the back of the house that jutted out as a gable at the oldest part of the farmhouse and at the head of the bed was a secret door. I suppose it couldn't have been all that secret if we knew about it, but we were never allowed to fiddle with the panels behind which the door reputedly lurked. It seems that a small staircase ran from this room to emerge in the dairy on the ground floor. We invented lurid stories of a blood curdling nature involving priest holes and smugglers, but it is far more likely that it had been used by the poor dairymaid early in the morning in order not to disturb the rest of the household.

Situated opposite the large gate of the farmhouse was a charming little granary perched on staddle stones which was one of our favourite play spots. It was divided into stalls which were filled with wheat, barley, and a fair sprinkling of harvest bugs that just loved a visit from any glackity child who couldn't resist romping in the grain. We would emerge at meal times covered in hard red bites that itched maddeningly. No amount of scolding and uncomfortable nights ever stopped us from sneaking into the granary, and from harvest time onwards we each looked as if we'd caught the plague.

I have an odd feeling that we were probably more effective at repelling unwanted visitors than a pack of pit bull terriers! Unfortunately for me, I have always been a magnet that attracts any insect inclined to bite and so sported ten red blobs to everyone else's one. Even today, in middle age, I am the one that emits a message to winged and hopping horrors and can get severely bitten while others walk about completely unblemished. Life is *not* fair, I've realised by now.

All things considered, we children were so lucky to have had part, however minor, in Liddon's long history as a farmstead. We were loved, extremely well fed, had very little pocket money – but as there were no shops it made no difference – clad in clothes suitable for the sort of life we led (extremely casual), and very happy, at least until it was time to leave. We remember hedgerows that didn't look like a row of shaving brushes and small lush, flower filled pastures that was home to the elegant Jersey and Guernsey cows. No-one can deny that making a living was very tough but the work was shared and the family was strongly bonded and content. It is the quality and beauty of the countryside that has vanished in so many ways and a sobering thought that contemporary youngsters have no conception of what has been snatched away from them.

In the early twenties the Guv'nor was the proud owner of a large and, judging by old photos, hideous Ford van. Prior to this astonishing acquisition, all the farm work and transport had been carried out by horses and an old bike that was built on the lines of an iron bedstead. The latter was used to ferry the Guv'nor back and forth to the village pub in the evenings, while the horses coped with everything else. Lord knows, he was a big enough menace riding his bike as it seemed to have no brakes and could build up quite a speed in a grinding sort of fashion while going downhill, resulting in an occasional disaster. The main danger spot was a sharp right hand bend at the exact bottom of the hill (return journey from the pub) coupled with a five-barred gate exactly positioned to receive the unwary traveller if the steering and no-brakes were at odds. The Guv'nor either forgot or ignored it, paying the price with several monumental crashes. If it was one of his luckier evenings, he would sail right over the gate landing on straw piled for the cattle. On the other hand, on less fortunate ones he collided with the gate that had been constructed to keep the cows in and the Guv'nor out. The funny thing is that the bike didn't seem to suffer too much, though apparently it was difficult to tell, unlike its owner who had to limp home and report to an exasperated Gran for soothing witch hazel and butter for bumps.

It is not difficult, therefore, to appreciate the alarm felt by the family and local people when, out of the blue, the Guv'nor came home one day from a farm sale proudly, if erratically, driving a huge and lumbering Ford van.

Somehow or other he managed to square up the van with the drive gate and came triumphantly to a halt just in time before the steps stopped him. The young uncles were highly delighted with this huge leap into the technological age, but Gran and little Aunt Della, though wildly interested, were apprehensive for everyone's safety. With good reason.

The van must have been an amazing machine. It was made to fly over ditches like a horse, charge across ploughed fields (also like a horse) and trundle down little lanes, taking up the entire width of the road and making unfortunates who happened to be using the same stretch dive into a ditch or scramble up a bank out of harm's way.

Della tells me of the time that the Guv'nor loaded the whole family in the van along with a tremendous stock of home produce and lots of mouth watering dishes made by my talented grandmother, and off they set to visit Gran's relatives in Leicestershire. It is quite a tiring journey nowadays, even with (or because of) motorways, and it must have been much more so then in that unsprung, unpredictable early vehicle, captained by an even more unpredictable driver. However, all went fairly well for some distance and the passengers relaxed enough to have a snooze. It can't be proved, but it was the common belief that the driver also snoozed while on duty: hotly denied, of course, by the Guv'nor. At all events, and assuming that he had momentarily closed his eyes to rest them, something must have awoken him and he responded by jamming the brakes on hard. Unlike his bike, the van brakes worked well. It was utter chaos in the body of the van as the carefully packed and stacked goods went flying along with a mixture of children and their mother. Della was practically knocked out by a very large cooked gammon which, having struck her a glancing blow on the temple, finally came to rest in her lap. She claims it was a jolly good thing it was a glancing blow because the gammon was about three times the size of her head.

A roll call and inspection discovered that everyone was present, if not correct. The Guv'nor meekly received a considerable tongue-lashing from the usually placid Gran, the goods and children were brushed down and restacked, and off they set once more. Very carefully this time, and to everyone's relief, they eventually arrived safely in Gran's old home town with a flourish of klaxons that brought children running into the street under the impression that a circus had arrived. They were very nearly right, with the Guv'nor in charge!

A quirk of fate decreed that the only other Ford van in the area belonged to a gentleman who lived in Chichester and he fancied a drive through the country lanes one beautiful spring morning. The Guv'nor had loaded up his van with farm produce in readiness to take them to a number of local small shops. So there we are, Chichester gentleman putting his foot down to take the rise towards Liddon and the Guv'nor backing down the drive with his view of the road completely obscured in both directions. He had never bothered to poke his head out of the window, as his theory was that anyone could hear him coming and would get out of the way, if they had any sense. This rule of thumb had worked perfectly prior to this beautiful spring morning, mostly because the few people who lived at Liddon had developed the sensible habit of disappearing into thin air when the Guv'nor and his van were teamed up. But, of course and sadly, the Chichester gentleman had the disadvantage of not even knowing the Guv'nor existed, let alone possessing a twin of his own van, and the inevitable happened with a most appalling crash. Amazingly neither driver was hurt, except pridefully, but the damage sustained by both vehicles ensured that peace was restored to Liddon for many years. Poor Guv'nor. He was a broken man for about a week and then he took up inventing tools and handy gadgets - very interesting for him but rather a trial for Gran.

The years rolled by with many happy times and some very sad ones. One excruciatingly sad period was the wholly unexpected death of my Uncle Ted, still in his early forties. Ted had inherited all that was best in the characters of Gran and the Guv'nor and his loss struck at our very vitals. Gran's health declined from that moment and my unselfish parents gave up what they were doing and came to care for her and the Guv'nor. Even though Gran suffered several strokes she lived to a ripe old age, surviving the dear old Guv'nor. It is equally sad to think that the grandparents' illnesses took a similar toll of my parents, and then it was the turn of Ray and me to try and ease their last years with immense help from our much loved Della.

A great urge to see Liddon again beset me after the death of my parents when I desperately needed a link with our mutual happier past. I couldn't feel the great joy of getting closer and closer to the farm as I did in childhood, of course, but nevertheless my heart stirred in the old familiar way as Keith and I rounded the bend at the top of the hill, and there was Liddon.

The first thing that hit me amidships was the empty space where the granary used to perch so invitingly and, secondly, that the wonderful very old barns aren't wonderful at all now. The farmhouse is much changed with 'improvements' and Gran's colourful flower beds have vanished. The most striking thing of all was the utter quiet. The only visible sign that someone actually lived at Liddon was the curtains at the windows. No children, cows, pigs, chickens, three geese, two dogs, and a varying number of cats; just a stillness and sensation of pause, as if the house was waiting to absorb vibrant life once more. It was very strange; it was Liddon and yet it wasn't, and then I realised that, yes, there was one child here, if only briefly, and that was me, even if I didn't remotely resemble the young hooligan of long ago. The past was reaching out to touch the present and no-one could take that away.

I found my link in the beautiful copper beech on the lawn, that had been planted by Gran and the Guv'nor on my mother's fifteenth birthday because it was the same colour as her hair. Now the tree stands proud and strong and in its prime while she has had her life and departed, a magnificent memorial to her and a heartening message to her daughter. The Liddon of our youth has no place in today's world; I should keep the memories, good and bad, but leave it behind and get on with my life.

CHAPTER 2

As if life isn't complicated enough on its own account, there appears to be a mischievous and sometimes malignant force at large only too happy to shove a spanner in the works to show who's boss. For the want of a better name I call him Old Sod, though he has been called worse when really on form. A visit from this ubiquitous gentleman is a rather common occurrence and not one that is greeted with enthusiasm by the unfortunate recipient. Generally, Old Sod will hurry to a likely locality that offers sport in the shape of a cat (particularly a kitten), dog, child, dear old lady or gentleman with plenty of time to spare, self-opening supermarket doors that don't, and practically everything that modern man has devised to plague his fellow beings. I now offer a few examples of my sufferings through the years, some of which may have a familiar ring as Old Sod doesn't belong exclusively to me.

Who, for instance, would have imagined that the dainty electronic keyboard could wreak such havoc on the poor operator's fingers, wrists, arms and shoulders? I pounded a heavy manual typewriter for years without so much as a twinge - in the arms at least - a headache from the machine-gun rattle, yes. I'm told that a possible colleague of Old Sod thought up a magic gadget to record the number of strikes on the keyboard per day, i.e. ten trillion at 9.00 a.m. to arrive at zero by 5.30 p.m.: diabolical thinking and completely in character. How can we poor innocents get our own back and, most important, how do we get in touch with Old Sod to gather a few good tips? Naturally he is not available on the very odd occasion one would like to pick his devious brains.

He is practically always present in the kitchen when friends are coming to dinner. I can panic quite easily, thank you, even when he is engaged next door, so I can see how tempting it must be to pop in to see how Peg's programme is working out and wave the spanner about. The Titanic cake is a good illustration and went thus. Hoping to show off my dubious skills with exotic puddings a little, my menu included a spectacular upsidedown cake, tastefully and artistically embedded with fruits, almonds and walnuts. To the uninitiated in this ambitious field, I have to mention that it is absolutely imperative that the USDC is tenderly tipped out immediately after removal from the oven, otherwise it is stuck forever to the base of the cake tin or tinfoil.

On this occasion Old Sod wandered in through the kitchen door and watched the proceedings with interest, no doubt. Certainly the smug expression on my face was a little premature. Rarely have I produced such a magnificent dessert; the design would probably have made Picasso wince a little but Laura Ashley would have adored it. Keith was as impressed as I was and while he was in the act of saying, 'My word! You have excelled yourself, dear wife,' or words to that effect, we simultaneously noticed that the circular pineapple slice in the centre was engaged in a disappearing act, and I think I heard a sardonic chuckle in the midst of my despairing wails. Not only did it sink but it must have achieved a world record for speed and depth. I think I should add neatness, as the cake area outside the pineapple appeared to be perfectly cooked and firm. Very strange.

Keith is quite familiar with my not infrequent disasters and remained calm while trying hard to keep a straight face. His mighty brain had already worked out a solution. Let the cake cool, dig out the centre, fill with whipped cream, place the pineapple over the cream, and - dah dah - call it Pineapple Surprise; simple. Which it was. Our guests were thrilled with it and asked for the recipe. I provided it, of course, but left out the dramatic bit, pretending that this was the only way to do it as the pineapple would automatically turn it into a ring cake, ready for the cream. A few weeks later my puzzled friend phoned to ask my opinion as to where I thought she may have gone wrong, as the wretched pineapple wouldn't sink no matter how hard she poked it. Oh, well, there was only one answer, commiserations with this failure and better luck next time.

Again in the kitchen came success for him in the form of a tasty snack prescribed by Clement Freud in the days, long ago, when he bombarded the viewing public with little gems to whet the appetite. In essence, all that was required was chunky cheese sandwiches cut into small squares, fried quickly and eaten right away. Though this was in our very early days of wedded bliss, I thought that even I could manage this ludicrously simple dish. Wrong again. I cooked a huge number of the little monsters and passed them on to Keith while frying frantically to keep up with the supposed demand. At last I joined him at the table expecting to see an empty plate. I was rather taken aback to see that the plate was still laden with Freud Specials and that the big satisfied grin was nowhere to be seen. Refraining with a little difficulty from comment, I popped one into my mouth and bit it in half. Firstly, the cheese was red hot and burned my tongue and, secondly, the taste was indescribably awful. Bitter words passed between us as I considered it was pretty mean to allow me to burn my mouth when he had full knowledge of the situation and could have alerted me beforehand. He then had the nerve to claim that he was so badly burned anyway, that it wouldn't have been possible, even if he'd wanted to. As an after taste, as if we needed one, the smell hung around our flat for days and did nothing to sweeten the rather strained atmosphere. Well, one up for Old Sod certainly, but on reflection I think Clement must take most of the blame and, anyway, he looks as if he is a blood relation.

I suppose it is a silly question to ask if you have ever been swimming in a sheepskin coat in February along Chesil Beach in Dorset. I have *and* it was Old Sod's fault. Keith and I were spending a week-end with our delightful friends, Sophie and Ben, and after a large lunch and discussion as to where we should go for a breath of fresh air, decided to watch the massive waves pound the enormous pebble ridge at Abbotsbury. It was a real struggle leaning on the wind to surmount this extraordinary barrier against the sea, but eventually we all stood puffing but triumphant on the summit, feeling as if we'd achieved the north face of the Eiger, when a sudden swerve of the wind sent me stumbling down the wrong side of the ridge. When I say wrong side, I mean towards the huge seas that broke at the base and then hurtled up the steep slope, returning with an awful sucking noise.

Desperately I tried to regain height and safety but a particularly vicious wave overtook me, knocked me as flat as a stranded whale and filled my sheepskin coat right up to the armholes. Perhaps it was the weight of water that slowed my slide into the icy Channel long enough for Keith and friends to haul me a few feet before the next wave roared in.

There have been a few occasions in my life when I have been badly frightened, but this time I confess that I was terrified and witless to a point where I did nothing to save myself and was completely reliant upon the others who, let's face it, were placing themselves in as much danger as I was in.

Brute force won the day and I was able to continue my stranded whale act out of harm's way at the top. I have since wondered what on earth I must have looked like, half-drowned, extremely soggy and probably white with fright and blue with cold, with, and this was the thing that gave them near hysterics, a large lump of solid oil firmly attached to each kneecap. We had spent many happy holidays together and it was a well known fact that four people would go to a beach and three would return bronzed and spotless while I would have to be hidden at the back of the group because I was covered in tar. Ben reckoned that these two lumps adorning my knees so prettily were the only ones along the whole stretch of Chesil Beach. You see, Old Sod's little joke again.

The Guv'nor was attacked by him many years ago at Liddon when a Bright

Young Thing with a raunchy sports car was staying as a paying guest at the farmhouse. She would roar around the lanes and sometimes try to turn round in a width not noticeably more than the length of the car. One particular day she was in a bit of a fix in this fashion half-way up a fairly steep hill, backing into the soggy bank, spluttering fiercely while see-sawing for an exit. It just so happened that the Guv'nor was walking down the hill and, as the road was fully occupied, took a by-pass along the top of the bank and then re-joined the road a few yards further down. Simultaneously the young lady succeeded in pointing her car upwards and roared off. Unbeknown to her, the exhaust pipe was plugged with wet bank and the next thing that the Guv'nor knew was a tremendous bang coupled with a hefty blow on the back of his head while his hat flew up into the branches. It was insult heaped upon injury to discover later that the girl had no idea of what had happened and refused to believe the concrete evidence of mud splattered clothes, a lump on the back of his head and a hole in his hat, and left in a huff (as well as a slightly rattling car). I'm not sure that I would have believed it either, except that I firmly believe in Old Sod!

As a child I suffered from reverse direction syndrome on occasion – that sounds impressive but only means that I think east is west and vice versa – usually at night when wakened during the black-out. One night, roused by distant gunfire, I took advantage to pop to the loo, still half asleep and, strangely, found my way there but not back. Well, I got as far as my bedroom and then got lost. Being a bit dopey I reasoned that if I took a flying leap at my bed it wouldn't have time to be somewhere else, so this I did and it did have time to move. After all these years I can vividly remember sailing through the air and landing with a terrific crash on Dad's metal-edged sea trunk. Fortunately my mother recovered very well from shock after a few weeks and no major damage was sustained by either of us, though I still bear a few scars. It is a very mean Old Sod to torment an innocent child and its mother, don't you agree?

Sometimes Old Sod comes walkies with us – in fact he seems to quite often – and then all sorts of situations can arise. Here is a mild one, but you will see what I mean. The spring of 1987 was most indifferent as far as the weather went, but one Sunday Keith and I braved the grey and abrasive climate to sample the delights of Slindon in West Sussex. It is very beautiful here and heaven knows there should have been enough to keep us happy in the village and forest. But, daft as ever, we spotted a folly on top of a great lump of a hill and decided to go and have a look. The footpath that would have taken us directly to it was impassable, because heavy rain and even heavier cows had combined to create an enormous yukky brown lake with no shoreline and we didn't fancy that slopping over the tops of our shoes and socks.

Keith, always ready for all contingencies, got out his monocle, cleaned it, and then consulted his map. After a brief study he decided that we could get to the folly from Eartham in a sort of long loop. So off we went in the car to Eartham, with its remarkable Roman Road, and it occurred to me while driving there that it seemed to be rather a long way from Slindon with the almost over-hanging strange building. Nevertheless, I trust Keith implicitly as he is much cleverer than me.

However, after more consultations with the map we struck off confidently along the Roman Road and then plunged into the woods as directed, and in very short order were forced to consider ourselves as missing persons. The funny thing about the South Downs is that it is always wetter and muddier at the top of the hills than it is in the valleys and we squelched and struggled through dripping woods and near-bogs for what seemed at least ten miles.

Amazingly, we did find the Folly, which was decidedly disappointing though odd enough to warrant its name, and - this is the good bit - found a well-worn footpath that took us back to the car with no fuss whatsoever. It was really infuriating that there was absolutely nothing to it; a ten-year-old child could have done it with a blindfold. I am of the opinion that if we could do things back to front life would be much simpler.

Slindon Forest was intact when we fought our way to that wretched Folly but was laid low a few months later by the October hurricane. It is believed to be one of the oldest beech forests in the land with the tallest trees and is now one of the saddest sights imaginable. The first time we saw the utter devastation jerked involuntary tears from my eyes and an ache in the heart. It was so unbelievable that our vast and beautiful woods had gone as completely as if a nuclear holocaust had happened. Perhaps with care it may recover for future generations, and much resuscitation work is taking place, but of course, the foreseeable forest is still just a twinkle in the National Trust's eye. You may have noticed that I haven't said a word about Old Sod and the hurricane - I'm a little too suspicious and cowardly.

Then there was Susie the cat. Susie and I met very briefly during Cowes Week in 1984 when Keith was crewing for a friend and I roamed around the Isle of Wight, mostly feeling hungry and trying to find somewhere to eat. This particular day I was wandering along a very pretty and old fashioned sort of lane with a few houses dotted at intervals and not a lot else; certainly not a tea shop that also sold food. But as you never know what is around the corner, I persevered in my urgent quest for nourishment.

What I did find instead of food was a garden wall surmounted with the funniest cat I'd ever seen. Very friendly and with a beautiful coat, she could have won a Cat Beauty Contest with no trouble, except for one embellishment, a Hitler moustache. Now I am a fervent cat admirer and said, 'Hello, Hitler!' affectionately, and was startled to get an indignant reply, 'Her name is Susie, not Hitler,' while a head popped up from behind the wall.

Naturally I apologised to Susie's owner who then asked why I'd called her Hitler. 'Um, well, it's the moustache, you see,' I explained rather lamely and was staggered by his next question, 'What moustache?' Fearing my eyesight had developed Hitler moustaches instead of floaters, I stole another glance at Susie, and sure enough, there it was in the right place just above her top lip, if it can be said that cats have lips. Susie's owner took off his glasses, peered hard, and then said, 'Good Lord! I've never noticed that before.' As Susie was definitely middle-aged and presumably had worn the moustache since a kitten, I couldn't think of a suitable response, so smiled weakly and set off once more.

Perseverance paid as I did find food and drink in a gorgeous castle about two miles further along Susie's lane. I have always considered the Isle of Wight to be a little odd, a place where unexpected things and places suddenly appear from nowhere, and wasn't unduly surprised by my good luck. This castle stands alone in rolling countryside and looks solemnly out over the magical Solent with the Hampshire and West Sussex hills in the background. It is easy to be fooled into thinking that the castle is reached long before it actually is, but this building is, in fact, a massive fortified stables. I paid my £1.00 entrance fee at the little wooden ticket hut and sped forth with renewed vigour, renewed because *I could smell coffee!* Oh! What bliss, and what a sanctuary. Wonderful ham sandwiches, mouth-watering cakes, and cups and cups of coffee. As Vená is wont to say through a mouth full of jam and cream doughnut, 'Oh, ecstasy!' and rolls her eyes about. Perhaps I had the same sort of expression on my face, because the nice lady behind the counter kept smiling at me, encouragingly I thought at first, but then noticed that she was having a terrible time trying hard not to laugh. It was impossible to feel miffed by her stifled giggles as they were so infectious but, longing to know what the joke was (apart from my hearty appetite), I took the bull by the horns and enquired. She pulled herself together with an effort and pointed to a spot over my head. Puzzled, I looked heavenwards and discovered that I was sitting immediately beneath an enormous stuffed warthog's head. Now that the reason was out in the open she explained that had I been sitting anywhere other than under the poor stuffed beast, all would have been mundane and normal, but as I was the only customer at that time and was tucking into my late lunch with such enthusiasm, she had been struck that Warthog and I bore a considerable likeness of expression. What a cheek, I thought, but I could see what she meant, and got my own back by threatening to write a book one day and telling the whole world about her rudeness to me. A little ambitious, I know, but it might just be Old Sod's day off.

I am slightly dubious about blaming events of Chernobyl entirely upon Old Sod as surely even he could not, I hope, be so entirely wicked as to be instrumental in orchestrating such horror. However, there was one Puckish incident that leaves room for a little question mark in my mind. You may recall that Government officials in this country listed areas, such as poor old Wales, where radioactivity had descended upon the earth beneath in showers of rain, and that the rest of us had escaped contamination. 'Anyway,' they gave us to understand, 'It isn't anything to worry about,' before promptly banning the sale of Welsh lamb. The south of England was apparently in the clear and we could carry on as usual with no risk to health, we gathered from the bland assurances. I rather wonder if that was so.

Keith and I were particularly keen to gather a harvest of dandelion petals as it makes a very acceptable wine, rather like a tangy sherry. I have to admit that we were only half convinced that no fall-out at all had taken place, but in view of the firm and reassuring statements from Whitehall, decided to go ahead. We found masses of these so-called weeds and twisted the bright petals out of their green bases until we had a very creditable stock to take home. I also admit that it had been raining just a few hours before we had denuded the West Sussex countryside of its wild flowers and that there was still an uncomfortable niggle at the back of my mind. Suppressing vague doubts, we spread the petals on trays to dry and left them on the already overcrowded bench at the rear of the garage. Everything that won't fit indoors finds a temporary home in the garage, sometimes making it practically impossible to get the car in. Drying usually takes about a week, depending upon the weather, but the very next morning Keith came back as far as the garden gate, yelling something about those bloody dandelions and come and see and got to go, goodbye. Husbands and wives very often speak in a kind of shorthand intelligible to themselves but probably not to anyone else. Immediate interpretation revealed that he didn't have time to stay for proper investigation, but there was something nasty in the woodshed that required my attention in his absence. 'My God,' I thought, 'I hope those dandelions aren't giving off a green glow,' and, picking up a pair of kitchen plastic gloves, made off for the garage and its hidden horrors. I took a deep breath in case it wasn't wise to inhale the trapped garage air, swung the up-and-over door open and wished fervently that Keith had given me a Geiger counter for Christmas instead of books and clothes. Peering through the early morning murk I didn't see luminous green trays; instead a pretty golden glow was lighting up the depths and sent a cold shiver down my spine. As Keith had taken the car I had plenty of room to make my way to this phenomenon and observed with amazement that whereas the trays had held petals to a depth of about one inch, they were now at least eight inches high and heaved gently, as if being consumed by maggots. It was a frightening and ghastly sight and I didn't know what to do. It's not as if one can pick up the phone and ask the Refuse Department to come and collect a load of radioactive dandelion petals; they would assume I was a nut case and shake their heads sadly.

Eventually I tore my fascinated gaze away, closed the garage door and withdrew to the house for a resuscitating cigarette and a bit of constructive thought. The best plan, I reasoned, was to trap it all in heavy duty plastic bags and then it could go to the incinerator with the rest of the rubbish and get burned out of existence (I hoped). After all, if West Sussex had been sprinkled with the stuff you could bet your boots that we had also, in which case this small amount wouldn't make much difference. Whitehall would definitely confirm that none had fallen on the south of England because I'd heard them say so on the radio.

There is one snag to this theory which made itself apparent a few weeks later. Dark green dandelion seedlings appeared in cracks in paving and concrete nearby and grew at a prodigious rate with funny leaves. With well protected hands I continually hooked them out and disposed of them in the (now) time honoured tradition of death by incinerator, and by the following autumn seemed to have won the battle. Well, Old Sod, was it your little joke, or were Whitehall's bland assurances incorrect? Surely not, on both counts!

Hospitals don't entirely close down at week-ends and although many non-urgent departments shut their doors until Monday morning, some have to stay in business in order to keep the vast majority of patients alive and kicking feebly. Just such a one was our laboratory which provided, among other things, blood test results for wards and surgeries. Accordingly, alternate Saturday mornings would find me pedalling away on my trusty bicycle in an effort not to be late and miss the coffee. A short distance from the entrance to the hospital there is a medium sized manufactory, quite close to the road, which also closed down for the week-end. Apart from the painter and decorator, that was. I could see him clearly through the large single pane window on the first floor, negotiating a cumbersome step ladder, a pot of paint and a brush. A second or so before I drew parallel with this little scene he accidentally let go of the step ladder which fell towards the window. In an obvious attempt to grab it he missed the piece he was aiming for and succeeded only in propelling it forward at about three times the speed it had already achieved. I also observed great globs of paint shooting ceilingwards which meant he had also dropped the tin but I don't recall seeing the brush perform any tricks.

Now had the ladder fallen at its own speed it would probably just have given the window a good old jolt, but as it was, a momentous explosion took place and shards of glass flew outwards across the forecourt, pavement and the normally very busy road. At this precise moment I was exactly in position to get shredded and heard the icy missiles ping through the spokes of my wheels, saw and heard them smash all around me and thought – I must have been cut, it's just that I don't feel the pain yet – in a bemused sort of manner and waited for it to assault me. I remember seeing the poor painter's horrified face staring out of the completely glassless window and hearing his trembling voice ask if I was hurt. There was no pain, nor blood, in fact, nothing untoward, unbelievable as it seemed. I shook my head in answer to his question and slivers of glass untangled themselves from my hair and fell to the ground.

'Yes, I'm okay,' I called. 'It's my lucky day and your unlucky one!'

I was thinking about his explanation for all that damage to an irate employer. After all he was probably only engaged to touch up a few grotty spots here and there with a pot of paint, a brush and a step ladder in the boss's office, and it now looked as if he'd had a mad bull to help.

It is incredible just how much glass constitutes a large shattered window. It was spread in generous quantities across the full width of the road and cars were scrunching their way through, unable to take avoiding action. I sincerely hoped that the motorists would check their tyres as soon as they could, though they would know soon enough by punctures if misfortune as well as glass had struck. Which reminded me – I should check my own tyres. This I did and was alarmed to see several dart-like pieces embedded in the rubber. 'Ye Gods!' it occurred to me, 'My skin isn't quite as tough as those tyres – what an escape!' Thoughtfully, I left a few shards in place, really as evidence that this dramatic event had actually happened and of the danger I had survived. I know of old how my sometimes sceptical husband automatically subtracts 50% or so of the facts as I see them, and a few large slivers of glass wouldn't come amiss, unless they fell out on the way home, which would be just my luck.

I received the same 'Oh! go on with you!' attitude from my colleagues in the laboratory until someone noticed yet another piece of glass nestling in my hair and advised a good shake outside in the car park. I took this opportunity to show off the wounded tyres and then at last convinced them they were lucky not to have to cough up for flowers, either in a ward or at my pathetic graveside. This sounded so poignant that tears welled up in my eyes and I was hastily given coffee for belated shock. The remainder of the morning passed very pleasantly with repeated accounts to interested poppers-in and stoppers-for-coffee and then it was time to go home. I hasten to add that tons of work were dealt with while enjoying my brief moment of fame.

My tyres seemed to be hard enough to pedal home and so bike and I wound our way through the hospital and thence on to the homeward bound highway. At the scene of the great drama I paused to see how things were getting on. With astonishment I saw that the window had a new pane and every scrap of glass had vanished from the road and, in fact, there was nothing whatsoever to corroborate my version of events. How had this come about? It normally takes weeks to get the simplest task done in our town and someone had upset our tardy record by working at frantic speed to repair all the damage. Perhaps the painter? No, unless he was Superman in disguise and besides, he had all that paint to get off the ceiling and probably the carpet as well. At first I was so impressed at the speed and efficiency that all I felt was admiration, and then I began to feel rather cross. What was the good of having a rattling good story to tell anyone prepared to listen if all the evidence is swiped from under one's nose? It's not good enough. Somehow the wind had been taken out of my sails and I barely mentioned it to Keith and, anyway, even my own evidence had dis-appeared by the time I got home as the shards had fallen out soon after I started. I have my own theory, of course. It was my old friend Old Sod having yet another joke at my expense. On the other hand, I had escaped unscathed while the painter had been left with complete chaos, had a terrible fright and maybe the sack to finish off a really spectacular morning's work. This is the real answer, I think. It was the painter's turn for a brush with Old Sod and I just happened to be passing at the time. I wish I was convinced.

If ever there was an Old Sod situation, it was the Betsy affair. It bears his hallmark perfectly and, true to form, leaves everyone feeling slightly uneasy. As if one of me wasn't enough, there is a lady hereabouts who bears an uncanny resemblance to me. I call her Betsy because it sounds cosy and nice, like me. The penny didn't drop for a long time that Betsy actually existed and seemed to have more friends than I have. I admit to being puzzled by the number of complete strangers greeting me warmly and then becoming slightly hurt by my polite smile and feeble 'Hello'. This usually happened in our local supermarket but neither was I immune at antique fairs or any old local gathering. You know how it is: apart from semi-familiar faces that live locally, there are so many people to meet at 'Friends of . . .', Associations, etc., that I can never be quite sure if a greeter is a friend of mine or of Betsy. Anyway, I was wondering if everything had become too much for me and if I needed a kindly and understanding psychiatrist to unravel this mystery for me.

I hadn't mentioned my new circle of Betsy's friends to Keith as it sounded so ridiculous, until *he* reported that one of *his* colleagues had observed me sitting on a bar stool, dressed in a bright red leisure suit, and hadn't seemed at all pleased to see him, let alone recognise him. Fortunately Keith knew Betsy wasn't me as I don't possess a bright red leisure suit, but nonetheless he was rather intrigued. This seemed a very good time to acquaint him with all the weird and strained conversations I'd been subjected to in the recent past and, to my relief, actually remembered a couple of occasions of mistaken identity when we had both been present. The kindly and understanding psychiatrist is now on 'Hold' and with luck will stay there. The most upsetting incident had been when a lady that I didn't know from Eve approached me with a beaming smile and immediately hurled herself into a sort of familiar monologue that I supposedly would know all about. I didn't, of course, and I didn't have a hope in hell of breaking into her one-sided conversation until she realised that my response was one of embarrassment only. 'Oh well,' she said, her face assuming an acid film, 'If that's your attitude and you don't want to speak to me - then don't,' and turned sharply away from me, leaving me prey to the curious stares of other shoppers. I will go so far as to say that she stalked off in high dudgeon, whatever that may be. Did she ever speak to Betsy again, I wondered, and how many of her friends had I insulted, and (even worse) how many of mine were getting the same treatment from her? Neither of us will ever know, I suspect.

Betsy obviously leads a carefree and jolly life as I've been spotted in all sorts of places that Keith and I can't afford to go to and some that we certainly don't want to visit. I wonder if she is puzzled by being seen in mundane places like garden centres by her friends.

We may have passed each other like ships in the night one blowy and rainy day when I was walking southwards through our shopping precinct and she (perhaps) was walking northwards. As the maybe Betsy was battling against the weather she had her umbrella lowered to protect her top half while mine was sheltering my back. In an unthinking moment I watched my reflection approach automatically until I suddenly realised that a reflection in the middle of an empty precinct is not a sensible conclusion. It was startling because she was wearing blue slacks and short jacket, as I was, was more or less my height and build and, to my fevered imagination, walked in a very similar fashion. The only difference between us was the colour of our umbrellas, and I felt the hair at the back of my neck prickle and rise. This surely must be Betsy and at long last we were face to face.

Something must have communicated itself as she raised her umbrella and for a brief while our eyes met. She could easily have been my twin sister and I even spotted what I thought were family characteristics, though that is going a bit far. Faced with such a confrontation so unexpectedly, neither of us was able to approach the other, I feel sure, and took the easy way out by quickly averting our gazes, hiding behind our umbrellas and hurrying off in different directions. The question I keep asking myself is, why are we so physically alike and why are we in the same vicinity? Could it be that we were related in a previous existence? If so, why do I feel nothing for her except a mild annoyance that we are so often mistaken for the other? A ray of hope seems to be peeping through. For the past six months or so I have not been approached or chided by any of her friends and I haven't been seen having a good time on a bar stool sans Keith, or anywhere else where I wasn't. So, Bye Bye, Betsy, Bye Bye, and I sincerely hope we never meet again. Somehow in the background I seem to hear that sardonic chuckle and hope I'm mistaken.

CHAPTER 3

It has been a considerable measure of success, I feel, to have lived this long, and is simply because my skull is obviously very hard as well as pliable. The very first attempt upon my life came from my poor exhausted mother who fell asleep while desperately trying to pacify her ailing and grumpy six-week-old baby and dropped me on my head. Well deserved, I imagine, but did more damage to my mother than to me as she subsequently excused my occasional bouts of bad behaviour by blaming herself.

I escaped further serious head injury right up to the age of three when my little friend Penny decided we would chop wood for Gran at Liddon. With her budding managerial tendencies in full force she organised that I should hold the piece of wood while she did the hard work with the axe. As with many situations, this was very good in theory but not so hot in practice. Her little arms managed to hold the axe briefly above the small crouched figure faithfully following her instructions, and, wallop, it fell blade side down roughly where my parting would have been if I'd had one - until then, that is. Fortunately as a child I sported a great mop of tight ginger curls which probably softened the blow a little and certainly mopped up the blood. For a whole week I was petted and pampered until it was noticed that I seemed to be perfectly fit and as unattractive as ever, so normal adult/child relations were resumed forthwith, even if I did have a large bald patch on top of my head.

During the next few years of childhood I fell off things, out of trees and into things, and always on my head. As a matter of fact, I rarely crash other parts of my body, apart from toes, knees, shins, etc.; it is my head that seems to act as battering ram and it's no wonder I'm a bit odd.

It did escape a slightly bizarre set of circumstances ten or so years ago - a near collision with a swan. Pedalling along like mad on my bicycle along a quiet road that joined a junction by a large lake, I observed with delight a swan also pedalling like mad across the lake for take off. Pleasure slowly turned to alarm as the swan gained a little height and ponderously flapped towards me. Have you ever been in a situation where you know avoiding action should be swift but for some unaccountable reason, don't? I know I was still pedalling while my brain was sending urgent signals to change course and maybe the swan was under the same hypnotic influence. An oncoming swan makes an enormous amount of 'swooshing' which added terror to my hypnotic state and froze all reaction. You have probably guessed that I didn't get killed, but it was a mighty close encounter, I can tell you. By the time our collision course had reached target, this huge and monstrously heavy creature was just a few inches above my head and a stunned passer-by, momentarily rooted to the spot with shock, almost fainted from relief when he opened his eyes to see me (belatedly) crouching over the handlebars.

'My God! I thought you were a gonner then. Why the hell didn't you get out of the way?' He should have asked the swan the same question as I couldn't give a satisfactory answer!

Only slightly less strange was an incident that, again, should have seen me off but didn't. Keith and I had just moved into our first very own abode, well, ours in the sense that we owned 1 brick to the building society's 999, and this des. res. included a coal bunker situated close to the back door. It was a perfectly foul day with a tempest raging that sent flurries of autumn leaves swirling and banging everything that wasn't nailed down and, of course, the coal scuttle was empty. The bunker was almost in the same state so that I was compelled to plunge head first into the depths brandishing a shovel, stabbing hopefully for a black harvest.

I truly do not understand what happened, but I heard - at least I think I heard - a clear and distinct message that went, 'I should come out of there.' Automatically I obeyed this advice and retrieved my head from the Black Hole of Coalcutta a split second before a tremendous gust slammed the heavy lid down with a resounding thud. There is little doubt that I escaped being squashed from the ears upwards yet again, though this time it would have been really messy.

I am not sure if the following gave me a headache but it certainly gave my long suffering mother one. At the tender age of five I was well aware that my bright hair colour was a disfigurement and a cause for shame. Consequently, whenever possible I hid it with any head cover that came to hand, which on one occasion was a lime green tea cosy. I can understand now the mirth this amazing sight engendered, but as that very morning I had been insulted by our butcher who had cheerily greeted me with, 'Hello, young Ginger,' it was the last straw to be laughed at for wearing a tea cosy. Something had to be done so that I could look like all the other children.

With this in mind I rummaged around looking for suitable head gear to hide every wisp of hair and happened upon a dark green beret, belonging to Mum, which would do beautifully. So, the next time she beheld her little daughter, certain changes had taken place. Instead of a little round face and freckled nose surmounted by a mop of ginger curls, this changeling had a dark green head with no forehead and ears, but did have two eyes, a button nose and a very pleased smile, and that was all. At last I was like other children and could now mix freely and wouldn't get laughed at.

This was the beginning of a very long and trying time for my poor mother and a very happy one for me. I absolutely refused to take her beret off and would scream blue murder if anyone attempted to do so. Apart from bathing and hair washing, and at nights when Mum would steal into my bedroom when I was asleep and remove it, that hat stayed on my head for nearly a year. A visit to a doctor was no help as he prescribed a good smack and confiscation of the offending head gear, and that didn't work. Though God knows what else he could have suggested, except perhaps dyeing my hair green which would make the hat unnecessary. I have not the least idea why I became hatless after this long period as I didn't ever think to ask my mother how it came about – perhaps it simply fell to bits. Funnily enough, I also have no recollection of presenting myself at school hatless and red-haired, which in theory should have been most traumatic after all that fuss and nonsense. What it all does prove is that it is not a good idea to chaff youngsters so that they think they are terribly different from the rest of the herd. I feel rather sorry for the silly young Peg and a whole heap more sorry for my mother.

I'm not really safe to be let out, which is why I spend so much time at home. I know that the unexpected should always be allowed for and definitely expected but never seem to learn from experience. Perhaps I'm just plain thick as even just going to a lovely wedding in London had its hazards, and that ought to have been safe enough. Here's what happened.

Keith and I were guests at this wedding which took place in Hampstead-on-the-Hill, a few years ago. The bride was as beautiful as could be, the bridegroom handsome and merry, it was a warm and sunny day, and there were many pleasant and interesting guests to mingle with. In fact, a scene so perfect that something was bound to go wrong. Not at the wedding, nor to the bridal couple, but guess who got it wrong again; that's right, it was me.

We had travelled to London by train and thence to Hampstead on the Underground. Incidentally, did you know that Hampstead is the deepest station on the whole network? I thought I'd mention it, because this sort of information comes in very handy as a conversation starter during an embarrassing lull in party chat. I haven't actually had to use it yet but it is tucked up my sleeve for emergencies. Anyway, back to the wedding. As it was but a short distance from the station to the church at the top of the hill we walked, noting how much Hampstead had changed over the years. It's rather posh now all over and definitely not the sort of neighbourhood to tolerate rowdy behaviour, by the look.

This was a Roman Catholic service and a completely closed book to us so we had to take our cue from the larger majority who knew exactly what to do and when. Our little friend, the bride, made a serene and smiling entrance on the arm of her father, followed by the bridesmaids. Why is it that the moment the bride appears, especially one as charming as Jane, a lump develops in female throats and an unbidden tear ruins the mascara? After all, this is a very happy occasion and not to be sniffed at. Much to our surprise, immediately after the bridal entourage started its stately procession, the doors of the church were slammed shut, almost debarring the bride's mother and certainly giving her delicious hat a good thump.

I fear the ceremony was slightly over our ignorant heads but was very impressive. Confusion did arise once or twice when it was time to sing a hymn; they sit down while we stand up, and until we'd got the hang of it the joint congregation must have resembled that old song 'Bobbing up and down like this'. However, by the end of the long service we were mostly at one but sometimes forgot to stand up to pray. When the ceremony was finished and the triumphant new Mr and Mrs came sparkling down the aisle, a hearty round of applause and cheering startled us and we joined in with squeaky cheers and hand claps. It was a lovely wedding, but feel we would have benefited from a rehearsal.

It was much later when we regretfully left the very jolly reception and, with a couple of friends and slightly unsteady steps, made our way gently down the hill towards the station. At this point piercing screams rent the tranquil Hampstead air in the most shocking manner, sharply reminding us that we were in lawless London where anything can happen. I won't go so far as to say that I was severely newted, just relaxed enough to fly off in the direction of the screams to see if help was required.

A sordid little scene was being enacted with a young girl pressed against a wall by a loutish character and watched by another young man who, I realised later, was looking rather embarrassed. Full of bravery and champagne I pounded on the lout's back and quavered the very foolish question to the girl.

'Do you need any help?'

'Stop it, you pig,' she was bawling, 'You've already 'ad it once today,' and then almost as an aside to me, 'It's all right, dear, 'e's me boyfriend.'

Well, really.

I suppose all this row was annoying the residents as, without warning, a bucket of water descended upon us from a higher apartment. The most unfair thing of all was that I received the entire waterfall with the exception of a couple of splashes on the culprits.

'Oh, my Gawd!' said the girl, laughing her stupid head off, 'You ain't half wet. It was none of your business though.' How true.

What a plight! Many miles from home with my lovely new outfit completely soaked, hair streaming with water and shoes that squelched miserably - to say nothing of my companions' disapproving expressions and hard words about my foolhardiness. In fairness I had to agree, even more so when fellow passengers couldn't believe the evidence of their eyes, seeing a party of three impeccable people and one who, presumably, had been dipped in a pond. It was easy to tell that they were dying to know what had happened as it hadn't rained for weeks and, anyway, it would have been a very localised thunderstorm to pick out one person only. At least the bucket didn't descend with the torrent and it could have been something other than water, so once again, I'm grateful for small mercies that this is not the age of 'Gardez-loo'. But then one wouldn't expect that sort of behaviour in Hampstead-on-the-Hill, would one?'

Experience shows almost all of us that life can be a bit of a struggle at times but does have its lighter moments as well as its puzzles. One that quickly springs to mind is the near impossibility of replacing worn out incidentals essential in carrying out life's little tasks. Take Keith, for instance - not literally, he's needed here - and Keith furniture, in the same sense that street lights and litter bins, etc., are called street furniture. Every day I am struck how immaculate and fresh looking is my beloved when he sets off to the daily grind. He is naturally fastidious (unlike his spouse) but it is the furniture that gives him trouble. The fairly new self-opening umbrella whose spikes have gone awry and opens with a great flourish to present a lop-sided square instead of round roof, is a good example. It also bulges with angular lumps and is quite a sight. Shoes are another problem. Here he is, spotless and well-pressed all the way down from his head to his ankles and then 10% has to be knocked off the total neatness score. The annoying thing is that it is not his fault at all. No matter if they are one week or one year in age, they immediately crinkle and adopt that 'lived in' look the moment he shoves his feet in. His metal half-specs case is also a problem. It is old, has lost most of the leather covering and is a definite health hazard to his fingers as the bare edge is razor sharp, removing bits of skin at regular intervals. The problem is that these items are always on our shopping list but we either forget or can't find suitable replacements. I maintain that the next time he feels he needs a pay rise he should present himself under his funny umbrella, so much the better if it is dripping, sit down with crossed legs to show off the crinkled shoes, and take his glasses out of the case, at the same time tutting and wincing, I can't see how it could fail to bring home extra bacon.

    I have disasters with Peg furniture, if I may call clothes 'furniture' and I don't see why not. Not so long ago I was about to emerge from the butcher's shop when I became conscious of a sliding sensation around my knees and discovered my (no, not my knickers) waist slip had reached my calves, past my knee length skirt. This predicament is very embarrassing in a crowded shop and so I had to relay an urgent message to the butcher that I needed to pop behind his counter in order to dispose of my underwear as discreetly as possible. He looked a bit flabbergasted but not as much as the customers and shop window gazers watching my mini striptease act. It was hard to bear leaving the shop to face the grins and whistles and, worst of all, *the* Striptease music sung in time to my walk which got faster and faster until I reached the blessed corner and disappeared. I haven't dared go back to that particular shop and now have to buy our meat from the supermarket. I call this sort of thing muddling through.

I didn't exactly muddle through this next little cameo - more like panicked through, but there were traces of muddle, nonetheless. We were spending a few days in the Isle of Wight and explored that wild and wonderful bit of coastline at Bouldnor. This area is far from any beaten track and from start to finish we didn't encounter a single soul. Spotting a nicely shaded and grassy bit of shoreline we decided to stop for a breather and wished an ice cream van would come tinkling through the dense woods, but as there was no road it wasn't surprising that our wish wasn't granted and we agreed to go without.

At the end of this fascinating conversation Keith's voice changed to a lower key. Is there an urgent key? If so, that as well.

'Don't move, whatever you do,' he said without moving his lips.

Naturally this instruction didn't entirely register inside my pea-sized brain and I shuffled my feet about and queried:

'What did you say?'

Even more urgently he repeated the 'Don't move' bit in his new funny voice and added, 'Stand still, for God's sake, stand still!'

I couldn't make top nor tail out of all this and lowered my head in puzzlement and saw to my utter horror that I was standing right alongside a coiled adder. Another half inch and I would have trodden on it. True to my usual form in a crisis I reacted with a strangled 'Aaarrgghh' and did a dance that likely resembled the Highland Fling, which must have given the sleeping adder the shock of its life. Poor Sid uncoiled himself, gave a terrified hiss and shot into the undergrowth before I could bite him.

The conversation that took place immediately afterwards was, I suppose, only to be expected and went thus:

Keith: 'The next time I say don't move, don't move, you silly ass.' (Shock I expect.)

Peg: 'Well, I like that! Why didn't you say I was standing next to a snake, ugh!'

Keith: 'Wouldn't have made a scrap of difference, now, would it?'
Peg: 'You are only cross because you might have had to carry me about five miles to the hospital. It's your selfish streak coming out, and don't shout at me, I've had a nasty shock.'
And so on . . .
However, that evening in the hotel bar I had a rare moment of glory and was treated as a heroine. Recounting our experience to the friendly lady behind the bar caused her to shriek which brought immediate attention from all within.

'We don't none of us go up to Bouldnor Woods,' she said, 'It's alive with adders and you're lucky not to get bitten and dead.'

In no time at all I was the centre of attraction because of my bravery and Keith, bless his heart, didn't explain the circumstances leading up to Sid's swift slither away from danger!

Nations also have a terrible time muddling through and, let's face it, most governments and large organisations would be at a loss to know how to produce a decent rice pudding. Take the Rochdale Council, for instance. Now Rochdale is the home of the British Cotton Industry, I am given to understand, and the Council decided to put on a big promotion exercise to alert the rest of the world to this fact. One advertising feature was the sale of special T-shirts emblazoned with information calculated to inflame the public into buying British cotton goods, but two things were at odds with the 'British' theme. Firstly, the T-shirts were designed in America and, secondly, they were made in good old Ireland. Now that is what I really call muddling through.

Our lady ex-Prime Minister got into a bit of a muddle not so long ago when she sent a letter to a Junior School in Bristol, declining to offer anything for auction at their school fund-raising venture. As it turned out, this was a bad move on her part, because the letter itself became a star item and the bidding was extremely brisk. Who says that our educationalists aren't bright? A brilliant piece of Thatcherism and she should have been proud of them.

It's funny how small mysteries set the mind wandering over possible explanations. Big mysteries, such as what has happened to all the monies collected by the sponge-like Government from taxes, VAT, etc., I can't cope with, and so concentrate on the odd little happenings that don't tie up. Like this one where, I suspect, a muddle may have occurred.

During the 50th Anniversary of the Battle of Britain, some persons, possibly an organisation, laid the most beautiful and touching floral tribute at the base of a very modest Memorial tucked away where few people would come across it. It consisted of a large flat rectangle depicting two Spitfires flying through white sun's rays, the sun itself incorporating the RAF badge and motto, and '50' in another ray, all against a blue sky background. It was an amazing piece of work which must have taken a very long time to create, as the picture was composed entirely of flower heads, a few laurel leaves and sphagnum moss. But what was it doing standing at the base of this Memorial to men lost in the Indian Mutiny and the First World War? We are not short of large and imposing Memorials in this town as there have been a great number of Military and Naval disasters hereabouts, all with local import, but to my knowledge, nothing much in association with the RAF. I searched our local paper for a clue but the newshounds hadn't spotted it either, which is not surprising, so I've made up my own explanation, and this is what happened.

A seventy-year-old spinster came to live in our town a few years ago, under the impression that it is a nice healthy spot to retire to. She wasn't to know that it is unwise to dip a toe in the polluted waters, breathe in noxious substances from incinerators and car exhausts, or venture out in occasional Force 11 storms that send trees crashing and debris flying. However, apart from these and a few more hazards, Alicia, for that is her name, was enjoying her new life here. She would sit at her window watching the big ships and small craft making their way across the blue sea and her mind would wander back to the desperate days of the war.

'How different it all was,' she said aloud, and then, 'Oh Lionel, why did you have to die?'

Still gazing at the peaceful maritime scene, yet not seeing it, Alicia remembered the fraught yet wonderful days when she and Lionel were both in the RAF and engaged to be married. They had managed to snatch a few precious and passionate days together in a shabby guest house not very far away from where she now lives. They were so very much in love and so didn't notice the grubby surroundings, fleas from the landlady's mangy black cat, or even the margarine at breakfast time, 'Gosh!' she thought, 'I must have noticed them otherwise I shouldn't be remembering now. Oh, Lionel, how I wish you were here by my side.'

As the Battle of Britain 50th Anniversary grew closer, her mind's eye clearly saw the handsome twenty-three-year-old pilot with the twirly moustache who had died so bravely while shooting down German bombers bound for London.

'I will make my own tribute – but where shall I place it?'

Alicia's eyes grew misty as she suddenly remembered the little stone Memorial close to where the guest house had stood (later bombed) half a century ago, and how it had witnessed the urgent kisses that Lionel had rained upon her eager lips.

'Oh, yes, of course!' she whispered, 'That will be perfect.'

And so it was.

An alternative theory was sparked off by this newspaper cutting: 'Truce cars. Courtesy cars at the Battle of Britain 50th Anniversary celebrations at Boscombe Down were provided by Volkswagen's Audi Group.' God bless my soul!

For obvious reasons the Germans didn't take too much public notice of the Anniversary, but it did give an uncomfortable twinge to their Government's conscience that, though they had actually been defeated in the last war, since then they had made a mint of money by filling our roads up with their cars.

One Government Minister thought it would be a nice gesture to present a splendid tribute to the brave few who had given their brave many such a rotten time. This idea was approved and the most acclaimed flower arrangers they could muster produced a flower scene depicting two Spitfires flying in the sun's rays. It was duly brought to England on the eve of the Anniversary but no-one quite had the nerve to take it to Biggin Hill so they left it, under cover of darkness, at the first Memorial they could find, and hurried home.

I think Alicia and Lionel's story is the more likely of the two; as their tale unfolded I cried a little, so it must be the true explanation - unless a good old muddle went on somewhere by someone entirely different.

Recently Keith and I attended the funeral of an elderly and very dear old friend who had suffered appallingly with cancer. It was, therefore, not as unhappy a situation as it might have been and we met several old friends from the past for our sins, well, mine at least.

'Well, I never,' said one called Percy. 'It's Peggy. What's happened to your lovely ginger hair? I shall be ninety soon.'

I found this statement quite amazing as he didn't look anything like this grand old age, but then he continued:

'Yes, I am eighty-two next birthday and I'm looking forward to my telegram from the Queen.'

I pointed out that as this occasion would take place eighteen years hence, it might be sent by the King.

'Oh well,' said Percy, 'I expect he'll do.' He sounded slightly put out by the very idea.

A further encounter with Joe yielded a similar response, hairwise. We had worked together in the distant past, Joe as a senior officer and me as an aspiring junior typist in an Admiralty research establishment.

'Good gracious!' said he, 'It's little Peggy.' (I am 5'7" in my socks, so I don't quite know where the 'little' came in.) 'What *has* happened to your gorgeous ginger hair? I hardly recognised you.'

All this harping on about my lack of ginger hair, gorgeous or not, must have flicked a raw spot in my conceit, as later on I approached Keith on the subject and asked him what colour he would call it. After a good old peer he said:

'A sort of orangey-yellow, I suppose.'

That sounded so revolting that I went to the mirror to see for myself. On reflection – literally – I am of the opinion that 'toffee' was the nearest shade and sounds much nicer: I think I can muddle along with toffee hair but orangey-yellow is a bit hard to live with.

Long ago and when my hair could never have been described as 'orangey-yellow', I was severely embarrassed by a muddle of my own making. Recently returned from our honeymoon I was out shopping for our very first Sunday lunch in our new joint home and stopped off first at the butcher's. Not the one where my slip fell off, you understand.

'A leg of beef, please, butcher.'

Butcher smiled pityingly at me and bellowed to his colleague:

'Here's another bride, Bert. This one wants a leg of beef!'

Not only did he tell Bert, but he also informed a shop full of good-humoured and chatty housewives who enjoyed the joke mightily.

'Never you mind, dear,' said one. 'We all have to learn. Have a leg of lamb instead, Hubby won't know the difference, or care!'

This witticism caused much noisy merriment among her companions and a scarlet face for me. And then in my confusion I made it even worse by changing my order to a pound of sausages and I am too much of a lady to repeat the sort of remarks that brought forth!

CHAPTER 4

If you have managed to wade through Vená's Interesting Part - according to Lavinia (who is now helping me), an introduction to Vená won't be necessary. However, there are always two sides to every story, and here is mine as her long suffering friend.

Although she is too modest to admit that this might be true, Vená is an extremely talented and artistic lady, and if you add a keen sense of humour coupled with a belly laugh that can stop a horse in its tracks at fifty paces, you will see that life is never, never, dull when she's around. Put it this way: I am richer in experience and appreciation because our paths crossed so fortuitously, even if she can make me wild at times. But then, I'm no saint, I'm told. She - and therefore all of us - suffers from extreme enthusiasm and if something takes her fancy and needs looking into, there is no holding her. When we both worked at our local hospital she was pitchforked into flower arranging and was so good at it she almost immediately became famous as a Flower Arranger proper and decided that her heathen colleagues needed tuition in this delightful art.

So it was that about a dozen or so of us attended Vená's Flower Art classes once a week in the hospital canteen in the evening, bringing great bunches of weird flowers and greenery, and tons of Oasis. At first we were as green as the leaves and watched our tutor's deft little fingers whizz about, popping a carnation in here and a wiggly twig in there, with mouths wide open. It was a complete revelation to us lesser mortals and fired us up into a fine old ferment. The moment Vená was switched into the 'teaching mode' she underwent an extraordinary personality change and out stepped Lavinia. It was rather like being back at school, unquestioningly giving our full attention to this (now) dignified and rather grand lady who was so kindly giving us the benefit of her brilliance and panache. Not that the dignity lasted long because between Vená, Lavinia and the class, some amazing interpretations on a theme were created, some of which were unwittingly very comical. Needless to say, there was a great deal of laughter during these sessions and it was fortunate that the canteen was situated a good distance away from our poor in-patients. Just occasionally one or other of us would accidentally contrive a mini masterpiece and Lavinia's face would be transformed with wonder and delight – rather like Vená's jam and cream doughnut 'Oh! ecstasy' expression – and the lucky pupil basked in high praise.

Nearing Christmas one year, Vená decided that her class would make a Nativity scene to greet our constant flow of trembling patients in the reception area.

'Oh, yes!' we all agreed, 'How lovely. That will take their minds off the nasty needles.'

I don't know about the patients, but the staff were almost taken to Casualty on the evening of the angel-making, owing to hysterics, and can only hope that the angels were as amused as we were. The class was instructed to bring a large apron, rubber gloves, as much cotton material as possible, wallpaper gunge, plaster powder, and the inevitable cardboard centres of loo rolls. All very Blue Peterish and we couldn't wait to get at it.

We were each assigned a particular sort of angel and splattered away happily and, believe it or not, actually produced some fairly recognisable figures, without wings at this stage. Except for Katie. Admittedly, her angel was taller and slimmer (rather like Katie herself) than those of the rest of us and she really looked too good for this world. Lavinia herself was busy concocting the Virgin Mary and the Baby Jesus and was most impressed with Katie's elegant creation. Having reached this stage, the angels with the Mother and Child then required a week to dry out and harden before they could be titivated up for their big appearance. Right on cue and at the precise moment Lavinia's face was glowing and complimenting Katie, the angel made a slow bow and gently sat down. Dead silence prevailed for about ten seconds after the angel's acknowledgement of her beauty, and then we exploded with mirth. It was unbearably funny and we suffered accordingly with pain-racked bodies and streaming eyes. We all agreed that there are times when Vená should be made to carry a Government Health Warning. There was no way of straightening the Katie-angel, so we decided to dry her out in her new and interesting posture. The drying-out process took place in the redundant and empty animal house and appeared to be doing just fine during that week. Someone did remark that there must be quite a draught in there because one Angel's skirt waggled about sometimes during an inspection, but no real notice was taken of a silly remark like that. It was a different story though when Vená and one of her pupils proudly went forth into the animal house to collect the heavenly host and ran back shrieking and clutching at their skirts. Poor angels, what they must have suffered. It was enough to make the blood run cold. For a solid week the poor things had had mice up their robes, nibbling away the wallpaper paste and making a fine old mess of their toilet roll backbones. Rescue was soon at hand by the kindness of a brave technician who risked life and limb by shaking the mice out of their skirts and returning them to the comparative safety of the laboratory. Apart from a few nibbled holes they didn't suffer too much damage, however, and soon they had toughened up enough to be clothed in holy-looking shifts and slightly cock-eyed halos. In the run up to Christmas they grew wings and every week saw an increase in the accoutrements necessary for a Nativity until it became apparent that we had a show large enough to lay out on a cathedral floor. Fortunately the reception area was quite big and we earmarked a corner with no doors by doubling up the patients' chairs around the rest of the room. In the meantime Katie-angel had set fast in her crouched and leaning forward position and, to be honest, we hardly dared look at her for fear of a return attack of hysterics.

The saga of the Nativity scene had intrigued both staff and patients and we had a constant stream of both eager to see progress and hear of the latest disaster (and then have a good laugh!), and eventually we were able to give a firm date when the assembly of the enormous display would take place. Under Lavinia's strict supervision it suddenly became a reality and was quite magical. Some of us even thought seriously about becoming nuns for a few minutes. Katie-angel was the star of the show: placed immediately by the side of the crib, she appeared to be bending protectively over the babe with a little secret smile on her rather red lips. It was most touching and had an effect on our more sensitive admirers, seen dabbing at the corner of their eyes with a handkerchief. We had more or less kept the Katie-angel cock-up a secret and were able to boast about how difficult it had been to achieve that attitude over the crib. We all felt justified in indulging in one little fib as it was Christmas and we'd worked so hard for the pleasure of others. I think it just goes to show that if something goes wrong in the making, don't chuck it away, it may be a Katie-angel in disguise!

I particularly remember one evening when Vená or Lavinia became extra dramatic during a class. With a flourish and a clearing of her throat, she waved some silk flowers in the air (they had only just been invented then) and in a throbbing, throaty voice, announced:

'Girls! I want to introduce you to [pause for effect] *the flowers of the future!*'

It was good meaty stuff and we duly did rather pretty-pretty dinner table arrangements until Vená or Lavinia reverted to flowers of the past. We privately thought that they might even reach into the future. I'm certain that she found the 'future flowers' rather boring after about three minutes but didn't say so, having been so enthusiastic and having spent a small fortune providing them for her class.

I have attended a variety of evening classes over the years, ranging from Geology to a particularly difficult and complicated Word Processing course, and Vená's Flower Art classes stand high on a pinnacle of pleasure and sheer enjoyment to me. If I had to miss a meeting for any reason it was a matter of great regret, whereas I invented several possible fatal illnesses every Friday night when I should have attended Word Processing. Keith cleverly put two and two together, and, to my joy, said it was worth the £25 for me not to go as I was making his life a misery from Wednesday until Saturday morning every week.

Now, when Vená feels strongly about something she is apt to get up at about 3.00 a.m. and dash off a poem about whatever is on her mind. I will attempt to do the same, except that it is about 3.00 p.m.

> Dear Vená with her face aglow
> Would teach her class the way to go
> To study hard our flowers, etcetera
> And make arrangements so much betterer
> Than the last one.

And I mean it so sincerely

Various factors decided the demise of the Flower Art classes, the principal one being the decision of Vená to leave the Health Service and add a little oomph to the Education world and, from what I've heard, they too have never been the same since. I have to add that life wasn't quite the same, certainly not so exciting, in the department after she left, but then it couldn't be. My dear old Dad used to brag that he taught me everything I knew; quite a lot, I agree, but Vená/Lavinia has added a whole lot more.

Vená's husband Roy leads a very exciting life simply because he has no idea what on earth is going to happen at any time. This has drawbacks as well as advantages and it has been known for strong words and hurt looks to pass between them. However, this is superficial and transitory as, despite their sometimes differing views on a situation, they enjoy similar basic characteristics and therefore each other's company – well, nearly always.

Roy's proudest boast is that he is a Grade 1 Miser, which takes many years to achieve. Not wishing to hurt his feelings, I almost believed this claim though it is true to say that I had a few doubts, until I actually witnessed his miserly ways in action. We happened to meet outside W.H.'s in our shopping precinct one Saturday morning and Vená and I were catching up on the latest gossip when Roy popped out of the aforementioned shop like a cork out of a bottle.

'Cor crikey!' he said with a wealth of disbelief in his voice, 'My *Aircraft* magazine's gone up to £1.75. I'm not going to buy another. Hello, Peg.'

'You say that every time it goes up,' said his wife unsympathetically, 'I bet you do.'

He pondered for a few seconds and said, 'Well, if I don't I shan't know what's new, shall I? I suppose I'll have to,' accompanied by a deep sigh.

'Never mind that,' said Vená, a bit on the abrupt side as if she'd heard it all before, 'You said you would buy me some daffodils. Get me a bunch from that stall over there.'

'What! I can't afford blasted daffodils now. I came out with a £5 note, bought one magazine and now I've only got £3.25. It's disgraceful!'

Vená took absolutely no notice of these mutterings; she had a faraway thoughtful look and then said:

'They have some lovely tulips. Oh dear, I don't know which to have.'

Roy was wearing a close-at-hand long-suffering look and bade her make up her mind before he forgot the whole idea. Eventually Vená settled for daffodils and Roy set off to the flower stall. We chattered on for a minute or two, before suddenly realising that we were three again and that the third one was carrying a large wrapped bunch of flowers.

'Oh!' exclaimed Vená in delight, 'Daffodils and tulips - you are lovely, Roy, thank you.'

The Miser shuffled his feet and gave a sheepish grin.

'Would you like some daffodils, Peg?' he asked.

I was stunned by this miserly generosity and for appearance's sake demurred before accepting his kind offer.

'That's all right, Peg, it's a pleasure,' he said. 'I expect Keith buys you flowers sometimes, doesn't he?'

I was able to answer 'Yes' quite truthfully as Keith had indeed bought me a bunch of snowdrops one spring many years ago.

He departed once more and Vená started to giggle.

'Don't take any notice of him. He loves doing things like this, really.'

'Are you sure?' I asked, 'I'm standing here feeling sorry for his £5 note.' We were still laughing when the self-styled miser returned staggering under the weight of an enormous bunch of beautiful daffodils. He didn't look as miserable as one would expect under the circumstances; in fact, his bearded face was grinning happily as he transferred the armful to me. Later, when tastefully arranging the fifth vase of daffies I mused upon the merits of being a miser and pictured Roy carefully hoarding the 5p change from his £5 note. I even pondered upon the possibility of becoming a miser myself but decided I couldn't afford it and would stick to my non-miser rather mean way; it certainly makes a £5 note go further.

With the inevitable reminiscing that has taken place during the gleeful compilation of events in our lives, Vená was moved with a burning desire to take part once more in big Flower Art competitions. She had dipped her toe in the water the previous year and walked away with several prizes but wanted to beat her already formidable winning record by getting First Prizes for everything. Vená, being Lavinia as well, entered for everything that was going, including the Photographic Competition which was a little ambitious as she had only ever taken about three snapshots in her entire life, but as the theme was Parks and Recreation Areas, she couldn't resist the challenge. So once again she (and Roy!) were hurled into the bustle and excitement of big shows with the usual pre-competition tension and headaches for both. It was a coincidence that Keith's mother had entered several bottles of her famous home-made wine and detailed us to take them to the big tent and to collect them after the show was over, so we were able to keep a watching brief on our friend's entries. We were amazed how many there were – how does she do it, we wondered. Anyone else would have entered a couple of things and been grateful to have won a Third Prize, but I suppose they haven't got a Lavinia supercharger.

As the show was ending Keith and I struggled through the massive crowds to the big tent and were delighted to discover that Mum had very nearly swept the board with her wine entries, and then wound our way to the Flower Section to see how Vená had fared. We were greeted with a doleful look from Vená and an edgy one from Roy.

'It was *disaster*!' she cried from about ten yards distance, 'I didn't win a thing.'

I was staggered at this news and couldn't believe my ears. Vená/Lavinia prizeless, no, surely not. Roy intervened.

'Don't be silly, Vená. It's silly to say you didn't win anything – you did! You won one First and two Seconds for your photographs, a First for that funny Dressed Vegetable, and a Third for your Orchid, so stop being silly. It's really silly the way you're carrying on. *And*' (here his face broke out into a big beam) 'don't forget you won £58 for your photographs. You are silly.' He finished this little speech on a triumphant note. I could tell that these achievements meant not a jot to Vená; never have I seen her so depressed and close to tears.

'Maybe I am silly,' she said, gulping a little, 'But I've lost my touch and I shall never compete again. All my arrangements were ignored, totally ignored and passed by, and I can't understand it.'

We tried to cheer her up but she was so immersed in grief (and dramatics) that we might just as well have held our breath. Roy did cause a fleeting lightening of her dark mood by telling us how the other photographers had crowded round her asking terrible technical questions like, 'What make is your camera?' and getting the answer, 'I don't know. It's a black one.' She probably felt better the next day when she went out and blew all her winnings in one go, despite the fact that when I asked her what she had splurged the £58 on, she couldn't remember. Poor Vená, and Lavinia was

missing now that the going was getting rough. Typical!
Just a matter of weeks later she said:
'Guess what Peg, I've joined the Horticultural Society and I'm going to enter their Competition in September.'
I can't say I was terribly surprised and said absently, 'Ooh ah' or something similar, and got on with my boring bit. September has now come and gone and I am compelled to report that she won the following:

>Two Firsts for Flower Arrangements
>One Third for 'A Rose'
>One First for Rose Buttonhole
>Two Silver Cups
>One Silver Basket

One Silver Cup caused slight mirth as it was awarded for a four inch square miniature arrangement and stands eighteen inches high. Oh yes, and Lavinia is back, bragging away as usual.
Speaking of Lavinia – she did threaten to help me with my boring bit and because I am toddling along in my own sweet little way, she is getting to me by other ways. Keith is in the process of re-designing and labouring away in our kitchen, and to our horror we heard scratching noises overhead between the kitchen ceiling and the bedroom floor. Thorough investigation upstairs drew a blank until we spotted small lumps of chewed plaster by the side of the loo and our worst fears were confirmed; we had taken in an unwelcome lodger named Mickey. Further proof, if any were needed, was the extraordinary sight of the back half of a mouse disappearing through a wall in the larder. Curiosity overcame natural reluctance to get too close to the fearsome beastie, and I peered round the door, wondering where on earth it had gone. A small crack between the wall and the door frame was all I could find and that looked impossible for his or her little plump body to squeeze through. Admittedly it had disappeared sideways with two little pink feet and tail waving agitatedly as it went, but what a party trick, which made me believe in levitation. However, party trick or not, mice carry nasty diseases and this one was going to live in our larder over my dead body. Keith went to his garage and came back with his gun. Not the kind that fires bullets, you understand, but the sort that squirts silicon cement stuff into holes that need filling up. Work on the kitchen was further delayed while we had a brief conference on the best course of action and resulted in me detailed to ring the Environmental Department the next morning. And this is where Lavinia comes in. Having got to the main switchboard in Civic Offices, I was waiting for someone to pick up the phone in the Mouse Department and something came over me. A disembodied voice asked me how I could

be helped and I heard my own voice get lower and throb and say:
'I have to report an infestation of vermin.'
'Oh, my goodness!' replied a startled one, 'Whatever is it?'
'There is a mouse in my cupboard,' I throbbed.

There was a slight pause at the other end of the line and then a hand was obviously placed over the mouthpiece while she unsuccessfully tried to disguise a hearty laugh.

'I'm sorry, Madam,' she lied, 'I had to sneeze.'

I could understand her predicament; I should have done exactly the same myself. Anyway, she kindly arranged for a pest control man to call and distribute bait in little heaps, and while we haven't seen Mickey again, neither has the bait been disturbed, so we shall await events. A sequel to this stirring tale reveals that a neighbour who also had a visit from a mouse (and we hope it was ours), sneakily put some biscuit crumbs in a paper bag and waited to see what happened. He didn't actually see it go into the bag but heard rustlings and so gave it an almighty crack with a broom that happened to be handy, and that was that, one full up but dead mouse. And as for that wretched Lavinia - I shall have to have a word with Vená, as I now have a reputation of being over-dramatic in the Mouse Department and probably won't be taken seriously again, should the need arise.

CHAPTER 5

We first met Sophie and Ben many years ago in Ibiza, were immediately bowled over, and developed a friendship that is strong and family-like. To everyone's intense sorrow Ben died a few years ago and now we continue as a threesome and an unfillable gap. It was sheer coincidence that we met in the first place as we weren't even planning to go to the particular part of Ibiza that Sophie and Ben had booked for their holiday, but there was a last minute muddle with our travel arrangements and we found ourselves on the same plane, bound for the same hotel. As we hit it off so well it was a joy to discover that we lived in adjoining counties, they in Dorset and we in Hampshire, which meant that it would be a simple matter to keep in touch. They were a handsome and striking couple and incredibly full of beans, making that Ibiza stay the holiday of a lifetime.

We learned that they had both been married previously and had also been childhood sweethearts. Sophie's first husband had died shortly after their marriage, while Ben's wife died leaving two small children motherless. Unpredictably, here they were, first loves reunited in a second marriage that was celebrated after a year by the birth of a son. Now we also have him and his lovely wife as friends. Four for the price of two, you might say! Sophie has a medical condition that, in theory, makes daft things like having babies, flying, swimming, drinking, and all the intensely interesting things in life, quite taboo. In practice she ignores these restrictions and lives exactly as she wants to. They live in the pleasant town of Hardy's Casterbridge (Sophie on her own now), both convinced that this is the best place on earth. The fact that they are both Dorset born and bred may have a little to do with this opinion, but they aren't far wrong. So many happy week-ends we spent with them; not exactly sober ones as Ben made gallons of potent home made wine that was guaranteed to put a smile on anyone's face. This craft is carried on as he taught me how to brew buckets of the stuff and now I'm nearly as popular as Ben was. I should also add that Sophie is carrying on the tradition with a pretty mean tipple that ensures a steady stream of friends calling at the door.

An incident related by Sophie was, I would say, fairly typical of the sort of silly situations that seemed to occur at irregular intervals. She and Ben were having a wow of an evening at a fairly posh dinner and dance and both were getting as happy as newts, owing to a low pressure area nearby or something, and the orchestra struck up the opening bars of that spine tingling number 'Jealousy'. Sophie herself is, and more definitely was, a very graceful dancer but Ben had two left feet and no memory whatsoever for dance steps. This small matter did not deter him in the least and he swept Sophie on to the dance floor with a flourish and whizzed her across with tremendous panache. Other couples dissolved into the background, thinking that some professionals were about to give an exhibition of the tango and must have been much surprised as Ben knew three steps only and repeated them in a straight line until he ran out of dance floor. Somehow they got through the tables and then disappeared through the door, never to be seen again that evening as they didn't dare go back. The shortest Tango Exhibition ever staged, I should imagine!

We were present on another hilarious occasion, this time in Menorca. I believe that this island is relatively unspoilt even today and when we went some sumptuous hotels had only just been built to attract holiday makers, but as they hadn't yet arrived in force we had the run of most of them and were made very welcome. So welcome, in fact, that another low pressure area developed making us feel just a little lightheaded and happy. You see, there was this really beautiful hotel in splendid isolation on the wonderful Santo Thomas beach and not a soul about with the exception of us four and the hotel staff. We were made such a fuss of for such a long time that we were in no fit state to undergo the conducted tour of the hotel suggested by the equally merry manager. Fortunately for us, all the staff had been making a fuss of themselves and so we all laughed a lot at each other's jokes which no-one understood. All went well until we were shown into a room that was furnished with valuable *antiquos* that included an ancient looking cane settee affair. It must have looked very inviting to Ben who approached it very carefully and then sat down very uncarefully. *Antiquo* it certainly was, as Ben's unexpected landing caused it to give an agonized creak and then subside gently to the floor with its poor legs flat at different angles. For a few moments there was an awed hush at the extent of the disaster while we gazed down at Ben sitting in the collapsed *antiquo* murmuring compliments about its comfort. I can't remember who giggled first (it might even have been me) but then we all roared and shrieked with laughter. Never in my entire life have I witnessed anything so funny, although the hospitality may have had a little to do with it. All I know is that I laughed so hard I put my bladder in dire straits and was forced to dash to the loo. When I returned the mirth was simmering down a little and by popular consensus of opinion we decided to make Ben's comedy act a grand finale and leave while the going was good. How lovely the Spanish are; they actually implored us to come back as soon as we could. We did think about it but decided perhaps it would be wiser not to accept their invitation in case another *antiquo* bit the dust.

I don't wish to give the impression that we always staggered around looking happy, far from it. It was just that whenever we met it was a celebration of friends being together and celebrations called for a glass (or two) of whatever was going at the time.

Keith and I got to know many beautiful and wild places in Dorset by visiting Sophie and Ben and they in exchange were enchanted by some of our Hampshire and West Sussex favourite haunts. Picnics at Bosham were popular, especially when we perched in a row on the sea walls that stop the incoming tide invading the waterfront gardens.

At high tides the road is impassable and it is a picnic with a difference when you can toss a bit of sandwich to a passing crab and watch him tuck in with relish underwater on the road.

Our very first Sophie-and-Ben-conducted tour in Dorset was not entirely without incident, now I come to think of it. This introduction to the wilder parts of Dorset consisted of walking to Whitenothe the civilised way and back to their car parked on the high Downs the hard way. I thought the civilised way was fairly tough, though quite delightful, but the return scramble up the near-mountain was rather like a Commando assault course. The Dorset Division took it calmly in their stride while the Hampshire Layabouts puffed and moaned. In amongst all the wilderness we came across a gate and lots of barbed wire that separated us from the next stretch that looked much smoother but which had small blobs in the distance that looked rather like cows to me. So long as there is a barrier between me and them, I am fond of cows and will even pat their wet, slimy noses if they look friendly. There was absolutely no way of telling if these dots were friendly or otherwise at this range, but, having been assured very sincerely that Dorset cows are all sweet natured and that bulls were definitely not allowed to roam freely in fields, we agreed to be big and brave and go forth.

At the point of no return I couldn't help noticing that one of the cows was approximately three times the size of the others and was watching our approach with some interest.

'Sophie!' I croaked, 'Surely that's a bull?'

'No, dear,' she replied; until this very minute I hadn't realised that she was a bit short sighted. 'It's just a big cow,' and then, peering hard, said, 'Oh yes! It is a bull – isn't he a beauty?'

How anyone could describe that fearsome beast as a 'beauty' was beyond me, but I have been informed that beauty is in the eye of the beholder, and judging by the beam on Sophie's face, apparently he was gorgeous.

'Don't run,' we were advised by Ben. 'Just walk slowly and he won't take any notice of us.' Fat chance with Sophie cooing, 'Who's a handsome boy, then?' and making clucking noises. Bovril the Bull raised and lowered his head several times as if enjoying Sophie's admiration; or was he, perhaps, practising to take a lunge at us?

Keith looked nearly as worried as I felt and even Ben didn't look too happy.

'Come on, Sophie,' he said, quite sharply for him. 'For heaven's sake stop mucking about and let's get moving.' I had the impression that in the scaredy-cats league I was the winner with Keith slightly behind, Ben some distance down the scale and Sophie nowhere in the running at all. Sophie received Ben's message clearly and, muttering apologies, she quietly turned and walked away from Bovril. The next few minutes were agony wondering if we would hear him thundering in our wake, but all was still, and after what seemed a year later we leapt over a gate and then turned to see if he had been following. No, he hadn't, and once again the herd were dots in the distance but this time we could definitely see that one dot was pretty enormous. It was then that Sophie made one of her famous 'not quite right' remarks.

'I can't think what all the fuss was about,' she said, looking quite hurt. 'Fancy being cowed by a bull!'

The years slid pleasantly by with many happy meetings and holidays and then Ben's erstwhile robust health took a dive. It seemed incredible that this larger than life and big-hearted friend could be vulnerable to ailments that plague the rest of us, but obviously no-one escapes for ever, not even Ben. Sophie was magnificent during this upsetting time and as far as she could made sure that life went on as normally as if Ben were still fit. Ben also tried very hard and nearly always succeeded. He was cracking a joke with Sophie just minutes before he died.

It was a forlorn congregation that gathered to say goodbye to Ben, and if it was unreal and nightmarish for us, what must it have been like for poor Sophie? As usual, with her great courage she comforted the rest of us and then set about organising the next part of her life. We are as close, if not closer, than before, and even now, after some years, when detailed to 'Lay the table, please, dear', I find myself picking out four knives and forks from the cutlery drawer quite naturally. It still hurts a little, but at least I can grin as I visualise Ben saying, 'You silly old fool, Peg!'

Sophie has had quite a few adventures on her own, including a trip to Russia and getting into difficulties with the Soviet immigration officers by accidentally removing part of her Visa document, and a champagne-and-violin-assisted flight in a hot air balloon over the Dorset countryside, and tootles around Dorchester and its environs on a small motor bike. She tends the large garden, continuing Ben's well tried and tested gardening techniques with amazing results, and has swept through her house like whirlwind, redecorating and improving. Quite a gal, our Sophie, and you should see her onions.

Quite a few years ago, for no apparent reason, Keith and I developed an urge to find a new home, but in the same town. What started off as a whim quickly became a secondary occupation; it was fiery and addictive stuff, this, and also taught us a thing or two about our fellow citizens. We soon learned to decipher the estate agents' blurb, substituting descriptions like 'compact, suitable for small family' with 'just right for dwarf with tiny wife', or reading, as did happen, 'character villa with large garden (etc.) in Conservation Area at a reasonable price', which was absolutely true. What they hadn't mentioned was that the new owner would have to spend at least £50,000 to replace the sagging roof, combat dry rot, immediately dismantle the rather dangerous garage, re-wire, install central heating and proper plumbing, re-decorate very heartily, remove many tons of junk from the garden, and last but definitely not least, call in the rat catcher.

On occasions such as this, upon return we would gaze lovingly around our own fairly clean and bright abode and think we must be simple-minded to go and look at someone else's hell hole, but still we persevered. I don't understand why, but once bitten by the moving bug there is no escape. It is more powerful than cocaine and much more interesting, I should think.

Sophie and Ben happened to be staying with us when we were going to view an apartment in a very nice sea front area and were both keen to see if we had been telling the truth about some of our experiences.

'Oh, this one will be all right,' I said airily. 'It's in a luxury block in a posh area and the rates are horrendous.'

We were actually only going to see it to indicate to the agent that we were deadly serious about moving, as the price was astronomical, unlike our joint salaries. So off we all went in high spirits, fully expecting a pleasant tour of a beautiful apartment with a large balcony overlooking the sea, to be followed (perhaps) by a nice cup of tea and a biccy. Information given to us by the agent had indicated that the gentleman owner was temporarily living in Hong Kong and that his niece was occupying and looking after the flat until it was sold. Well, that seemed fair enough - people do go and live in Hong Kong and allow relatives to use their premises while absent - very sensible. Having gained admission via the security system and been wafted up to the fifth floor in a rather sumptuous lift, we walked through an extremely pleasant corridor and found the number we were looking for. The only thing was, this door looked different somehow. Whereas everything we had encountered *en route* gleamed with cleanliness (and slight opulence), this one was dingy, battered, and decidedly out of place.

'Ooh, crumbs!' I remarked. 'Here we go again, I reckon.'

There was also a rather strange odour seeping into the corridor and, having sniffed experimentally a few times, I came to the conclusion that it reminded me of a not too fussy fish and chip shop. I could tell from their expressions that Sophie and Ben were also getting keenly interested now that all was not what it seemed, and couldn't wait for someone to open the door when all would be revealed.

They weren't disappointed. After a few minutes and a second knock on the door, it opened and a pretty face framed with beautiful, long blonde hair appeared, smiled and bade us enter. The smell was much stronger now; in fact, it was nigh overpowering. We followed her through the little hall and into the lounge. Well, I suppose it was a lounge, but to our astonished eyes it looked as if burglars and vandals had moved in and taken up residence. There was so much clutter, muck and unsavoury clothes spread around that our mouths dropped open with shock. The girl seemed to be completely unaware that anything was other than normal, and to her, perhaps, it wasn't. She was so attractive and clean looking, rather like a lily on a dungheap. She smiled at Ben and Keith and told us that her uncle would soon be home from his travels and that she, therefore, would be trying to find another flat. She seemed to me to be looking at us, or rather at the men, hopefully, as a homeless Persian kitten might do, or an appealing puppy viewing a likely sucker to take it home. In my mind's eye I was seeing a trail of ruined flats and houses wherever this weird girl had happened to land. And what of uncle? Was he of the same ilk, or would he die of a heart attack when confronted with the nice tidy apartment he had left in her care? Or was he, indeed, her uncle at all? It was very intriguing and we all longed to know the answers.

Bearing in mind that this was a lounge that had large windows with a balcony beyond and the sea bobbing about in the background, it should have been bright to the point of being glary, but no, it was quite murky as the windows, inside and out, were black with grime and heaven knows what. I started to feel itchy and scratched my leg. She then led us into a bedroom that could only be described as catastrophic (briefly) and then another. The second bedroom was almost neat and clean by comparison so, presumably, she didn't use it much. The kitchen was next on the grand tour and was also the source of the unpleasant smell. I swear upon the Bible that I have never encountered anything so awful in my life as this squalid room. The windows were in the same condition as those in the lounge, the sink was full of dirty pots and pans, and the cooker and the wall behind it were hidden beneath about an inch of grease, old bits of chips, curry and things unidentifiable. It was entirely gruesome and Sophie looked a little pale. We edged towards the door and freedom but the girl quickly darted ahead of us to show us the bathroom. Fearing the worst, we gingerly peered through the half opened door and saw rows of dripping jeans of varying sizes, and very little else.

The human frame and sensibilities can only take so much and we had all reached our limit. Fortunately the front door was close at hand and we made our escape to the nearest pub for medicinal purposes. After a prolonged recovery period we felt strong enough to conduct a post mortem with vigour and thoroughly enjoyed ourselves exploring various theories as to what had been going on. Obviously we could never know the exact truth of the matter but one over-riding feeling was immense sympathy for the poor uncle – if he was! Of course these forays were very much in the minority, which is why they stick in the memory, and most of our appointments with destiny were very pleasant in nice houses owned by nice people. We did our best to assure Sophie and Ben that this was so and almost convinced them.

One Saturday afternoon we kept an appointment to view a period house in a delightfully quaint little road (rather scarce in our city) and promptly fell in love with everything, including the owners. We quickly became on Christian name terms with them, discovering that they were Naomi and Chris who didn't want to leave their lovely home at all but circumstances demanded their living in another area. We were very keen to buy their house; it was more or less within our price bracket, supposing we could find a buyer for ours. As always, the people that really wanted to have ours couldn't sell theirs, and so on. I am sure this is a very familiar story for most folk and is madly frustrating. Reluctantly we had to admit defeat so that Naomi and Chris could inform the next on the list of prospective purchasers. A few weeks later we appeared to be in a good selling situation and hastily contacted them, just in case they were having the same problems that we were experiencing. Pipped at the post, we were, by a whisker, to the chagrin of all concerned. Still, that's the way it goes and now we can't imagine living anywhere other than in the dear little house we did eventually find.

Naomi is small, brunette, and the lucky possessor of beautiful and unusual eyes, while Chris is tall and handsome in a whimsical sort of way. Put together, they are a very attractive and charming pair – a perfect foil for Keith and me, only one of which can be described as attractive, charming etc., and I will leave it to you to guess that it isn't the one with gone-off ginger hair and tousled look! However, and putting a brave face on it, I fully realise that we can't all be good looking and three out of four is pretty good going.

At this time Chris had unexpectedly been made redundant by the large oil company that had employed him for some years; this fell like a bombshell, shattering the fragile security we all seem to share these days.

Perhaps there never was total security in the past, just a false impression of the 'good old days' when life seemed more stable. After some disappointments, anxiety and heart searchings, they entered a new phase in their lives when they were chosen by the National Trust to take up an appointment in one of their wonderful properties in Suffolk. As Keith and I have been keen 'Trusters' for many years, we were naturally thrilled to bits with this exciting piece of news and followed their adventures and progress avidly.

Even more thrilling was an invitation to spend a week-end with them in this imposing and beautiful house. For some reason we had never visited Suffolk before, imagining, I suppose, that it is as flat as a pancake and cold, so that the lovely rolling countryside and hot sunshine was a delightful surprise. Visiting one of the National Trust Houses as a member for an afternoon is one thing, bowling up to the front door and unloading suitcases is another. Thank God it was me and not Vená. Lavinia would have taken over in short order and then who knows what would have happened. Actually, I can see her transforming herself into Vita Sackville-West at Sissinghurst and reorganising the gardens on a grand scale. Week-ends at the Houses are very busy, so after a very warm welcome and refreshments, we made ourselves scarce by exploring the property while they attended to the many visitors. It was like suddenly being dumped in heaven or winning the Pools and we scampered around the grounds in sheer delight. Much later, after the House had closed and the tremendous amount of security had been put into action, we were at last able to get together properly for our first meeting since they had left home.

We had already been aware that National Trust staff work amazingly hard, but being witnesses at close quarters we began to appreciate just how hard and enormous is the responsibility for countless treasures. Awesome, that's the word for it. Despite it being business as usual, we managed to spend a lot of time together, trying hard not to get in the way and even managing to help here and there in a minor sort of way. How on earth they remembered all the hundreds of things that had to be done, I'll never know, but then nearly everyone is more intelligent than I am. The evenings were nicest, enjoying a delicious supper miraculously provided by Naomi and then relaxing by the fire with such good friends and much laughter.

Like exotic gypsies, they moved to different Houses in different counties and we were privileged to stay with them in each. It's queer how magnificent buildings and the odd Reynolds hanging about on the brocaded wall very soon become almost natural and homely, and it is only upon return to one's own little front door, small (in comparison) sitting room and tiddly kitchen, that realisation dawns that the whole of our house could easily be fitted into one of the stately rooms with even a bit to spare. It takes at least a couple of days to readjust to mini-surroundings, but on the other hand, there's not so much dusting to be done here.

Like all of us, Naomi and Chris have gone through bad times as well as good ones, and one of the worst was the severe illness suffered by Chris which resulted in heart surgery and early retirement. They have exchanged mansions for a picturesque cottage, but still in delightful surroundings, and have down-graded an extremely hectic life to a merely hectic one, and we still enjoy an occasional happy reunion despite the many miles that separate us. You see how very interesting house-hunting can be. Had we not viewed their house – even though we didn't manage to get it – we should never have stayed in the wonderful big houses or, worse still, even known that these two dear and gentle people existed. Take the rough with the smooth, is my advice. You are bound to come across the odd house or flat of horror but, on the other hand, if it's your very lucky day, you may even meet a Naomi and Chris.

CHAPTER 6

While Keith and I have enjoyed many visits to the Channel Islands, two trips stand proud of the rest in my memory and both, as usual, for silly reasons.

The first of these we shared with friends Erica and Peter in Guernsey and had booked flights from our local small airport with a sprig of a larger airline that operated on the Channel route. This was quite a few years ago and was much more of an adventure than in these casual days of hopping in and out of planes with not much clear idea of where one is off to. So, when the great day came we were all tingling with excitement, though the men wouldn't admit to it, of course.

When we arrived at the airport it was a little disconcerting to detect an air of suppressed outrage and couldn't-care-less attitude amongst the airline staff. In fact, it rather matched the weather which was very blowy, dark and raining: just the way to start off our little holiday! After a very long wait in the lounge we were herded into a medium-sized plane and eventually took off. Buffeted by the strong westerly wind we climbed in lumps and seemed to be grinding along rather painfully. I am not a lover of air travel at the best of times and tend to keep a wary eye on the wings and nuts and bolts, just to make sure that nothing is falling off, and while performing this little duty observed that the same piece of Isle of Wight scenery was passing for the third time. Though hyper-sensitive where personal danger is involved, I bravely didn't mention this to Keith in case it worried him, only to hear him say, 'Hey! We're back at the airport - I wonder what's wrong with the plane?'

We landed in a disjointed fashion; Peter asked a passing hostess for the reason and received the standard reply on these occasions, 'Slight technical problem, Sir,' before she buzzed off.

If I remember correctly, there were roughly twenty passengers, and we were all keen to know why we'd had three trips around the Isle of Wight instead of one straight one to Guernsey. We four had noted while boarding the plane that the tyres looked sad and bald, but that couldn't have been the reason because a message from the Captain asked us to fasten our safety belts ready for take off. This we did, but not so happily as the first time.

The second attempt was more successful and we ground our way across the heaving Channel, shaken to death by the increasing wind. It was a relief to see the familiar and beautiful coastline of Guernsey and even more so when we bumped down on to the runway. All the passengers huddled in a group in the lounge, some looking a bit sick, and we set about trying to find out what on earth was going on. After much probing we were informed that the large airline had pruned this sprig and we had been privileged to travel on its very last flight. No wonder the staff had looked (and acted) so miserable, and thank God they didn't feel suicidal – there had been plenty of opportunity.

After this ill-tempered and rather frightening start to our long awaited holiday, it was a pity that we couldn't know how good it was going to be. We had booked accommodation at Guernsey's oldest inn, The Yacht, which is situated on the outskirts of St Peter Port. Apart from being old, it was definitely and enjoyably quaint. It was draughty, rambling and creaky, with very few of the refinements we expect now in the modern purpose-built monolithic hotels, but was miles ahead in character and a genuine welcome. Most of the guests were quaint also and we had some rather hilarious evenings in the bar after dinner. One quainter than usual guest was a dear old gentleman who immediately fell in love with me and desired to adopt me, promising me wealth and happiness. He was much too nice to laugh at so we laughed with him and, perish the thought, he may have been pulling my leg. I am not convinced that this was the case, though, as his face would light up when I hove into viewing distance and from then on he didn't take his eyes off me. I was astonished because I've never had this effect on anyone and was inclined to agree with Peter who said, unkindly I thought, that the silly old fool must have forgotten to bring his white stick with him.

He had stayed at The Yacht for so long that he was considered a permanent guest and was held in great affection by the proprietor and staff. I was strongly advised to get adopted as, they said, he would make a lovely rich daddy. I suppose it says quite a lot for my dear Keith that he looked down his nose most decidedly at this suggestion. It was really sad when we left and I felt a little like an errant daughter (adopted) deserting her loving and dear old dad (also adopted). I don't know what the law is in Guernsey on this subject – I don't suppose it crops up often – but in English law it is not permitted to adopt a married woman, so that was that.

The weather cheered up considerably after our peculiar journey to the island though the wind persisted from a westerly quarter. The seas around the Channel Islands are very clear and of a beautiful greeny-blue shade, so that whipped-up rollers topped with spume create an invigorating and colourful seascape. It was on one of these high wind days that we decided to take a boat trip to the little island of Herm that beckons so seductively across the short strip of water to St Peter Port's visitors. Also, the sea looked fairly calm on this side of the island, which was a good reason for going. Keith and Peter sat in the stern of the small passenger boat and Erica and I faced them amidships, and chugging out of the harbour was rather like gliding over the Mediterranean on a calm day. As we left the shelter of the high stone harbour wall we were suddenly transported to Cape Horn conditions on a rough day, which tossed and pitched us unmercifully. It was just as well that the crossing was so short, but a large breaking wave caught up with the boat as it slowed approaching Herm's little landing stage and hit the stern with a resounding thud. Now, Erica and I have always maintained that it was most unchivalrous of our men to duck at that precise moment and, predictably, this reasoning is dismissed as nonsense. It must have been Old Sod at it again as we both clearly remember two hastily bent heads and half a ton of sea curving over them to land squarely on Erica's head. Gasping and spluttering, she hung on to the bobbing boat while the rest of us tried unsuccessfully to mop up streams of sea water running down her neck and tried to forgive the ripe comments issuing forth from blue lips. As she said, it wouldn't have mattered so much if it had happened on the return journey but to have to creak around dear little Herm dripping with water and bits of seaweed, was too bad. I agree.

However, in the warm sunshine and brisk breeze she dried out somewhat, though it was difficult for her to keep up with the rest of us as her clothes were stiff with salt. She coped with this disability by adopting a slinky looking gait to avoid severe chafing, but when we reached the famed Shell Beach she forgot her straitjacket clothes and dashed about finding treasures at an alarming speed. By the time we returned to the landing stage for the homeward trip, the high tide rip had subsided, the sea looked as flat as a mirror and not a single drop of sea came inboard to dampen our dry but stiff friend, as Peter pointed out unwisely. 'Huh!' said Erica, and there was a wealth of meaning in that single syllable. The only thing that surprises me is that it was Erica who copped the top of the wave and not me. I can only think that perhaps Old Sod didn't quite have time to direct it a foot or so to the left, or port as we boat people say.

We did a tremendous amount of exploring around Guernsey's spectacular coastline and, of course, it was my turn to be the victim. You see, I love to wear sandals whenever possible and I don't always pay attention to where I'm going. Consequently, it is quite usual to see one or other of my toes encased in a strip of plaster. Imagine a superb and exciting beach strewn with granite rocks and me leaping about happily: a perfect recipe for disaster, I fear. My feet so often seem to arrive at a destination before my brain catches up with them, and on this occasion a trap for the unwary in the shape of a limpet-encrusted rock neatly removed the top of one of my big toes. I would have thought that a little sympathy would have been in order, but no, used to my disastrous gambollings, all that was offered was mild amusement and sarcastic remarks, the swines. And did I need sympathy! The initial numbness soon vanished leaving a pretty sharp pain in its wake. Not one of us could produce even the scrappiest piece of plaster for temporary repairs, which meant that the raw wound was in constant touch with sand, shells, seaweed, and all the junk that normally loafs around on a beach. We had hired a little white Mini for tootling around the island, so at least I had transport back to The Yacht. Rather like Guernsey folk, it had definite character. Though young in years, it had received the very minimum of attention throughout its short life and, very endearingly, grew tufts of quite long grass in the metal strips along the doors, rather like an upside down grass skirt. By the time I scrambled out at the Inn it was further embellished with about a pint of blood, inside and out, and it occurred to me to wonder if the car hire firm would make discreet enquiries as to whether one of their customers had been murdered. Probably not; in Guernsey people live their own lives and let others get on with theirs unhindered.

Once cleaned up and a toe-pudding applied, I felt strong enough to hobble to the bar for a much needed gin and tonic, and in this convivial atmosphere received more than enough sympathy to make up for the earlier lack. My adoptive dear old daddy was very concerned and thought I should nip up to the hospital to get the gash stitched, and I had to tell him that there wasn't anything to stitch up as I'd left it on the beach and it had probably been eaten by a crab by now. I did notice at dinner that no-one ordered crab!

The rest of our holiday passed very pleasantly, though I took great care not to put my toe in danger and tended to stay put in some lovely spot while the others did athletic things. It was certainly no hardship to commune with nature on some sheltered cliff, waving now and again to the three little ants on the beach below, who were going to have to climb all the way up to my niche that was filled with wild flowers, butterflies, bees, and (if I hadn't drunk it all) some left-over Martini. It was quite the life, really.

There is a sequel to the bashed toe saga. When at the airport for our return journey, I was still nursing it and screeched if anyone came within a yard. A last minute trip to the loo was necessary and I limped across the lounge and into the Ladies - and quite failed to see a metal door stop which took the top off my other big toe. There was no time to get it patched and I had to limp with both legs on to the plane. I have no idea which airline took us home; all I do know is that I christened it redly and it probably never looked the same again, like the Mini.

CHAPTER 7

A few years after visiting Guernsey with Erica and Peter, we suddenly had an urge to return to the Channel Islands and thought that Alderney might just prove to be interesting. Reports of a free and easy lifestyle appealed and it seemed like a good idea to go and find out if this island was as quaint as had been painted. Decision made and bookings confirmed, we made our way to the same little airport, with bag and baggage and a good supply of sticky plasters (at Keith's insistence). This time we flew in one of those special inter-island planes that have an engine tucked under each wing and a spare on top of the fuselage: very reassuring, I thought, and was the only flight that I have ever enjoyed. It was a little like sitting in the cockpit, as the plane was just two seats wide and either we were part of the crew or the pilot was a passenger who happened to be driving it at the time. He was a big cheerful man who chatted away to us clear across the Channel and obviously enjoyed this air taxi work very much. The only unnerving moment was landing when it looked as if we might be crashing into the side of a cliff, but we cleared the top by about six inches and that is where the runway starts. Alderney is only one mile wide and 3½ miles long and can just about cater for small aircraft, and as it was our plane seemed to require more runway than that provided. However, with a great squeal of brakes and wheels we came to a halt with another six inches to spare. It's quite exciting and makes the adrenalin flow nicely.

It was clear from the start that this was going to be a holiday with a difference - the trouble was we didn't know if that would be good for the better or bad for the worse and only time would tell. The small airport building was so incredibly relaxed that it was a wonder it stayed in one piece, and of formalities there were none. We used the phone to order a taxi and then waited - and waited. After some considerable time Keith rang a second time and was informed that, yes, he's just coming to get you, shan't be a minute. The next half hour gave us an indication of how long an Alderney minute is and then we heard a grating, scraping noise. The one and only member of staff said, without looking up, 'Here's Bill now. Have a nice holiday - see you when you go home, 'bye.'

The car's appearance matched its mechanical music and Bill jumped out, greeting us cheerily and bundling us and our luggage into the clapped-out vehicle. Bill himself wasn't all that smart and looked as if he'd just returned from a fishing trip (which he had) and off we rattled. He plain ignored the fact that we'd waited for the best part of an hour and chatted away, finding out all about us in the process, until we reached the hotel.

Having read and heard reports of an intriguing nature about Alderney and its off-beat inhabitants, we didn't know in the least what to expect. The hotel we had chosen is situated practically on a beach and looked normal enough, so we risked going in and signing the register and then settled ourselves in a rather basic bedroom. These things attended to, we decided to do a little island exploring and leg stretching. The hotel layout was rather confusing and we missed our way. After a few false trails we detected a subdued racket that seemed to emanate from a door named 'Lounge' and, being curious, opened it and went in. Well, we went in for a couple of steps and stopped dead. What a scene! The room was filled to capacity with people sitting, lying on the floor, draped over things, all drinking, smoking, laughing, and generally having a pretty jolly time. As this was a Sunday afternoon at about 4.00 p.m., we were somewhat taken aback. One or two prone figures waved with floppy arms and bade us, 'Come in, come in! Join the party. Somebody give 'em a drink.'

As we were slightly suspicious as to what sort of 'party' was going on, we declined graciously and withdrew. The funny thing is, except for one person whom we got to know very well, we didn't see any of them again for the entire holiday. Who were they, and where did they go? After all, Alderney is so tiny and under-populated that the chance of not meeting them again in some bar or other was pretty remote.

However, having shuffled off a bit sheepishly, we had a wonderful afternoon discovering the superb coastal scenery with its dramatic and savage cliffs. It was enchanting. Much later we returned to the hotel with enormous appetites, really looking forward to a hearty dinner. Another surprise awaited us. Alderney shuts up shop after lunch on Sundays and the bar wouldn't open, even to residents, until about 9.00 p.m. Even worse, the restaurant was closed and we could see through the glazed door that the tables were laid ready for breakfast. *Breakfast!* Oh dear! It's one thing being half starved knowing that a large meal is in the offing after a refreshing gin and tonic, and quite another kettle of soup having to cope with the dawning realisation that neither will be made available as there is, apparently, no-one on this island apart from ourselves. It seemed a bit silly to wander out of the hotel, along the sand covered road and up the steep hill to St Anne's at the crest, in our (fondly imagined) smart evening gear - we might have frightened the rabbits.

Mournfully we repaired to the lounge, now empty of bodies but still full of the remains of a riotous party, and passed the time listening to the not very tuneful duets performed by our rebellious stomachs, wondering if we'd done the right thing by coming to blighted Alderney. After what seemed about a week we became conscious of far away voices and little sounds of human activity and sped hastily in the direction of the bar - just in case. How wonderful - it was open and occupied by a couple of clients and a barman pouring drinks into glasses. They all looked slightly startled at our 'dressed for dinner' clothes, as well they might, as they looked as if they'd just stepped ashore from some grotty boat or from fishing off the beach. They had, of course. We learned very quickly that Alderney is classless so far as dress is concerned; everyone looks the same, be he or she a millionaire or dustman. It cuts no ice whatsoever if the posh frock has been donned for dinner and, in fact, I needn't even have bothered to comb my hair. I could live here very happily.

A couple of drinks uncreased our strained faces and we asked John the barman if there was any possibility of food to go with them. He was shocked that we had missed lunch and arranged for sandwiches to be sent to the bar for us. I wouldn't have swopped those gorgeous sandwiches - great chunky things full of cold roast beef with stinging blobs of mustard - for a ten course meal. Fisherman's Specials they were called and guaranteed to keep the wolf from the door for at least twenty-four hours. It was then that we both decided that Alderney was pretty good and fully expected to enjoy our holiday thoroughly, and, as it turned out, it exceeded our high expectations.

The one and only survivor from the afternoon party wandered into the bar and greeted us, 'Oh, there you are then! You didn't come back - what happened? We missed you.' That really did amaze us as we hadn't realized anyone was sober enough to recognise us, let alone miss us! Our new friend was a large, lumbering man with an awesome pot belly. Aged about the latter middle years with a weather beaten face and long, rather straggly ginger hair, his was a presence not to be ignored. He introduced himself as Len and told us he was a Guernseyman over here on a fishing holiday. It was instant friendship all round and in no time at all we were as integrated with this hub of the universe as if we'd lived there all our lives.

There were such extraordinary characters on Alderney and they all seemed to have a second home in John's bar. Kate, for instance, lived in a cottage a short distance up the hill from the hotel and her mode of transport was a moped-type bike. Nothing very strange about that, you may think, but Kate was a large lady who dressed only in men's trousers with the flies tied up with a shoe lace, shirts and large boots. Unfortunately, she suffered from several fairly severe illnesses and drank like a fish. After about three minutes when she had got to know us better, she told us her life history and we were fascinated to learn that she had been a racing driver in the 1920s. This obviously stood her in good stead when wobbling around on her bike, because the only way she could get the tiny machine to climb the hill to St Anne's was to descend to the hotel, make a precarious U-turn and gather enough speed to get a run at it. It was advisable on these occasions to stand well clear of her turning spot as she required the whole width of the sandy road to change direction and invariably it looked as if disaster would happen. It never did, at least, not while we were there.

Kate had spent her misguided youth having a whale of a time hobnobbing with many famous and infamous personalities of that decade. She was, she said, the last in the line of a well known and rich family and never did explain how she came to be living in Alderney, of all places, in straitened circumstances but thoroughly enjoying it, having changed her vehicle from a Lagonda to a moped. I suppose this sounds a little sad, but not so; her gruff laugh through the inevitable cigarette, accompanied by a large gin & Cin, proclaimed a woman who was more than content with her lot. She was fond of saying, 'I wouldn't give a shit for the Mainland,' and this made eminent sense to us at the time as we were rapidly becoming Kate-like and partisan. Even Len, you see, had to get away from the hurly-burly of life on Guernsey to recuperate on this neighbouring island with his fishing rods and relaxing spells in John's bar, so it was easy to feel panic-struck at the thought of going all the way across the Channel to that hell-hole called the Mainland.

In addition to us (temporary) Alderney folk, there was a constant coming and going of boat people calling in for a respite and a much needed bath, and it was interesting to note how quickly they adjusted to the general atmosphere of 'tomorrow will do' and stayed longer than intended. Perhaps the size of the drinks had something to do with it. Keith and I discovered that, miraculously, drinks got longer and cheaper as time went by and wondered if it was just as matter of time before John paid us to drink them. It was no wonder than Kate had settled down so happily here; she didn't often have to actually buy her favourite tipple.

Alderney has some of the most incredible cliff scenery that we have ever encountered and we spent many happy hours completely engrossed in the wonders wrought by nature. We picked beautiful mushrooms on the lower slopes of the coastline and our talented chef was highly pleased when we took them into the kitchen. He could have had tons of them free gratis and for nothing if anyone had bothered to pick them, but no-one seems to gather anything that grows wild. Blackberries as big as damsons were in abundance everywhere and fed birds and small furry creatures until they must have been bursting, but at no time did we spot a human with a bucket and red fingers. Now this we could *not* understand because the Alderney wild fruit is succulent and sweet and surely someone living on the island must have fancied a blackberry and apple pie or a pot of damson jam. I accept that there was no necessity to make wine as the place was awash with every sort of alcoholic beverage known to mankind at remarkably cheap prices, but I was puzzled by the way they treated their potatoes. We often came across fields of them that should have been picked as they were turning green in the strong sunlight and therefore unmarketable. Why go to the trouble of planting them if it's too much hassle to get the school kids to gather them in? The Alderney potato is superb and quite the best either of us had ever tasted, and that includes the famous Jersey Royals. Still, that's Alderney for you and perhaps it's not possible to relax so thoroughly if one has to keep rushing out to pick spuds, mushrooms and blackberries, and 'tomorrow will do' nicely.

There are grim reminders of the German occupation in the form of ugly concrete coastal fortresses and literally miles of rusting barbed wire waiting to snare the unwary walker. Alderney people don't talk of those days, presumably because many of the civilians were transported to Guernsey for the duration of the dark days, while prisoners of war from many countries, including Russia, were half starved and worked to their deaths constructing the defences. Time must have softened the effect of so much evil and suffering as, strangely, there is no miasma of the recent past to haunt us. Oddly, there is more 'atmosphere' surrounding the tall standing stones on the high part of the island.

Len, when absent from John's bar, spent all his time fishing from various beaches, and it was always a welcome sight to come across that now familiar figure with the amazing outline when we rounded a cove or spotted him standing on the end of a jetty. He was very good company. Uncompromising and most unsentimental, he also possessed a pithy sense of humour that appealed to us. Not one to suffer fools gladly, he could deflate a windbag in ten seconds flat, but on occasion showed a much softer side to his nature when hobnobbing with his own kind. He obviously considered us as his own kind and displayed kindness of a sort, not a balanced recipe for the thin skinned, however, more of a take-the-rough-with-the-smooth, with more of the former than the latter. His fishing skills were legion and he seemed to dine exclusively on the catch of the day, as did other selected guests at the hotel. Alderney had an enormous crab and lobster store close to the jetty where Len caught most of his fish. It was not very visible at high states of the tide and shortly after we returned home we heard on the radio that one of Her Majesty's rather larger ships had crashed into it, demolishing the structure and, worse (except for the crustaceans), releasing every single would-be succulent dish. We thought of Len and wondered what he said on hearing this terrible news - not suitable for my ears, no doubt.

When the sad day of departure came, I was most touched when Len shoved a grubby piece of paper at me and gruffly asked to be informed when we were coming back. This request was followed by a bit of a hug and a bit of a kiss for me and a crippling handshake for Keith. He wheeled quickly and stomped off towards the beach and that was the last we ever saw of our extraordinary friend. We corresponded for quite a while and were delighted when we found a marvellous birthday card depicting a big, fat man with ginger hair, complete with fishing rod, which we sent to him. Back came a typically rude reply which in Len language meant 'Well done, kiddo'. One Christmas we didn't receive his usual card and could only assume that something had happened and, not knowing his circumstances, thought it wise not to enquire further. If he went to heaven I just bet it looks like Alderney, has lots of fish eager to be caught, and John's bar is open all day. I'm going to try to get there, too.

Over the years we have, from time to time, thought about a return visit, but without conviction. Kate would be long gone and probably Len; the hotel surely must have changed hands by now - any old excuse. The simple truth is that neither of us want the memories of that crazy short holiday to be tampered with and a second visit could not possibly resemble the first.

Our plane took off and wheeled around the beach and jetty favoured by Len. Dashing some stupid tears from my eyes I looked in vain for the familiar portly figure, but all was completely deserted. Perhaps he was wishing us God Speed by raising his glass in John's bar. I hope so, but his absence made a final curtain on our little escapade and caused a few more tears to trickle down my cheeks.

It is very strange how, when taken out of normal routine and you find yourself suddenly in a different environment, the routine becomes remote and unreal while the present becomes reality. Equally, once back in the old system, after a few days the reverse happens. It has to be so, I guess, otherwise we would all be in a bigger muddle than ever. Would we really want to live on Alderney, as we once thought? Certainly it is the first place that springs to mind in idle contemplation, but our roots are firmly embedded here with a network of family and friends and who do we know on Alderney now? On reflection, it is safer by far left in the memory compartment marked 'Nostalgia'.

CHAPTER 8

A favourite haunt of ours is situated between Compton and Walderton on the borders of West Sussex and Hampshire, full of mystery and set in wildly forgotten park-like gardens, alongside which runs one of the quietest footpaths in the South Downs. We marvelled at this delightful playground and wondered why no-one was ever encountered on our lengthy visits. Admittedly, if one is blessed with good eyesight, a sign warning of danger and also starting 'Private', could just be discerned through the thick foliage, but that only added spice, naturally. We christened it 'the house that wasn't there'.

For years the only evidence that a house had actually stood in these grounds was a large area of mellow old-fashioned bricks neatly stacked and covered with blackberry bushes that produced the most succulent of fruit. The supposed site of the house was surrounded with flint and brick walls, many exotic semi-wild shrubs and trees and a veritable jungle of flora peculiar to chalk downland. We once discovered a hidden wall grotto made of white marble with amazingly bright and clear water in its shell-shaped base. The overall design of the house suggests that it was fronted by a small park with imposing brick steps rising to a higher open space with specimen trees that included cedar of Lebanon and mulberry. At the top end of the garden were more steps leading to an enclosed formal, though incredibly overgrown, garden complete with a dilapidated summer house arrangement tacked on to the end of an old and very handsome large barn. A large coppice of beeches, elder, bamboo and holly completed our imaginary estate.

The danger sign was entirely justified as deep pits lurked under rampant vegetation and hidden heaps of rubble were a decided hazard to the unwary wanderer. The most interesting and picturesque part was a courtyard converted from stables to - now, if I say 'garages' it will convey entirely the wrong impression - so a stables for early motors is about the nearest description applicable. The three-sided arrangement of buildings had obviously housed staff as well as conveyances, and the main centre block was beautiful, if crumbling, and surmounted by a clock tower with an elaborate weather vane. In fact, the whole complex was in a perilous condition and each time we visited more tiles and flints had crashed to the ground. However, this mattered not a jot to us as the biggest and sweetest blackberries flourished within its confines, to say nothing of the glorious elderberries. The best red wine I ever made came from here.

The footpath that skirts the grounds sweeps grandly up to a fairly steep hill, rather like an avenue, as it is flanked with magnificent beeches and provides the sort of lovely views that only the South Downs can furnish. Eventually, having puffed a bit climbing the sharp rise, an ancient woodland was ours to enjoy, again in solitude. Considering that we live in a most highly populated part of the south coast, I have never understood why this little paradise was so deserted. We have our fair share of Ramblers Clubs and week-end walkers, but perhaps we have imagined the whole place and it doesn't really exist.

There was once a notable exception to the solitude rule. A warm and sunny afternoon saw us traipsing up the hill armed with flasks of tea and painting gear. Having picked the exact spot to produce masterpieces, settled ourselves and waved exploratory thumbs in the air to get scale, we decided that the ground was much too hard to sit on unaided by cushions for long. The snag here was that the cushions were in the car and the car was about a mile down the hill. Fine going, rotten coming back. 'I'll go,' said one, 'No, I'll go,' said the other, and in short order Keith had won and loped off on the cushion trail.

Sitting there in the shade, watching the young green corn ripple idly in the breeze, I daydreamed ideas rather above my station. Instead of getting on with my own crabby efforts at painting, I thumbed through Keith's sketch book and pretended that his undoubted talents were mine. I went further into the realms of fantasy and considered that I must look a little like that girl in the chocolate advert on the telly before it rains and makes her poppies all blobby. A man's voice in my ear nearly made me jump out of my skin.

'Excuse me,' it said, 'I hope you don't mind. I just wanted to see your picture.' And then, as I was still speechless with surprise, 'My goodness! What a beautiful watercolour. You are very talented, congratulations.'

I thanked this nice gentleman prettily and after a few more compliments he strode down the hill and I heard him say 'Good afternoon' to Keith, plodding upwards. Sneakily, I've always hoped that he didn't put two and two together as that was the very first time in my life that I had received glowing and sincere admiration for creative work. Just goes to show how good Keith is, I suppose, but Lavinia would have been proud of me, I bet!

The first sign of impending doom was the sudden and complete disappearance of the stacked bricks and a half-hearted attack on the brambles and undergrowth. This was very worrying but as time went on and nothing else happened, we concluded that the owner - and there must have been one somewhere – had simply sold the bricks and that would be that. We could rest easy. Unfortunately for us, this was just the beginning of a major change. A wide track was forged through the trees and shrubs to the stables and the delicate ironwork gates were barricaded against the likes of us and bore a more threatening notice to clear off than the old flaking, but more polite, 'Private' sign that we had always chosen to ignore. It is said that trees transmit messages to each other when under threat, and I am quite prepared to believe it, because the atmosphere was charged in some undefinable way, quite unlike the old cosy unruliness that used to welcome us. We could also see that demolition work had started and that something awful was about to take place. What did happen is that the stables are now rebuilt into Yuppie-type dwellings surrounded by smooth green sward, and practically everything we held so dear has vanished.

At around this time of despair the south of England was struck by the 1987 hurricane and this particular part of West Sussex took the full brunt of that maniacal storm. Most of the woodlands were destroyed, resembling a giant tree graveyard with their huge chalk embedded roots acting as headstones, and later the massive machinery used to clear the stricken beeches made short work of the grassy avenue footpath. In a trice our fascinating retreat had gone for ever.

We seldom go to 'the house that wasn't there' these days; it feels uncomfortable and is tidied up in the ugly fashion of today. And, of course, it is scarcely likely that our presence would be tolerated by the new occupiers. Not that I can blame them; after all, their new homes probably cost a King's ransom. I have a few relics that bring back pleasant memories: two small triangular-shaped pieces of white marble that I use with flowers, a piece of plaster adorned with a Victorian design from the demolished stables, and a twisty piece of ivy trunk shaped like an abstract headless otter with folded arms. Silly these things may be, but they remind me of so many happy afternoons just mucking about and, in particular, sitting on the steps in the overgrown formal garden in the sunshine surrounded by primroses on my birthday, one spring. Ah, well!

There is a surprising Stop Press to this sad tale. We were driving past this large and spreading property about a year ago and noticed signs of activity in the area where we had always assumed the house may have stood. 'What's going on?' we wondered, and the very next time we drove past, to our great amazement there stood a massive house, very imposing, with enormous Palladian columns, looking as if it had been there for centuries. It was rather like being in a time warp and I tried blinking to see if it would disappear. It didn't. Just this autumn Keith and I, armed with our blackberry buckets, wandered along our old footpath just in case a few bushes had been spared or had re-appeared, and naturally we stopped to have a look at the new house. So far as we could see it was completely empty and unoccupied. I imagined that it looked uneasy, as if it didn't know what it was doing there and, indeed, for how long might it stay.

Over the years I have resisted researching into the history of this extraordinary place as I really wished it to remain mysterious, but now I am so curious that I think I shall have to see what I can find out. Anyway, it's not 'ours' any more, so it won't matter quite so much.

Vená would call this next strange episode 'an adventure', and I suppose in a way it was. It all started when Keith and I were enjoying a stroll along the bank of the River Itchen at Brambridge one warm and sunny Sunday afternoon, blissfully unaware that a very peculiar and rather sinister turn of events was about to take place and keep us guessing for evermore.

Rivers are always fascinating and a joy to the soul - except those poor little trickles tamed by Water Boards - and we were walking along the left bank towards Winchester. This side of the river was fringed with woods and river bank greenery that precluded long views of the straighter sections and was surprisingly deserted for a warm Sunday afternoon. Perhaps most people were still recovering from a large lunch. In ordinary circumstances, striding along is out of the question, as there is so much to stop and investigate, and our attention was entirely focused upon river life, punctuated with brilliant conversation like, 'Oh, look at that dear little crocodile paddling along, isn't he sweet?' to be answered by, 'Don't be so bloody daft, and get moving for heaven's sake.' There are no prizes for guessing who said which.

We continued strolling gently alongside the river with more inconsequential chatter to annoy Keith until a thudding noise made us stop and look at each other.

'Whatever is that . . .' I began, and had my question answered by the appearance of two men running furiously towards us. Startled, we melted into the greenery as it was obvious they weren't slowing up at the sight of two people walking towards them and there certainly wasn't any room for four abreast on the narrow river path. It was also obvious that these men were very frightened indeed, judging by their deathly white faces. They were also rather rough looking characters and definitely not the sort one would tap lightly on the arm and ask, 'I say, old chap, what's the matter?' Discretion and invisibility were much better ploys, and so we stayed half in and half out of a bush. Apart from being a bit scared, we were astonished at this turn of events as we had never encountered anything more untoward than a wet dog shaking himself over us along this delectable stretch, and here we were, crouching in a bush and affected by the tangible smell of fear.

The two disappeared around the curve of the river and we picked bits of twig out of our hair and tried to collect our wits. Almost immediately and to our great consternation we heard yet more thuddings ahead and I heard myself whimper in dread. It was all so uncanny and I had difficulty in believing that all this was really happening. It was happening all right, for a whole group of men, plus a large Alsatian straining on a leash, thundered towards us. In addition to this frightening sight, the man with the dog was brandishing a long, carved cosh, and they were all wearing some strange sort of not-quite-military uniform.

Once again we dived into that poor bush (that now had a large hole in it) and pretended to be part of the foliage as they passed. Perhaps we hadn't had sufficient practice in camouflage because they all ground to a halt some yards ahead and looked back at us and, horrors, the man with the dog pointed that cosh at us. It was rather like an evil eye and twice as effective. That did it. Four scared eyes met and Keith jerked his head in the direction of the trees and, for once, fear lent wings to my heels instead of paralysing them. We fled through the trees and undergrowth and for two weaklings attained an incredible turn of speed; I doubt if even the Alsatian could have caught up with us.

When relating this little yarn we say (casually) that we went back to the village 'the pretty way'. It was rather a long way, probably in the region of five miles, through woods and fields, and even freely roaming cows didn't deter us – and that speaks volumes! The village was about as peaceful and normal as it is possible to be, with little groups of Sunday strollers chatting away happily; absolutely no sign of drama anywhere. The very least we had expected was police cars and ambulances, but there was nothing at all to suggest that an incident had just taken place.

It was only later that we realised that at no time did we hear voices or anything at all except the footsteps and the rasping breath of the pursued and the pursuers, and that is very strange when you think about it. It still sends a shiver down my spine to recall the terror of the two hunted men and the very sinister presence of their hunters. I think in retrospect that Keith and I were really lucky not to have ended our day out by floating out to sea face down, via the river.

Little flight of fancy here – we might have starred in a Murder Mystery as the foully done-to-death witnesses to a heinous crime and become famous, but that's no good if we are dead, is it? Naturally we listened to the radio and television news and read the local paper in case two bodies had been found, but nothing was ever reported. And that is terribly frustrating.

From time to time we visit the river at Brambridge which is still peaceful and beautiful, except, sadly, that most of the bushes and trees have been ripped out from the banks. Now I maintain that those bushes and woods might just have saved our lives, and what thanks do they get?

CHAPTER 9

Just as I was blessed with my dear, funny and unpredictable grandfather, the Guv'nor, so Keith was equally so with his. He was a small mischievous man with a remarkable history. I loved him dearly and still miss his company and fund of amusing anecdotes. He was the son of a locally well-known boatbuilder and, having joined first the Army and later the Navy, eventually settled down to become an extremely talented yacht designer and boatbuilder. He married Keith's gentle and blue-eyed little grandmother and they and their family went to live in a large Georgian house that was complete with a boatshed-cum-workshop at the rear. This sounds very grand but the property was incredibly cheap by today's standards and as they were raising five boys and one girl, they required a sizeable house. In fact, after the deaths of the grandparents just a few years ago, the house was sold for £18,000, and that buyer now has a property worth well in excess of £250,000, which shows how crazily money has devalued in a short time.

The house still stands today only by the skin of its teeth: firstly by Hitler chucking bombs at it and missing and secondly by the post war era when so many beautiful old houses were demolished to make way for brave and brash new schemes. It is scarcely recognisable, though. In Grandad's day it was a straightforward and 'no nonsense' working home, not entirely pleasing to a critical architectural eye, but nonetheless possessing a certain charm of its own. Today it is painted a strawberry ice cream pink, has modern bay windows and is crowned with a dark grey Mansard roof. Let's just say that it fits in with the new houses further down the road!

There is no doubt that times were hard when they were bringing up the children and the waterfront folk eked out a precarious living with a bartering system - mostly with fish - and somehow or other survived the harsh conditions. Old photographs and sketches show that the area was packed higgledy-piggledy with picturesque dwellings, mostly very squalid, and dozens of highly dubious ale houses. It must have been a fascinating little town but highly dangerous as there was an ever present risk of catching cholera from the sewage-infected well water. 'King Cholera' claimed literally thousands of lives here and in the latest documented epidemic of the 1830s, the authorities ran out of burial space, which makes gardening very interesting nowadays as you never know what you may find stuck on the end of the garden fork. All this is going back long before Gran and Grandad lived and worked here but, even so, there were many of the very old houses still standing and lived in right up until the Second World War, when so many of the timber framed houses were destroyed by fire bombs and land mines.

The grandparents' house was a powerful magnet to Keith and me (as well as many others) and we spent countless happy hours either in the house or bobbing across the Solent to the Isle of Wight in one of the family boats for picnics on summer Sundays. How lucky I have been to have had Liddon and Keith's grandparental home to provide a kaleidoscope of memories so varied and comforting.

There was nothing Grandad enjoyed so much as a good old chinwag, which usually took the form of holding our entire attention with some outrageous prank or other that he or others had perpetrated, his eyes twinkling, having to stop now and again for a hearty laugh. One of my favourite stories took place in 1919 when the country was struggling to survive after the appalling war and money was in hideously short supply. Not so man's spirit, cheek, and sense of humour, and Grandad's little story illustrates this well. It is the tale of the wherry *Flying Cloud*, owned by a local business man, and Grandad's challenger, *Sportsman*, in a momentous race.

For many years *Flying Cloud*, built at the end of the last century, was the undisputed champion in local waters and had triumphed in some sixty-three races, but shortly before the First World War it had suffered defeat at the hands of Grandad's father with *Bird of Freedom* in a local regatta. *Bird of Freedom* was smaller than *Flying Cloud* and it was agreed that the race should have two oarsmen instead of the customary four, and as *Flying Cloud* was considerably heavier than her opponent, her unbeaten record was over.

After hostilities had ceased, in 1919 life slowly picked up momentum and Grandad had the bright idea of challenging *Flying Cloud* in a four-handed wherry race. The winning stake was £25, a very large amount to gamble with. Grandad, well known for his sometimes slightly warped sense of fun, built a new wherry, to be named *Sportsman*, for the race. It had been agreed that the owner and crew of *Flying Cloud* would be at liberty to visit Grandad's workshop loft while *Sportsman* was being built, to ensure fair play. *Sportsman* was painted a darkish green inside and a heavy-looking grey on the outside, making her appear to be very solid and sluggish. Grandad had a little (and fiendish) trick up his sleeve, however, and this was to drill two holes in the loft floor, attach thin wires to the bow and stern, thread the wires through the holes so that they protruded into the workshop, and then hang two half-hundredweight iron pigs from them. This cunning device was masked from inquisitive eyes by arranging heaps of wood shavings at the incriminating spots in the loft and making sure that the pigs were hidden from view in the workshop amongst the masts and sails. So successful was this devious scheme that *Flying Cloud*'s crew were completely taken in when they tried to lift her, with the result that her owner immediately raised the stake to £100, otherwise the race would be cancelled.

After much worry and two sleepless nights, Grandad agreed to the new terms. £100 was an enormous amount of money and clearly, were he to lose the race, he would be in great trouble. He finally decided to go ahead because, having implanted the 'evidence' of a very heavy boat to be rowed, he would have the advantage of knowing that his wherry had been dismissed as a serious contender, and carelessness on the part of his opponent was a viable consideration. It was sound in theory but it didn't stop him worrying. When *Sportsman* was ready, the crew practised at night by lantern light, using *Bird of Freedom* as a pacer and exchanging crews for the return journey. To the delight of Grandad and the crew, it was immediately obvious that *Sportsman* was an exceptionally fast boat and, as Grandad said, 'She went like a shot from a gun, my gal!', chortling happily at the memory. The only people who knew her true capabilities were Grandad's brothers and a few local involved boatmen who were keeping quiet for betting purposes.

The great event took place on Christmas Eve, a perfectly foul day of blustery winds and cold rain. The entire crew of *Sportsman* had been picked for their light body weight, the boat herself floated high, and the adrenalin was flowing nicely. There had been a great deal of interest in this race and the foreshore seems to have resembled a watery racecourse, with bookies doing brisk business with the odds heavily in *Flying Cloud*'s favour. It later came to light that about £12,000 had been laid out in bets and most of it was on *Flying Cloud*. Though confident that *Sportsman* would put up a strong fight, Grandad reluctantly decided not to risk any more money on a side bet, just in case things went wrong. News of this race had spread far beyond local limits and a vast crowd had assembled to see the fun; by the commencement of the race, excitement was at fever pitch.

Sportsman and *Flying Cloud* slowly and majestically got to the starting position and both were forced to battle against the strong wind and tide to maintain weigh, awaiting the signal that the race had started. At long last the pistol shot rang out and immediately *Sportsman* was in the lead, much to the amazement of the spectators. The agreed course was long and punishing for both contestants, but much more so for *Flying Cloud*'s crew who had to propel the extra weight through choppy seas and a vagrant wind. The gap between the boats widened as they battled along and at the finishing buoy *Sportsman* was the winner by at least 500 yards. All through the race a muttering roar had percolated through the wind and across the waves from the thronged shore and it didn't sound good to Grandad. He was aware that trouble in a big way was looming so, wisely, the moment he and his crew scrambled ashore, they beat a hasty retreat for home and safety. He was right! After a stunned realisation by the vast majority of spectators that they had lost a great deal of money, a great roar of rage thundered through the Old Town. Fighting broke out between *Flying Cloud* and *Sportsman* supporters and indeed the situation got very close to becoming a riot. The few policemen in the area were unable to control the angry mob so, like Grandad, did a disappearing act while the going was good. There were, apparently, many sore heads and empty pockets to be nursed for days after this eventful Christmas Eve, and Grandad admitted (with an infectious chuckle), 'I wasn't much of a Sportsman, was I, my gal?'

I can't argue with that, Grandad, but I wouldn't have had you any other way.

These particular wherries seem to have vanished entirely. In Grandad's more robust times they were used as supply, trading and ferry boats – not to mention a little smuggling when appropriate. The technical description describes them as having two stepped masts for sailing, and being oar-powered and sprit-rigged. Some years after the infamous race, when boats became power driven, the wherries were no longer in demand and Grandad gave *Sportsman* to the local Sea Scouts for seamanship training, but didn't know what happened to her after that. But during her day, *Sportsman* was renowned as a fast boat and was much in demand by local watermen and visiting ships, made famous (or infamous) by her extraordinary debut. There have been many rotting boat ribs sitting starkly in the harbour mud over the years, looking like the remains of stranded and doomed whales, and it is possible that *Sportsman* is amongst them somewhere; there is no way of knowing. As for *Flying Cloud*, she never raced again and, like *Sportsman*, has disappeared into the mists of time.

I remember so clearly listening to Grandad's vivid accounts of past demeanours and misdemeanours, watching him re-live the prime of his life and seeing the twinkle in his almost blind eyes while we laughed together. I can also hear his signature tune in my mind's ear, 'Heave away the *trawl*, lads, heave away the *trawl*, etc.', sung in an untuneful and slightly cracked light baritone. I have never known if Grandad made this peculiar song up or if it's a recognised sea song – I hope not, because it's pretty awful and not for those of a nervous disposition.

Grandad's boats, designed by himself and built by him and his sons, are still renowned and working today and it shows a measure of his reputation that shortly after he retired, he received a letter from a large organisation in Japan requesting his services. The punch line is that the envelope simply stated his name, Yachtbuilder, UK, and the Post Office delivered it within days of the Japanese post mark. Now that really is fame.

CHAPTER 10

A considerable number of years ago when Erica, Peter, Keith and I were a lot younger, we spent a great deal of our free time together mucking about in boats. Along with their jolly little dachshund named Heidi, we were all members of the same homely and slightly grotty sailing club that embraced a variety of craft that would have made an old sea dog yelp with surprise. Erica and Peter were the proud owners of a Caprice sailing cruiser that rejoiced in the name of *Mudskipper*, while Keith and I made do with a small all-purpose day boat, whose name I can't remember. Most of the Club membership could have been described as 'salt of the earth' types, like wot we are, though a few appeared to be quite well off while retaining the earthy-salt flavour. The Club House was a fright. A large wooden building badly in need of a lick of paint, it squatted cosily in a dip in the long shingle ridge and resembled, so I fancied, an elderly lady caught in the act of having a pee.

The interior was equally frightful but was beloved by members who could splosh straight in encased in soggy waders without having the bother of hooking off seaweed, etc., and head directly to the bar. This accomplished, knots of wader-wearers were at liberty to discuss in animated fashion the day's catch and the simply enormous one that got away. Every word was Gospel truth, judging by the sincere expressions that accompanied the wide stretched arms and, being terribly naive, I was suitably impressed by their skill. It was just sad that there never seemed to be a decent sized fish available for envy and admiration, but as an audience, I was very popular, which made up for the lack of evidence.

I liked to fish, and often Keith would drop me off with my rod and bait tin on to a pontoon moored in the harbour, while he indulged in his favourite pastime of dinghy sailing. This suited us both well, providing the weather didn't deteriorate, leaving me stranded and wet in a hostile environment waiting for him to return and rescue me, and fortunately, nine times out of ten I provided our supper of succulent freshly caught fish. If the wind force was less than two, I was happy enough to accompany Keith and was put in charge of the jib, but that meant that we had to forego our fish supper and needed serious thought before making a decision. On these occasions we might well be missing from civilization for many hours, drifting or spanking along the many creeks that afforded such abundance of beauty and wildlife, and a very full up waterproof container of life supporting essentials accompanied our every trip. By the time I had packed coffee, many sandwiches, cake, bananas, wine and glasses, chocolate, peppermints, extra thick woollies, buoyancy jackets and waterproofs, and Keith added his contribution of oars, sails, outboard motor and petrol, there wasn't a lot of room left for the captain and his crew (me). However, after a wobbly start while getting the sails up, we were free to skim the waters in tune with the musical zizzing and slapping of waves that assaulted or aided our progress. I was quite clever at getting port and starboard mixed up in response to a shouted order from the skipper and I fear there were slight altercations if my jib sail didn't snap smoothly into place with split second timing. Why we can't just say left and right is a mystery to me and it would most likely side step glowers and bitter words on board. Not all the time, maybe, as I have also been known to get the humble left and right reversed, but certainly not as often as port and starboard.

Many summer Sundays we spent aboard Erica and Peter's posh *Mudskipper*, climbing the Upmarket Ladder by at least five rungs, and were able to look down upon lowly day boats from at least six feet. I tried hard not to let this sudden jump into elevated company go to my head but have to confess that my friendly wave to less fortunate week-end sailors became a tinge regal. *Mudskipper* was so big that she had a deck and a downstairs out of the rain and spray and two bunks. Talk about luxury. The only snag was that Peter liked to sail her heeling over at an alarming angle and that upsets me and makes me gulp. Erica pretended to like it but I could tell she didn't really by the change of colour in her complexion. Heidi didn't mind unless an extra boisterous wave slid her off a bunk on to the cabin floor, and then she didn't look too pleased and grizzled to Erica. The facial expression rota went like this – on wild and windy days two male faces wore delighted and evil grins while the female ones of a slightly pea green hue could, at best, manage only the slightest hint of what might be loosely termed as a smile; on flat calm and sunny days merely substitute the gender and retain the description.

Occasionally there was a day that suited us all and just such a one involved another friend named Edwin who owned and hurtled around in a catamaran. I have stood upon the shore and held my breath expecting to see the entire craft and crew take off like a sea plane and disappear into the wide blue yonder when Edwin was in charge of that stick-thing at the back of the boat; he would also be bellowing incomprehensible orders and messages to his petrified crew, which didn't appear to help much. Until this nice day that suited us all, Edwin had never invited Erica and me to get anywhere near his Cat, and I don't blame him in the least – just relieved – but perhaps he had run out of people willing to risk all and had to lower his sights until they rested upon Erica and me.

'I say, you two,' he greeted us cheerily, 'How would you like to float about on the Cat today?'

Needless to say, neither of us had the slightest intention of 'floating about' on his wretched Cat, and anyway, we were strictly booked up by Cap'n Peter and First Mate Keith as galley slaves aboard *Mudskipper*. The plan was to venture out of the harbour and spend the day gently bobbing about in the Solent sipping wine and munching sandwiches and definitely not risking life and limb with madcap Edwin.

'Oh dear, what a shame!' lied Erica, 'I'm afraid we can't - we're needed as crew on *Mudskipper*. Thank you very much, though, and we would have loved to come.' (She will never get to heaven.)

'Tell you what,' exclaimed that traitorous but eager to please Peter, 'If you girls want to go with Edwin, we'll all go out together in the two boats and scoop you off the Cat outside the harbour. How's that, Edwin?'

'Oh great! Come on, girls, get your knickers on and let's go.'

Poor Erica and I could have killed both Edwin and Peter on the spot and our only help lay in the slightly doubtful expression on Keith's face. We gazed at him pleadingly but could see that he didn't know how to get us off the hook without hurt feelings and uproar, and we resigned ourselves and our fate to the Gods. Ever since I'd known Edwin I'd noticed that not one of his crews wore that silly happy look of men who are about to get soaked and bruised while leaping about in a boat, but I daresay he'd never had such a miserable looking crew as this one. It was the 'scoop you off' bit that worried us. I mean, could the silly fool stop the Cat at the right moment exactly alongside tall *Mudskipper*? I doubted it very much. Reluctantly we scrambled aboard and set off, fearing the worst, and were pleasantly surprised to find that we were floating gently owing to lack of wind. Oh well, perhaps it wouldn't be as we had feared. We passed *Mudskipper* about half way down the channel and waved to the men who had promised to protect us from all evil, shouting insults as we overtook. They grinned encouragingly back at us; relieved perhaps that we were taking our unexpected adventure so well. Edwin was stretched out flat on his back with the mainsail sheet in one hand, an idle toe steering the Cat by means of poking the stick thing now and again, and wishing that he'd thought of bringing some grapes for us to peel and drop into his mouth. It was idyllic and we were thoroughly enjoying ourselves, though a little lightheaded with relief.

As we approached the harbour mouth a slight cross wind filled the sails and our speed increased through rippled waters. Edwin sat up and became businesslike. Our smiles wavered and finally disappeared as orders were rapped out, followed by exasperated bellows when commands were executed incorrectly. *Mudskipper* was some way astern, so Edwin somehow managed to make the Cat do a circle and when she was within hailing distance he yelled, 'GET THESE BLOODY WOMEN OFF MY BOAT!'.

There was no time to feel resentment at this appalling ingratitude of the skipper, but it was certainly noted for airing in less fraught circumstances. The wind died away and we and *Mudskipper* were drawing close together ready for scoop-off time. Though neither of us were looking forward to the actual event, we couldn't wait to be shot of that blasted Edwin and his temperamental boat. We slid alongside and were ordered to crouch on the hull nearest *Mudskipper* ready for haul-up by Keith. Erica was first in line; she did a sort of half leap as the two hulls were more or less parallel and, with a few grunts, was successfully landed in *Mudskipper*'s cockpit like a two-legged mermaid. With Erica's weight suddenly missing, the Cat's port hull lurched alarmingly, almost unseating me into the sea, made even better by Edwin describing a second circle and bellowing across the void, 'GET THIS BLOODY WOMAN OFF MY BOAT!'.

As we approached *Mudskipper* for the second time I observed Erica's head appearing over the gunwale and two round eyes stared down at me as if in shock while she rubbed her shoulder. That didn't look too promising to me but if the same treatment would deliver me from a mad boat and a crazy owner, I was more than prepared to take a chance; in fact I was welcoming it. Anger at everyone except Erica took precedence over fright and I am proud to report that for once I was level-headed and almost intelligent. Helped by a friendly smooth wave that lifted the Cat by a couple of feet, I launched myself in the direction of *Mudskipper* and required very little assistance to clamber aboard. Contenting myself with shaking a fist threateningly at Edwin, I turned my back and henceforth ignored him while listening to his shouts getting fainter and fainter as he drifted away from *Mudskipper*. I didn't care if he was screaming for help or merely wanting to know if his former crew had landed safely. So far as I was concerned he could have gone on forever like the Flying Dutchman and I wouldn't have batted an eyelid. Perhaps it was just as well that my fist was on *Mudskipper* while Edwin was bobbing about elsewhere in the Solent.

Heidi was pleased to see us; she had been watching the pantomime from the stern, whining and looking anxious. She knew full well that if Erica and I weren't rescued there would be very little chance of any lunch and was wishing us God Speed accordingly. The same went for the men (we suspected), because barely had we drawn great breaths of relief than our new skipper said:

'I reckon it's about time we had some lunch, don't you?'

We all agreed, really, but only Heidi was brave enough to be vocal about it!

Apart from high jinks on the briny, we had quite a jolly social life in the tatty old Club House. We had marvellous and colourful friends and were always sure of a warm welcome. Admittedly, sometimes it was a good job that the Club was stuck miles from civilization as we weren't exactly quiet when gathered together, and I look back with longing and much affection for the sheer unaffected and spontaneous fun and comradeship that we all shared. Even Edwin got forgiven for his frequent near disasters, and that says everything! Nothing stays the same for ever; some members left and others joined and gradually the new and more trendy ones outnumbered the originals. There was talk about a splendid new Club House, an electric winch for hauling boats up the slipway, bigger car park and compound, and much bigger fees. Eventually all these things came to pass and the only things that got smaller were the informality and fun. The Club survives still, long after the dear, shabby old Club House was demolished, still boasts many colourful characters - though rather richer-looking than in days of yore - and still embraces a variety of craft that would make an old sea dog yelp with surprise.

The Boat Show at Earl's Court was a yearly feature that we all looked forward to - particularly Erica and I as there wasn't much chance of drowning there - which made the men's eyes light up with interest when something incredibly boring-looking but obviously invaluable they couldn't possibly live without, was discovered in a stand. The normal practice was for Erica and me to stick close to Peter and Keith and not get lost, as demanded by them. Usually there was plenty for us to be interested in, so that was no problem so long as we were treated to occasional snacks and cups of tea, but one notable year things went terribly wrong. Having been admitted and ordered not to get lost, we obediently followed our protectors for about three minutes and then spotted a stand that was full of the most gorgeous sweaters.

'Hang on a minute, lads,' one of us chirruped and we both disappeared into the racks of woollies. We didn't notice that Peter and Keith hadn't followed us (for a change) for some little while and then, of course, it was too late. Once parted at Earl's Court, that's it unless a meeting place has been pre-arranged. A thorough search proved fruitless so we thought it wise to toddle around and look at the things that were of more interest to us, punctuated with cups of tea. The time went rather quickly and we were surprised to see that it was about time we should be leaving Earl's Court to get to Waterloo Station.

'Oh Lor',' said Erica, 'I bet they're pretty cross by now - what shall we do?'

And then she had a very bright idea.

'Let's go to the Lost Children Station. That's the sort of place they might think of. I don't think there's a Lost Grown-ups place.'

We managed to find the lost kids' haven and had just settled ourselves when we espied two rather fraught faces bearing down upon us. Erica gave me a quick dig in the ribs.

'Where have you been?' she said accusingly. 'We've been waiting for you for ages, haven't we, Peg?'

'Yes!' I chipped in, 'You could have looked for us instead of leaving us on our own all day, and we thought this would be the very first place you would go to.' I felt quite indignant while spouting these lies and both Erica and I were gratified to see a small spark of guilt flit across their faces, confirming that they had lost track of time just as much as we had, only we had got in first and that was very satisfactory. Of course, a dead giveaway was the enormous load of brochures and pamphlets, not to mention a couple of boaty gadgets, collected during the time they should have been trying to locate us, which made us feel quite virtuous and hard done by.

'Gosh!' said Erica much later when on our own. 'That was a close shave, wasn't it? But you see how attack is the best form of defence - I always do that. And haven't they been nice to us ever since?'

She's absolutely right and I have used her tactics a thousand times over the years with confidence and resounding success.

Now that we are all firmly ensconced in our middle years of life, our friendship and love has never diminished though one important member named Heidi is missing. She is remembered with so much affection. I'm told that dachshunds can be temperamental but this one was sweet tempered all her life and loved nothing better than that we four should be together engaged in some mad caper or other. Perhaps I should have said 'five' as she joined in any fun wholeheartedly. Resembling a well stuffed Hoover with four little short legs instead of wheels, Erica didn't really need any other sort of cleaner as the minutest edible crumb was swiftly discovered by Heidi's liquorice black nose, and the long pink tongue took the place of a suction nozzle. Apart from craftily and mysteriously removing food from our plates at a distance of three feet, her only sin was her love of a beautifully sploshy cow pat to roll in and then she was unbearable. But nobody's perfect.

CHAPTER 11

If there is one thing that intrigues me it is mysterious and odd occurrences that never end with an explanation. Over the years I have collected accounts of strange goings-on, in a haphazard manner, some of which seem to be of a paranormal persuasion while others are just plain funny. The one thing they all have in common is that they are bizarre, and unfortunately, unexplained and maddening.

I am mindful of a serial account of the poor guy whose very modest current bank account was suddenly swamped with massive amounts of money from an unknown source. Alarmed by this inexplicable wealth he pleaded with his bank manager to find out what was happening and who was sending it and why. At first glance it sounds a lovely way to get rich; just sitting back in a favourite armchair while other kind souls make sure that one won't be short of a few millions to stuff in the old sock. It doesn't work like that in practice. Firstly, the manager was unable to gather the slightest clue as to where it was coming from, except that it appeared to have been channelled through various international banks and organisations; secondly, the detective work cost a lost of money and Mr Poor Guy couldn't afford it; and thirdly and much worse, the Inland Revenue had to be informed. I listened avidly to the radio for the next thrilling instalment for about three weeks, and having got to the stage where the Inland Revenue were considering the possibilities of sending Mr Poor Guy a bill for a couple of million (who was having a nervous breakdown, understandably), phut! no more episodes were broadcast and not one more word was ever heard. It was infuriating but I have my own explanation, for what it is worth. Someone, somewhere, was busily engaged in tapping out huge amounts on a computer when the phone rang. 'Damn!' he or she said and, having dealt with this infernal interruption, swung his or her swivel chair back round to the computer and tapped '5' instead of '6'. A simple error that went unnoticed, it diverted a large chunk of those vague 'invisible earnings' from the Treasury coffers and plopped it into Mr Poor Guy's unwilling pocket. An official from the Treasury was shaving and listening to the radio one morning and was much amused by this financial cock-up, chuckling at the thought of how someone would receive the rocket of a lifetime when the truth was revealed. At the back of his mind a little niggle wormed its way to the front. Now, what was it old thingy had said the other day about a sharp drop in invisible earnings? No, surely it can't have any connection . . . can it? Perhaps I'd better go and . . . Unbreakfasted and with a pale half-shaven face, he drove to his office earlier than was usual and had much trouble getting in because the security arrangements didn't expect him until 10.30 a.m. His startled secretary hastily contacted the key personnel he wished to see and then made herself scarce but available, as a good secretary should under iffy circumstances. Hours and pots of coffee later the meeting broke up and there was a great flurry of agitated activity while the secretary put her boss through to the BBC. Meanwhile, back at the bank, another computer was receiving instructions to dematerialise Mr Poor Guy's amazing bank balance and substitute one that was, hmm, well, marginally larger than it was prior to '6' becoming '5'. Mr Poor Guy was doing very well in hospital, hoping to be discharged in a day or so when the course of injections had dealt with his silly fixation that he was drowning in £50 notes, by blanking out the immediate past. It seemed kinder, the psychiatrist said. As for the bank manager, he took early retirement and went to live in the Bahamas at the age of thirty-three with a sizeable sum replenishing his account every month, but couldn't remember why. There! That's that little mystery solved and sounds reasonable to me.

In 1977 I was rather tempted to answer an advertisement that appeared in a newspaper and went thus:

'Capable girl to live in and help with children and general housework by family group interested in philosophy and self-sufficiency. Write Box No. . . .'

I could picture the scene and just wanted to see if my suspicions would be confirmed. I saw a biggish, rambling and inconvenient sort of house that the previous owner could no longer afford to maintain and had sold to a dreamy looking pair with tied-back long hair and lots of beads. Shortly after this transaction took place the neighbours were disconcerted to see a large van draw up and disgorge *three* dreamy looking couples with tied-back hair and lots of beads, plus about a dozen gruesome and runny-nosed children. Open-mouthed, they noticed piles of large cushions, long low wooden furniture that still bore the fruit importer's name and emblem, and a mysterious something that looked rather like a totem pole. Mrs Worthington-Smythe, who lived next door, didn't like the look of this invasion at all and was fearful for the continuation of the high value of her property. Nevertheless, nothing as exciting as this had ever happened in the sleepy village so she remained glued to the netted window to watch developments. The totem pole had taken three people to carry it round the side of the house and curiosity drove her to peer from a back window. There, in the middle of the large lawn, one gowned man was digging a large hole while the other two were gathering large rocks from the rockery. She waited until the hole was deep enough and the pile of rocks high enough with bated breath, and was rewarded by witnessing the three men carefully plant the totem pole in the hole and place the rocks around its base. Next there was a low moaning sort of chant in what sounded like a foreign language and all three prostrated themselves at the foot. Mrs Worthington-Smythe gasped in amazement and rushed to the telephone to tell her friends and neighbours of these strange events.

She had occasion to rush to the phone again later in the dusky eventide when, hearing an excited babble of voices, she observed the whole group (bedecked with flowers) gathered together and holding hands in a circle around the pole. In ecstatic voices they chanted:

> 'Oh pale and crescent moon above
> Like a wondrous turtle dove
> Shine and kindly beam on me
> While I sit and have a think.'

followed by:

> 'Oh, totem, totem, in the hole
> You have such a great big pole.'

'Oh, Tarquinne,' exclaimed Imogena, her eyes misting over with emotion, 'The Leader is so mystical and clever with verse. And wasn't it a philosophical price?'

And the capable girl to help with children and general housework said:

'Sod this for a turtle dove!' and drove off at high speed in the old van. Who can blame her.

An intriguing report came to light way back in 1967 of a blonde woman vampire, dressed in a mini-skirt and black stockings and with long pointed teeth. Nothing too strange about that, you may think, but the hospital at Manaus, Brazil, received an influx of patients with puncture marks on their necks and suffering from blood loss. Every case claimed to have been attacked on a certain popular beach. The police also received a great number of complaints and the beach grew deserted, especially at night. Public feeling was running high, and reluctantly the police chief ordered that a thorough investigation take place at the beach in question. As no volunteers came forward, thirty men were detailed to report at the beach at 10.00 p.m. (a most popular time for blood sucking) the next day, but the exercise had to be called off as no-one turned up for duty. Every man jack seemed to be ill that evening and made a miraculous recovery the next day. It could have been termed 'preventive medicine', couldn't it? Search as I might, no further reports came my way so, gentlemen friends, the next time you are tempted to try the pretty blonde in a mini-skirt and black stockings, get her to smile first before you both dash off hand in hand into the night. 'Sucked dry by a vampire' would look remarkably silly on your medical records.

Magistrates aren't usually renowned for a sense of humour, but one in London did, in my opinion. It seems that a ravenous traveller on British Rail purloined a sandwich and ate it. Unfortunately for him he was apprehended in the act and spent the next four weeks in custody. When his case came up before the magistrates, his lawyer recommended to the bench that his client should be released because 'eating a British Rail sandwich was suffering enough', and after a hearty laugh from one of the magistrates, the man was released without further penalty. I've always thought that British justice must be unique.

A sense of humour in the Church also was apparent, owing to a misprint in a parish magazine; it caused inadvertent mirth and had them rolling in the aisles (as you will see!). The misprint was a 'g' which should have been an 's', thereby making very interesting reading and a long queue at the door trying to get in. It read:
  'Mating has gained in strength and enjoyment since worshippers came up to the front pews. How wonderful if this could happen in both Churches at Evensong. Singing, prayer and friendship all gained enormously.'
  This should not be taken as a recommended aphrodisiac.

There doesn't appear to have been a sense of humour attached to a Jehovah's Witness a few years ago when he was remanded in custody, charged with assaulting a woman with a bag full of bibles. The swine! But I do wonder what she said to merit a sharp clump around the ears with a bag full of bibles; it couldn't have been a message from above, could it?

My blood ran cold in 1960 when I read a report that was headed 'Deadly Water – A New Discovery'. 'Oh Lor'!' I thought, 'Some more rotten bugs in the tap water to plague us,' but no, it wasn't as simple as that. Just listen to this and you will see why my blood ran cold and my hair stood on end, and it didn't seem worth the while to rush out to make a will because there wouldn't be anyone here to squander the £3 10s. 0d. left over from my funeral expenses. Perhaps you should take an aspirin before reading the following, to settle your nerves; I've just taken one to stop my fingers trembling and making typing errors by the dozen. The report said:

'Australian scientists have announced the discovery of a new type of polywater by accident – a substance which an American scientist has claimed could destroy all life on earth. [The aspirin hasn't taken effect yet.] Polywater was discovered by a Russian scientist in 1962. It keeps its properties to about 1,000°F. and well below freezing point. Dr Frank Blank of Pennsylvania has warned that it could destroy all life on earth and claimed that if it got loose and combined with normal water the earth would become a hot, dead world like Venus. British scientists discounted his warning, however.'

Thank God for British scientists. But what is this stuff? Does it turn all the world's water into jelly with poor us stuck on the surface like flies on the golden syrup tin lid? Or perhaps it evaporates water into steam which shoots off into space. I admit it is very worrying, but as this discovery is thirty years old and I can still splash about in a bath and drink a cup of tea, perhaps I can stop taking the aspirins.

And what about these circles and patterns in the corn? I haven't actually seen one myself but my mother did while tootling around the countryside in a coach.

'Gosh!' I said, terribly impressed. 'What was it like and what did you think of it?' Mum was famous for getting under-excited at all times.

'Oh, it was nothing much,' she said. 'It was just a circle in the corn. It was round.' I suppose that *is* the perfect description of a corn circle even if undramatic! I always want to know more than available information provides. After all, Mum's corn circle must have happened somehow, created by someone or something, and the big question of why, is to date unresolved, at least to the likes of me.

This year on television two men were demonstrating how they made hoax circles with a funny little loop hanging down from a basketball cap and a strip of wood to squash the corn. Okay, so it worked, but there was a crudity about the finished object that simply shouted, 'I'm a hoax, I'm a hoax.' Apparently these two fellows had been stomping around on corn for years in the middle of the night and I couldn't help wondering, what on earth for? It's much nicer to be tucked up in bed snugly asleep than creeping around in the dark of the night and treading in wet cow pats, I should have thought.

The patterns that have appeared more recently are quite breathtaking in complexity and beauty and as some of them are huge, it is difficult to imagine how hoaxers might accomplish such a clever trick. One scientist tells us that he is very puzzled because his sophisticated equipment used for measuring levels of this and that showed that the actual molecular structure of the flattened corn had reversed and, as I understand it, it is about as startling as coming across a patch of anti-gravity. In other words, if I knew what I was talking about, my mind would have boggled beyond redemption. In the absence of a plausible theory to offer, I contacted my old friends, Imogena and Tarquinne, for their views on the subject. They took a bit of tracking down as they no longer lived next door to Mrs Worthington-Smythe and, although the totem pole was still proudly erect, it had mysteriously moved into Mrs W.-S.'s garden.

'No,' she fluted, 'I'm not quite sure where they live now. They thought about finding a squat in Glastonbury about a year ago - I don't know if they did. I say, my ladies are joining me shortly for our Zenyuppa ceremony round the Totem - would you care to participate?'

I thanked her and expressed regret at having a previous engagement. As I walked away she called after me:

'The poor things couldn't get any reliable help, you know, and one can't be self-sufficient and philosophical if one has to do housework and look after children, can one?'

No, I suppose not, I thought, and headed towards Glastonbury.

I eventually found them in a large crumbling manor house, quite close to the magnificent Tor and, following sounds of activity, discovered them in the old stables manufacturing totem poles. Though they were a quarter of a century older than our last encounter, they looked much the same, except that their tied-back hair was sprinkled with grey and they looked sleek and richer somehow. Still delightfully naive, they knew nothing of current upsets and disasters and had never heard of Mrs Thatcher, and as for paying poll tax, they innocently said they weren't thinking of keeping a parrot so they wouldn't have to pay any. I made reference to the large heap of totem poles and Tarquinne said, 'We have such a job keeping up with demand. Mind you, they are a real snip at £500, don't you think? Would you like to buy one? This one is a little cheaper because my chisel slipped and cut off his . . .'

I interrupted by asking if he and Imogena had any idea what was making corn circles. Imogena answered, 'Yes, of course we do,' her eyes misting over with emotion again. 'That's why we are selling so many totem poles. We told all our friends that if they sang the totem song an answering sign from Zenyuppa would appear in corn fields, and they told their friends, and their friends' friends told . . . and pretty soon we had to employ about twenty people. The only trouble is we don't know where to keep all this money; the cellar's full and it's such a trek up to the attic. I shall have to give it some thought.'

I left shortly after this enlightening and philosophical conversation, and as I drove down the drive I heard Imogena singing 'Oh, totem, totem, in the hole . . .' while Tarquinne lit a large cigar with a £10 note.

I also was giving their theory some thought. After a while it sounded quite reasonable to me and not in the least far fetched. What happens is this. Tarquinne and Imogena sell a totem pole to a gullible client, they make a note of the area in which it will be planted, send a couple of the twenty employees equipped with funny little loops hanging from basketball caps and a strip of wood, and Zenyuppa!, another mysterious corn circle appears. All that nonsense about a puff of wind and UFOs. It simply doesn't hold water.

Speaking of UFOs, this is another phenomenon that I haven't encountered personally. But here again, I am deeply interested and believe implicitly that they exist. It would be too silly for words to think that Earth is the only planet in the universe capable of supporting intelligent life, though I do sometimes wonder if the 'intelligent life' here deserves that title.

According to my scrapbooks, 1967 was a marvellous year for reports of UFOs and practically everyone who saw one said, 'I've never seen anything like that before.' This is strange because 99% of reported sightings could be describing the same object. Just occasionally a really fancy UFO makes a visit and briefly causes a stir, and then Official Sources seem to step in and nothing more is heard. My very favourite attempted 'put down' by officialdom concerns a sighting in Brixham, Devon (and here I shall be terribly precise) at noon on 28 April. The object was observed by seven coastguards who watched it through high-powered glasses for an hour or more. It was described as a giant cone-shaped craft that slowly revolved, revealing some sort of door in its side. Oh yes, and it hovered at 15,000 ft. During the time that the coastguards were keeping this strange object under surveillance, they were surprised to see an earthly aircraft approach the cone and fly around it. So someone else had spotted it as well, hadn't they? Some little while later the cone upped anchor and climbed to 20,000 ft. before vanishing behind cloud.

Police stations along the Devon coast were inundated with telephone calls from people reporting the spitting image of the coastguards' sighting, and the coastguards themselves sent a report to the RAF at Plymouth, who immediately passed it on to the Ministry of Defence in London. Quite a lot of people were involved by now and shoving it under the carpet was going to be difficult. But they did have a go. Firstly the Ministry denied ever having received such a ridiculous report and then a few hours later it said, well, yes, we did receive such a report, but somehow it was not logged. And then it went on to say, 'We can only suggest that the object may have been a reflection of car headlights or some sort of meteorological phenomenon. I cannot comment further.'

The seven coastguards had a good laugh. A little later a senior RAF controller at Plymouth said:

'We reported all the details. I cannot tell you where the aircraft came from, and you will have a job to get anyone to admit that one was sent up. I understand the UFO was also tracked by radar.'

The seven coastguards had another good laugh because it sounded as though the Ministry of Defence had been stabbed in the back by the RAF. A few days later the coastguard station had a VIP visit from an Air Vice-Marshal and was shown a detailed drawing made by one of the coastguards. His comment was most interesting. He said, 'Most interesting!' He was quite right but should have been more enthusiastic instead of suddenly discovering that he had another engagement elsewhere and having to dash off. It didn't ring entirely true.

My final delve into the unexplained concerns apparitions and is not for those of a nervous disposition. Again, I cannot claim to have seen one myself to my knowledge, but I know plenty of people who have, including Erica and Peter. Both of these dear friends could be described as being very down to earth and fairly sceptical about unexplained phenomena, but even they were not immune on one occasion.

Along with a group of friends, they were enjoying a canal long-boat holiday, chugging contentedly through lovely countryside and having lots of fun. When they came to a longish and, consequently, rather dark tunnel, one or two of the party decided to hop off and nip to the other end to photograph the boat as it emerged with its grinning crew. Erica did tell me later that it wasn't very nice in that dark, dripping hole with a small light in the distance and that she rather wished that she had hopped off, too. However, as she couldn't change her mind half-way she had to grit her teeth and put up with it. Slowly the boat approached the widening circle of light and one of their friends stationed himself at the bow to take pictures of what he hoped would be a dramatic subject. Just how dramatic he didn't know at the time. Without warning the figure of a girl with long hair appeared, standing in the water, which could be seen under the surface as well as above. Erica, slightly petrified, was struck dumb, and as no-one gasped or said anything, she remained silent. Some time later when she and Peter were alone, she asked him if he'd seen anything peculiar in the tunnel and was rather relieved when he confessed that he had, but hadn't wanted to say so in case the assembled company rushed him off to hospital.

A few weeks later when everyone's colour slides were back from processing, an evening was arranged to show off photographic skills and have supper. The strange experience in the tunnel had faded a little in Erica and Peter's minds and they weren't prepared for the shock that was in store. When the tunnel picture appeared on the screen there was the girl with long hair who could still be seen through the water. Their photographer friend said, 'What the hell's that?' which let forth a deluge of confirmation that everyone had seen it at the time, including the ones on the tow path with cameras poised, except the poor chap that took the picture. I bet that wouldn't have happened if I'd been there; I would have screeched in fright, clutching Keith, and then everyone would have been able to have an 'Oh, my Gawd' session there and then, and not have to sneak around thinking it was an attack of the DTs. But then I'm not the strong and silent type!

Naturally we can't go through life without something odd and/or sinister happening to us, and Keith was subjected to almost having the living daylights squeezed out of him by me in terror shortly after we were married. As we were saving up madly for a deposit on a house we didn't have a car and travelled by bus and train. My parents lived in the same village as they did in later life, but their house was on the outskirts, and, boy, was it dark on moonless nights. When visiting Mum and Dad in the evenings – which was usually the only time we could manage – the golden rule was to take a powerful torch, otherwise a tumble into a ditch was a distinct possibility. One particular evening when we were in even more of a hurry, we forgot to snatch up the torch, an omission that was bitterly regretted the moment we left the brightly lit bus at the village. With all the light scatter from well lit towns and roads nowanights, it is well nigh impossible to remember just how pitch black the 1950s were in the winters. We could see the lights from Mum and Dad's windows, but to get there we had to climb a hill lane and then turn left along a track. It was a cheery beacon but it took us a long while with clasped hands and shuffling feet to reach. However, once we got there, we spent a very pleasant couple of hours exchanging news and drinking whisky and then it was time to set off to catch the last bus home.

It took some little time to adjust our eyes to the stygian night, and we felt our way carefully down the hill and at last judged that we were at the road where the bus stop lives. There is no pavement on the left hand side of the road which is flanked by a tall flint wall with a few meagre tufts of grass in between. Having discovered the bus stop post by touch, we heaved a sigh of relief, reckoning that we had at least ten minutes before the bus was due. It was then that we became conscious of some very queer noises that appeared to be coming down the road towards us. Memory does play tricks, I know, and after all these years I can't be certain what these sounds were, except for puffing, panting, moaning and groaning, mixed up with thuddy footsteps. It was downright weird and I became terribly scared and shrank between Keith and the wall, that being the safest place I could think of at that moment, and anyway, he had promised to take care of me. Even more frightening was the fact that this 'crowd' of noises wasn't passing us; it was very, very close and not moving. I have no idea how long we huddled together, expecting to be attacked by someone or something, when a shaft of light appeared around the corner, heralding the bus. And the beam of the headlights picked out a completely empty road, even though the noises seemed to surround us at close quarters.

'Evening, folks!' said the conductor as we scrabbled on to the bus. 'Hey! What's the matter? Seen a ghost?'

No, Conductor, I should have said, we haven't seen a ghost, but I think we've just heard a whole crowd of them.

So often things aren't what they seem on the surface. I spotted a manufactured stone head in a junk-cum-antiques shop and fell in love with it right away. It was such a kindly old gentleman with a haughty long nose and a rather sweet and wistful smile on his pale lips, and, not being able to resist his charms, I asked Keith if he could take up residence with us in the garden.

'Don't you just love him?' I asked. 'And I'm sure he'll bring us good luck, he's got that sort of ambience about him.'

'Well, I don't know about that sort of stuff,' said Keith, 'But have him if you want him.' No sooner said than done, and I staggered home with him wrapped in newspapers, thankfully lowering him to the ground the second I got inside the gate. Considering he was only half a head (the sort that gets hung on a wall) he surely must have weighed more than a whole one and my arms were numb and aching. 'Blooming thing,' I muttered to myself, 'I should have waited until Keith could collect it in the car.' So I suppose it wasn't much of a welcome for the poor old soul to his new home and caused him to sulk.

It was a couple of weeks or so before Keith banged a nail into the brick pier that I had earmarked for him, and I was called to admire our new guest when he finally took up residence at about eye level to me. Only he'd changed. The nose had grown longer and positively supercilious while the rather sweet and wistful smile had turned into a sneer. Also, the blank stone eyes fixed mine with a 'I know something you don't know' expression that disconcerted me. His previous home must have been amongst the ivy, because fronds had left charming little trails across his chin and up one side of his face, which had looked attractive and interesting in the shop. Now, viewed from a distance of more than about a yard, he looked as if he'd caught some awful plague that might be contagious.

Having made such a fuss about wanting the thing, I didn't quite know how to confess to Keith that I'd changed my mind. I decided that I was being silly and should give the poor thing the benefit of the doubt and let him settle down in his new home before condemning him. And who knows, I comforted myself, his sneer might turn back into a sweet and wistful smile. It was a bit like whistling in the dark. I tried very hard not to meet his cold white eyes every time I popped out of the door, but it was no good, for they drew mine like a loathsome magnet and I knew with certainty that either he or I would have to vacate the premises. So plucking up my courage in both hands I made my feelings known to Keith (after all, this horrible thing had cost quite a lot of money), quite expecting to get tutted at.

'Thank God for that!' he said, 'The bloody thing gives me the creeps.'

We wrapped him in newspapers again, but not before a final glare from the stone eyes, and into the dustbin he went. Silly as it sounds, I wasn't entirely happy until the dustmen took him away and then I was able to walk past the dustbin instead of pretending I was in a hurry and having to run.

All this set me wondering about his past. How could something in a junk shop made of reconstituted stone smile beguilingly through the window and change character so completely while wrapped in newspaper and lugged home? While accepting that I can be a little foolish at times, that does not apply to Keith who is so level-headed it makes me sick, and he also rather liked him in the shop. Perhaps our surroundings weren't grand enough for him and he let his feelings be known, and if that is so he smiled at the wrong householders, because his next home was the Corporation tip, and serve him right! The rotten old snob.

Vená has the last word, as usual. Though, come to think, this will sound more like the budding Lavinia, as we float back in time to that crazy weekend spent camping at Durdle Dor thirty years ago, and has the outlandish Lavinia ring about a certain occurrence. Having spent a good part of an afternoon discussing and editing her recollections of life in a small tent in Dorset, we both pronounced it pretty good and the draft was left in my incapable hands to make some sort of sensible account. I typed and laughed my way through her scribblings and went on to the next chapter, quite pleased at the way in which her strange lifestyle was unfolding rather neatly. My pleased thoughts were a bit premature. At our next meeting we were engaged in something quite different when she suddenly squawked:

'Oh! Blast, blast, blast!' in her usual ladylike manner. 'Peg! I forgot all about my albatross.'

I sighed, sensing yet more alterations and additions.

'Go on, then, tell me about your albatross. Only make it quick, we've got masses to do.' Her face was assuming Lavinia's expression which meant even more trouble.

'You remember how I spent the night lying on the lounger in the van – well, I saw an albatross when I woke up.'

'No you didn't,' I interrupted rather rudely. 'You woke up when your friend wondered how long you'd been dead.'

'Oh, not that time,' she said impatiently. 'This was the first time I woke up, it was then I saw my albatross.'

Anyone other than Vená would have awoken to the chirps of a sparrow or blackbird, and stayed awake; Vená is roused by an albatross, of all things, and then goes back to sleep. This was getting much too interesting to ignore, so I apologised for being snappy and gave her my full attention.

'Well, I thought I must still be asleep. I heard this flapping noise and looked out of the window and it flew past the van. Then it went up a bit without using its wings and skimmed the edge of the cliff and then flew out to sea.'

I was slightly disappointed; all this sounded exactly like any old bird flying about on the top of a cliff. But then she went on:

'It was so *huge*' (and here she stretched her arms to their maximum), 'the wings were longer than this, and it looked just like a whacking great seagull.'

From experience I knew better than to disbelieve my friend. But it did sound a bit unlikely, so I parried with:

'Are you sure it wasn't a swan, Vená, they have an enormous wing span?'

'Nah!' she said scornfully, 'I know what a swan looks like, you burk. I tell you, it was just like a giant seagull, and anyway, when I told Roy about it at breakfast, he said it must be an albatross, so there!'

'But Vená,' I pointed out, 'There aren't any this side of the equator – they all live in the South Seas.'

'Well this one didn't,' she countered, 'It was down in Dorset.'

Later that evening I consulted my dictionary as I wasn't one hundred per cent sure about the location of their habitat, even though I'd probably sounded confident and cocky while contradicting Vená. It read: 'Large sea bird. Belongs to petrel family and is found in South Seas.' (Hooray, got it right!) 'Resembles exceedingly large seagull, and on rare occasions is seen round British Coast.' (Oh, bum!)

'Well, anyway,' she had said during our little exchange of views, 'Can you put it in the week-end chapter?'

'No, I can't. It's finished now and I'm trying to do my boring bit.'

I knew very well that I was being ungracious, so conceded:

'Tell you what – I'll try and fit it in somewhere if I can.'

She still looked disappointed and as if she didn't hold much faith in my sincerity. I suddenly felt rather mean and picky and made a note on one of the thousands of pieces of paper conspicuously, to show her that I really did mean it, despite my prune-shaped mouth.

It was after reading the description of the albatross that I realised that waking up in a van on a sun lounger and witnessing the amazing sight of this mighty bird flying past, really did deserve a spot on its own, and where better than to finish off a chapter about odd goings-on? After all, do you know anyone that has seen an albatross? No, I'm not surprised – it could only happen to my friend Vená!

CHAPTER 12

I can scarcely believe it, but at the time of writing, it is Census year, and I am astonished by the speed at which the past ten years have fled by while I am trying to catch up with everything that happens. Ten years is a hefty chunk out of anyone's life and yet it seemed such a short time since we were ploughing through the 1981 compulsory divulgence of personal details. I realise that I have slept through approximately one-third of the time but even so, the remaining two-thirds should have lasted longer, surely? Pondering upon this weighty matter, it came as a small shock that only just prior to the last one we were still living in our last abode and frantically trying to make it look as though two squeaky clean persons resided there instead of us. This, of course, was for the benefit of the very nice couple who were hoping to buy it. So many people have mentioned that the older one gets the quicker time flies, and at last I believe it absolutely. The more I thought about this the more it became obvious that quite earth-shattering things have occurred in this space of time, some altering our personal lives to an extraordinary extent.

At the time of the last Census Keith was slowly recovering from a very serious illness that involved a hefty operation and we were both suffering from shock as a result. As we can be just a little foolish at times, we were also in the throes of selling one bungalow and buying a house – hence the mad clean-up operation on my part, weakly supervised by one slightly impaired and valiant husband. Having been unsuccessful in the purchase of Naomi and Chris's house, we had looked around and eventually discovered a smallish house quite close to where Keith's grandparents had lived and decided that, warts and all, this was for us. It wasn't perfect by any means, but despite one or two drawbacks, appealed immensely and we commenced negotiations. After one or two false starts and a few aggravations, the whole chain of house-movers exchanged houses and front door keys on the same day, all fully occupied removing the remnants of the previous owner and sealing it with their own stamp. This strange practice (that we all undertake) ensures that the DIY stores get rich while the proud new house owner gets steadily poorer.

It is true to say that we both love this little house to the extent that the best part of a holiday is the coming home bit when our tired, travelled faces uncrease and light up in a smile. Why go, we ask ourselves, we are happy here, but we always think that a change will do us good and perhaps it does. Our favourite type of holiday is the mini sort when there is barely time to catch homesickness, and as we usually do this with a coach-load of dear local friends and go somewhere very nice, of course we do benefit as well as enjoy the change. It's still nice to come home though.

I was secretly rather worried about the amount of work in renovations envisaged for our new home in view of the delicate state of Keith's health, but was pleasantly surprised to find that our new surroundings had given him a new zest. I thought the tremendous amount of work he undertook quietly was a pretty drastic way of passing the convalescent period and was proved wrong, as he grew stronger and more confident very quickly. So well, in fact, that when approached by a friend who needed a crew member for yacht racing in the Solent, he jumped at it, performing very strenuous antics in the process and thoroughly enjoying himself. During this time we expanded our circle of friends considerably and settled into our new life like chameleons, and once having dealt with the first mad flurry of house repairs and improvements, were able to taste the real pleasure of living so close to the sea amongst so many nice new friends.

Just a year after our move, this country was plunged into war with Argentina in what was then termed the 'Falklands Crisis', and although geographically we were far removed from the war zone, this city was very much involved and Her Majesty's Ships were given a tearful and rousing send-off from the ancient fortifications that have guarded the entrance to the harbour for centuries. The city is a Naval home and a great many of the Navy personnel are local people so it was natural that a ripple of apprehension should affect the majority of its citizens. It was difficult not to feel emotional when part of the vast crowds that gathered to wave farewell to loved ones and friends, and many a bravely smiling face also had tears upon it.

As the Falklands War progressed and the list of casualties, of both men and ships, became shockingly intrusive into our daily lives, concern for those involved and their families increased as the dark days crept by. It was a strange time, fighting a terrible war using horrific weapons at such a distance, which was regularly condensed to a few feet by means of extensive and graphic television coverage which has now become the 'normal' method of news presentation. In times of stress and trouble, my mother had a little maxim that went, 'Everything passes, don't fret,' and even this conflict came to an end eventually. The homecoming battle-scarred ships received an ecstatic welcome from the townsfolk on the same fortifications and, once again, tears freely mingled with the glad smiles. It takes time to heal wounds but human nature is resilient, and while celebrating triumph in battle one felt somewhat chastened by the sheer random waste of young life on both sides. And life goes on for the survivors.

We had two further causes for anxiety shortly after the war ceased: my parents were visibly declining in health and our dear friend Ben had become ill. Sophie hid her own feelings very successfully by presenting a bright and cheery mien to the world, and I tried hard to emulate her courage rather unsuccessfully. It soon became obvious that with the extra demands that illness brings, it was sensible to terminate my employment at the laboratory, and this I did with much regret. Naturally there had been occasional differences of opinion among us over the years – I don't suppose that any organisation is sweetness and light all the time – but the overwhelming family feeling and so much fun was enough to sweep any little niggles under the carpet. I have to add that things had lost their savour a little after our star colleague Vená had so traitorously defected to the Educational field.

My brother Ray and I are much indebted to our little Aunt Della who took such a lot of daily responsibility off our shoulders. Along with her husband Ted, she was the firm rock that kept us all going during those last years of acute suffering for my parents. Of course there were lighter moments to make us grin, and one that occurred at the end of a particularly gruelling day was an encounter at Della and Ted's house with their grandson Donald, who happened to be staying with them at the time. Not exactly spotless (quite the opposite in fact), he shimmied through the doorway, presenting himself with a self-conscious smirk flitting across rather grubby features. Della looked disapprovingly at him and urged his absence to the bathroom and thence to bed. Donald was thunderstruck and his smirk gave way to an expression of amazement and disbelief at this command.

'What! But, Nan, I haven't had my supper yet.'

Della was having none of this nonsense.

'You've just this minute come back from a barbecue and I expect you've been eating all the evening.'

'Well, yes, I suppose so,' he conceded after a little ponder, 'But I didn't have my tea before I went, did I?'

He reluctantly admitted defeat after a while, having pointed out that it wouldn't be his fault if they found him dead in bed from starvation the next morning, and then, suddenly, his face lit up as he remembered something really important, and he removed one of his disreputable trainers.

'What on earth are you doing now?' enquired my exasperated aunt.

'Look, Nan! I won 50p.,' he said proudly, meanwhile shaking the coin out through a large hole in his sock. 'This was the only place I had to put it in and I forgot all about it.'

A little grilling brought to light that Donald had won a race early on in the barbecue proceedings and had continued competing (without winning) with this 50p. coin jammed into the arch of his foot and didn't even notice. Years ago I came to the conclusion that children are a completely different species from their elders and betters! What the child couldn't know, of course, was just how much he had contributed by way of lightening the atmosphere by making us laugh, or how he had somehow or other earned himself that large cheese and pickle sandwich to keep him going until breakfast, brought in by his hard-hearted but now smiling grandmother.

My mother had been living on borrowed time for some years, thanks to the dedicated care of the hospital, but the time came when she could no longer tolerate the massive blood transfusions and she was admitted into hospital where she died a few days later. The real grief of losing a loved one comes later when shock has diminished and we had my poor bewildered father whose memory was practically defunct to care for, which concentrated our minds entirely. It was only to be expected; he didn't understand for long what had happened, which was a mercy, as in six weeks he also succumbed and joined his beloved Meg. It comforts me a little to remember a tale that Dad was relating to Keith a few years ago which ended with . . .

'. . . and I said to Old Bert, we are so lucky, we've got four of the nicest kids in the world.'

As he and Mum had Ray and me only as offspring, it showed that they loved my Keith and Ray's Jan on equal terms, and weren't in the least surprised by the unselfish care and help that Ray and I received from our respective spouses. Whereas my mother had untied her earthly bonds shortly before she left us, Dad underwent the reverse and responded to our whispered love messages by saying:

'It's so nice to be loved,' and that was treasure indeed for his nearest and dearest.

It was probably just around the time that my parents' troubles were accelerating that a storm of a different species hit the southern counties of England with disastrous results. Keith and I spent that evening at a meeting held by our local 'Friends of Association' and had walked the short distance through moderate rain and a frisky wind. Nothing out of the ordinary at all to suggest that Madame Nature had a surprise in store for us - that is, not until we stepped out of the door at the meeting place to go home. Replacing the light wayward breeze and rain was a turgid stillness that was both warm and smelly. It also contained an element that we couldn't put a finger on at the time, and the only description that seemed to fit was electricity that wasn't there. Ridiculous as that sounds, it complemented the strange and unidentifiable smell. Not exactly sweet, it clung in the nostrils rather like rotting vegetable odour, and yet that wasn't quite right. We never did think of a suitable comparison and very much hope we don't ever smell it again, as we shall know we are in for trouble! It got even warmer as we trudged homewards. It was all very strange; we had set forth three hours earlier in normal slightly nose-blueing October wind and rain, and here we were returning in tropical mysteries. A considerable shock awaited us when we looked at the barometer in the kitchen. I don't think it was depressed about my latest sunken fruit cake, but it had gone as low as it was possible. A little tap upon its face made the needle jiggle about rather uncertainly before it decided it had to return to the original record low. Now, Michael Fish had said something about a bit of a blow somewhere around Biscay, but as we didn't live there, we had taken very little notice. Not a word had he said about hot pea soup weather that smelled so sweetly revolting and I can only guess that it sidled in when his computer was having a snooze or an oil break.

We stood at the door for a few minutes, uneasy about the eerie calm and yellowish lowering murk.

'Well,' remarked Keith chattily, 'I've never seen anything like this but I'm not going to stand here all night chit-chatting to the likes of you - I'm going to bed.' Which he did, and I went also. Some time later we roused from that first deep sleep, conscious of a faraway roaring that increased dramatically, even while we were blinking the cobwebs away. Like the smell, this noise was strange, and my first waking thought was that a Jumbo Jet was about to descend upon us. True to form in an emergency, I lay paralysed with fright for a moment or two and then clutched at Keith as a drowning woman would a straw. At that precise moment a gust of ferocious proportions hit the house and marked the start of the hurricane. Our bedroom window gave an agonised creak and groan as if it had been pole-axed and the wall itself seemed to move. After the initial shock of such a rude awakening, and the chances of an aircraft landing in the garden had receded, we got out of bed and bravely twitched the curtain at the protesting window. So far as we could see the world had gone mad, with missiles flying at great speed, the little crab apple tree bent double, and all viewed through a constant barrage of heavy sea spray, sand and pebbles. Lurid flashes of lightning, also yellow, lit the storm though, oddly, no thunder was heard at any time during the night: too much cacophony on earth to hear the celestial fireworks doing their stuff, no doubt.

If possible, the wind increased and there seemed to be a real danger that the window couldn't withstand such an onslaught for much longer and we deemed it prudent to decamp to the lounge on the leeside of the house. Not that there seemed to be a lot of difference in the intensity, as roof tiles bumped noisily down and smashed messily on the paving, causing me to squeak in alarm while jumping. Around 4.00 a.m. there was a slight lessening in the wind force and Keith decided to drag his tired body up the stairs and risk going to bed. That was too adventurous still for me to attempt such a foolhardy trick and I remained huddled under a duvet in my chair, falling into an uneasy light doze as the storm left us to devastate Sussex and Kent.

The sky had cleared by the time the sun rose and, bleary-eyed, we ventured outside to assess the visible damage. It was useless trying to see through the windows as they were covered in an admixture of sea, sand and mud, as was the entire brickwork. The debris that had flown around like feathers during the night now lay passive in heaps, revealing the enormous amount of damage suffered. The radio waves were crammed with graphic accounts of disaster and warnings of danger still lurking in the aftermath of the hurricane. Smashed roof and ridge tiles aplenty littered the streets and gardens and we thought ruefully about the rumblings and thumps of dislodged tiles we had heard while cringing in the lounge. It was difficult to spot a roof that didn't have a snaggle-toothed outline and there was evidence of much more serious damage. We particularly mourned the many huge uprooted trees that we could ill afford to lose in the city, and the sea itself, whipped to a frenzy, had wreaked havoc along the coast and in the parks and gardens. It was incredibly fortunate that almost neap tides were in operation for, owing to the extremely low barometric pressure and the extraordinary force of the wind, long before high tide that night the sea had risen far above a spring tide level and was rolling in waves up streets and across parklands. I shudder to think what could have happened if a spring tide had been calculated and so, bad as it undoubtedly was, it might easily have been similar to the infamous and terrible storm in Good Queen Bess's days when 8,000 souls perished hereabouts by drowning. But here we are, alive and kicking sufficiently to fill in the Census form which didn't ask:

'Have you suffered from wind during the past ten years?'

In between natural disasters and family illnesses we had settled down in our new home as if we'd lived here all our lives and enjoyed ourselves immensely. We both have a deep love for this house and it seems to quite like us and, it is true to say, we have spent a great deal of time, effort and money upon it and still have some things to do. When away, I am just as homesick for this house in middle age as I ever was in my youth for Liddon and have never felt the same for any other house I have lived in, with or without my dear Keith.

During the first half of this Census decade Keith was very much involved as a member of the crew of a friend's Victory boat and, having a 50% mix of sea water in his veins, relished every moment. It has never failed to amaze me how someone can stagger home wet through, stiff with salt, battered and bruised, but wearing the widest grin possible without actually splitting his face in two. It makes no sense, but apparently that has nothing whatsoever to do with sailing, and in particular, racing. Thursday evenings and Saturdays were inviolate and could never, never, be tampered with for any other frivolous (comparatively) engagement, and my life seemed to revolve around tide tables and getting the last lot of sailing gear dry enough for the next wetting. Another thing that makes no sense is the yellow welly language. Tell me, what springs to mind with the word 'sheet'? 'Sail' comes the answer, triumphantly. Wrong; it is a piece of string, and this is just an example of how easy it can be for me to put my foot in it, making Keith's salty colleagues feel sorry that he was so foolish as to marry me. In view of my landlubberyness it wasn't surprising that I sort of flitted about the edges of all this activity and kept my feet dry. I can't help thinking that this was a wise move anyway, because each time the race course included going round the sewer outlet, I could smell Keith's arrival half-way up the garden path.

'Hello, love!' he would greet me grinning and squelching, 'Had a nice afternoon? Give us a kiss then.'

The social calendar was more exciting, and in addition to dinners, barbecues, and the like, whole week-ends were arranged with a similar boaty fraternity in the Isle of Wight. Not that I saw a lot of Keith (except through binoculars) during the day's racing, but the Club's hospitality in the evening was really something. We even appeared on television once when BBC2 were filming the Redwing and Victory classes at Bembridge. Keith, being tall, handsome and very bronzed (due to searing winds and sewage) had a magnificent coverage of about three feet of film, and not to be outdone, there was a quick flash of me downing a gin and smoking a fag. When I saw this programme about six months later, I couldn't help but be reminded of Kate in Alderney and resolved to amend my ways. Particularly funny was the fact that Keith's father had kindly recorded this programme on video, in case we missed it for any reason, and while we were thanking him said:

'And what did you think of our television debut?'

They both looked at us blankly, wondering what the hell we were going on about.

'Didn't Keith look dishy?' I enlarged. I thought it best not to mention my own brief appearance.

'What do you mean?' asked Mum, looking both puzzled and bewildered.

A short explanation and two rather sheepish faces revealed that though they had watched the programme twice, neither of them had noticed their only son filling the screen nor had they spotted the Kate lookalike crouched in a corner. Can't trust anyone these days, not even parents! I thought that Keith looked so striking that he was bound to be snapped up for a starring role in *Howard's Way*, and eagerly rushed to the door each time the post dropped on to the mat, but, no, nothing has arrived as yet, and if his own mother doesn't recognise him, the chances of fame and fortune are remote, I think.

Accommodation had been organised by the Host Club for the visitors and we scattered around the area seeking our B & B establishments. Keith and I, along with Skipper William and his wife Rhonia, toiled up a long hill, turned left a couple of times and eventually spotted the address we were looking for. It was a nice Victorian house with an attractive winding path through the garden to the front door, and we thought, 'Gosh! This is a turn up for the book,' (we are used to very peculiar B & Bs in the Island), and rang the bell. A very little lady with the appearance of a scared mouse admitted us into the hall, squeaked something about getting Mrs McPlunkett, and scuttled off. A few minutes later Mrs McPlunkett herself creaked slowly along the passage way and eventually joined us.

'Guid afternoon,' she greeted us. 'The girrl tells me you've arrived.'

We agreed that we had, and after a few pleasantries that we didn't quite get the hang of, she announced,

'I'll get the girrl to carry your bags to your rooms,' finishing with an ear splitting shriek, summoning the unfortunate girrl to her presence.

I could feel a Vená-like explosion of laughter welling up and with difficulty almost stifled it by turning slightly and pretending to cough. The poor little thing was severely out of breath and received her instructions (in loud tones) with great attention and devotion to duty. Now that we had a chance to look at her, we realised that she was even older than Mrs McPlunkett, and it didn't seem in the least fair that she should be expected to lug all our gear up two flights of stairs, especially as her head was on about the same level as Keith's kneecaps. Obviously the others thought so also, as Keith and Skipper W. demurred and gathered up the baggage, while the girrl looked aghast, terrified that her 'programme' had been tampered with and now didn't know what to do. She looked imploringly at her employer and twittered something unintelligible to us, but which caused Mrs McPlunkett to dismiss her summarily to the kitchen. I was still struggling with hysteria even though it didn't strike me as being at all funny now and considered taking the poor girrl home with us to do my chores - at least I would supervise her more kindly. During our short stay at Mrs McPlunkett's establishment she brought early morning tea, served breakfast (probably cooked it as well), cleared the tables, dusted, polished, weeded the garden, and that was just the bits that we observed. I felt really tired by the time we left.

While the puir wee lassie was being hithered and dithered by her authoritarian employer, we, on the other hand, were leading the life of Riley, especially me. Especially me because I was the only one who didn't have to struggle into heavy weather sailing gear and then bail out or get cracked on the head with a madly swinging boom, as I was nobody's crew. I was free to wander along beautiful and exciting strands, littered with fossils and interesting flotsam, splash through rocky pools and chat with anyone who was prepared to listen (or pretend to), and it was blissful. Non-crews have to make their own way across the Solent from home, and during the nice sunshiny trip on the ferry I had struck up a conversation with a very pleasant retired gentleman, discovering that we were heading for the same destination. I had intended to take a bus from Ryde, while he had decided to walk as it was such a beautiful day, and after a little discussion, I was persuaded to join him. After all, he was in no danger as I was strong enough to defend him, if attacked, and we both thought each other's company would be nice, as so it proved. It was a long trek but a good part of it was along the sandy beaches before we struck inland through very pretty countryside. Fortunately we had encountered a café that featured good coffee and superb great jam doughnuts, otherwise I probably wouldn't have made it, and as it was, I was getting a little weary around the calves when the Host Club came into view. Surprisingly, I could see our crowd milling about and drinking on the Club's terrace. Strange, I thought, I'm usually miles ahead of the boats, glanced at my watch and found that we had been walking for nearly three hours. No wonder my calves were complaining – I only hoped that my husband wouldn't do likewise! He did look a bit straight-faced when I joined him on the terrace with my new friend-for-the-day, but it had seemed churlish not to invite him to have a refreshing gin and tonic after all those miles we had traversed. It turned out that he knew most of them, anyway, which created much goodwill all round and lots of gin and tonics. Sailing can be great fun, so long as one doesn't have to actually put to sea.

Other things in life caught up with Keith, including a much increased work load, family commitments, and absolutely no free time at all, which resulted in a very reluctant withdrawal from nautical nexus. I, too, was sorry he had to give up his favourite sport for mundane and less enjoyable ways of passing the time, but as Nature abhors a vacuum it was quickly filled, unrecorded because we can't remember with what!

Life in Britain during this last decade had altered radically from its predecessor. Gone, to a large extent, were the days of more easy-going and friendly comradeship amongst working colleagues which were replaced by the more ruthless methods of 'achiever' tactics, and a rather frightening worship of money became evident. This brought about a rapid rise in consumer prices and a widening gap between the well-heeled and the ill-soled. Despite a severe recession that started in October 1987, the gap grew larger still, and mute disquiet became more vocal when details of the poll tax were put before the public. In a word, Britain started to ferment. I strongly suspect that Old Sod had been taking a lively interest in this heady mixture and had been biding his time before the ideal opportunity presented itself. It came in November 1990 when the Prime Minister's popularity appeared to be waning and the Cabinet and House on the Conservative side were deeply divided upon certain policies.

'Aha!' said Old Sod to himself, with a pleased smile, 'Dear old Sir Geoffrey – just the job.'

Since his abrupt removal from the high office post that he had loved so much, poor Sir Geoffrey had slumped and glumped on the hard bench, raising the spirits of the Opposition and lowering those of his own party. Much too good an opportunity to be missed. Noted for his gentlemanly and mild manners, Sir Geoffrey made dramatic history the afternoon when he stood up and made the speech of his life, during which he quietly slipped a deadly stiletto between Mrs Thatcher's political ribs. It is quite horrifying to imagine what Sir Geoffrey had suffered and suppressed like lively wine in a tightly corked bottle. In the end either the bottle will shatter or the cork will pop and in this case the cork popped with devastating results for the Prime Minister. It must have been an exceedingly bitter moment for her when filling in this Census form to enter under 'Occupation' – 'Member of Parliament' in place of 'Prime Minister', and just goes to show that absolutely nothing should be taken for granted, especially in politics, and even more especially when Old Sod is waiting to pounce.

However, I have gone forward in time with that particular tempest and must revert to two of the natural kind that happened in the early months of 1990. The first one came roaring in from the west and performed a good job on weakened trees and structures left in a parlous condition by the hurricane. We are quite used to a good old blow in these windy islands of ours, but this one did border on the dangerous side and a lot of damage was left in its wake. Scarcely had we time to congratulate ourselves for surviving the semi-tempest, when the second one gathered strength as it crossed the Atlantic and the barometer once again plunged alarmingly. Storm No. 2 was of momentous proportions, taking life, property and trees with terrifying ease. Though not quite in the same league as the hurricane which was local to the south, this one shook the whole of the British Isles in a violent embrace and happened during daylight hours, which put many more people at risk.

Keith's parents were victims insofar that part of their tall Victorian house collapsed and caused tremendous damage and upset. Luckily, they were both a few feet away from the sudden deluge of brickwork and escaped physical injury, but the shock was dreadful. Naturally Keith and I took as much weight off their shoulders as possible during the spring and summer while the poor battered house was slowly restored, and they gradually regained confidence and health. So much so, that during our Saturday evening Newmarket gambling sessions after supper with us, they regularly and thoroughly cleaned us out, laughing all the way to the bank and back (knowing full well that more winnings would follow in seven days' time), and looking forward to the next marauding. There's gratitude, I must say!

Our friend Anna had a particularly frightening day during the worst of the storm. Her place of business is situated half-way up a high rise office block faced with mirror glass and steel, which started to perform a lively gavotte. Mesmerised, the staff watched their desks assume a life of their own by sliding back and forth and spilling the contents with a crash on to the heaving floor. And worse was to follow. It is bad enough to be seasick conventionally, tossed about on a lively sea, but the land is supposed to stay still unless in the midst of an earthquake, and several of the staff were suffering the same drastic upheavals of rebellious stomachs. It later transpired that a tremendous gust had collided with the bland exterior of the block, was sucked downwards and wreaked havoc at street level. From then on, until the storm abated somewhat, the building behaved exactly as if an earthquake was happening. Poor Anna and everyone else in the office block were trapped inside, unable to use the lifts, and had to try to grin and bear it bravely, which must have been extremely difficult. Keith and I had occasion to drive past this stricken building a few days after the storm, and were taken aback by its odd appearance. The entire mirrored face was crinkled and distorted, causing very queer reflections, and was a sober warning of the strength of the ferocious weather systems that seem to beset us more and more. I am happy to conclude that Anna (made of sterling stuff) weathered the storm magnificently and managed to stop trembling after a few days, which was a lesson to us all.

During the summer of 1990, Vená-Lavinia and I put our heads together and decided to compile our joint meanderings. Apart from our marvellously funny Ben, no-one has given me hysterics to the extent that Vená has induced over the years, and the thought of working with her kindled a flame of enthusiasm to start immediately, if not sooner. After all, not many people are privileged to partner an extraordinary woman who magnetically attracts strange and hilarious situations, and even if we don't become rich and famous at least we are having a wonderful time recounting some of our experiences.

Our working methods would probably drive a proper writer mad. We have frequent afternoon meetings filled with cups of tea and home made wine, shrieks of laughter, many reminiscences that we decide we'd better not reveal, hasty appraisal of each other's latest contribution, and then one of us dashes home to get the family supper and the other stays where she is and does likewise. No committee meetings, minutes, Filofax, tedious consultations, etc., just we two (sorry, three!), a couple of typewriters, lots of memories and a rather large heap of manuscript.

Today is Tuesday 19 November 1991, and the most marvellous thing has happened. Terry Waite has come home, and although the majority of us do not have the privilege of knowing him personally, many, many of us feel uplifted and thankful that this giant of a man is safe and home after five years of suffering and separation from his loved ones. The powerful address to his countrymen immediately upon arrival at RAF Lyneham drew admiration and awe, and has ensured him a high place in history and in people's hearts. Not the least for his ruefully humorous account of the difficulty in obtaining some sort of footwear for his enormous feet when (so he said) the RAF contacted the Navy, who came up with a couple of barges!

This event was, of course, outside the last Census decade and now, dashing away a joyful tear, I will return to the main object of this last chapter. As I was saying ...

So much has happened within this time, some very good and some very bad, and it did occur to me that practically nothing of life itself is recorded on the form. We have lost people we love dearly and we have gained some truly lovely new friends. Keith is much healthier now than ten years ago, and life is, on the whole, very good. None of this will be noted for posterity on a personal level. For instance – the very day before Census taking, the sun was shining brightly and it was warm enough in the garden, sheltered from a bitter north-east wind, to sit outside and drink coffee after lunch. While doing so I turned my head for some reason and was mightily surprised to see a tiny bird perched in the trellis, not more than two feet away. Its eyes were half closed and it rocked gently, as if with fatigue. It was so close that I could see its legs were no thicker than a thread and I wondered how on earth they could support even this tiny body. We identified it as being either a chiff-chaff or a willow warbler – they are very similar – which meant that it had battled against extremely strong and icy winds for maybe two thousand miles, and having made landfall, just happened to plop into our garden to recover. At least, I hope he or she did; we shall never know, of course. Now then, I would have loved to record this useless highly interesting snippet of information on the form, but it didn't cater for birds dropping in after lunch, just for people who dropped in after dinner and stayed for the night.

The Census decade started with a very violent war in the Falklands that claimed many lives and dreadful injuries on both sides and, ironically, ended with another. This much shorter one in the Gulf countries was even more terrible although our own casualties were surprisingly light. What the outcome of this war will be for the future is impossible to predict, particularly in the environmental sphere, and we simply have to hope for the best that our fragile earthly home is not irreparably damaged. And in between these two wars some amazing changes have taken place. Who could have guessed that the Berlin Wall, a dreadful and repressive symbol for so many years, would be razed and then sold in chunks as souvenirs at an astronomical price? Or that the Soviet Union no longer exists as such, and although there has been much trouble with break-away States and an excruciating economic crisis reigns supreme, the major part is now known simply as 'Russia'. One other unbelievable fact of life, but closer to home, is that Britain's well loved bangers cost in the region of thirty bob a pound, and my darling old Dad would never have believed that – everything else, but *thirty bob a pound* – never in a month of Sundays!

Perhaps it is the deliberate intention of official fact-gathering to collate the dry as dust details and leave the art of living to the individual, thereby preserving a modicum of privacy. If so, it has my wholehearted approval, and if not, please don't mind our business any more than is strictly necessary in the future. Just think, they've never heard of Lavinia, and I am perfectly willing to swear that she exists; in fact, she has proved it on many an occasion, ask Venà! A last thought on this subject: the very next counting of heads will take place in the twenty-first century. I wonder what it will be like.